T0240971

Re-Making Communication at Work

Re-Making Communication at Work

Jesse Sostrin

RE-MAKING COMMUNICATION AT WORK

Softcover reprint of the hardcover 1st edition 2013 978-1-137-33706-1

First published in 2013 by
PALGRAVE MACMILLAN®
in the United States—a division of St. Martin's Press LLC,
175 Fifth Avenue, New York, NY 10010.

Where this book is distributed in the UK, Europe and the rest of the world,
this is by Palgrave Macmillan, a division of Macmillan Publishers Limited,
registered in England, company number 785998, of Houndmills,
Basingstoke, Hampshire RG21 6XS.

Palgrave Macmillan is the global academic imprint of the above companies
and has companies and representatives throughout the world.

Palgrave® and Macmillan® are registered trademarks in the United States,
the United Kingdom, Europe and other countries.

ISBN 978-1-137-33707-8   ISBN 978-1-137-33276-9 (eBook)
DOI 10.1057/9781137332769
Library of Congress Cataloging-in-Publication Data

Sostrin, Jesse.
    Re-making communication at work / Jesse Sostrin, PhD.
    pages cm
    Includes bibliographical references and index.

    1. Communication in organizations. 2. Communication in
management. 3. Interpersonal communication. I. Title.
HD30.3.S655 2013
651.7—dc23   2013020510

A catalogue record of the book is available from the British Library.

Design by Newgen Knowledge Works (P) Ltd., Chennai, India.

First edition: November 2013

10 9 8 7 6 5 4 3 2 1

This book is dedicated to my late friend and mentor, Barnett Pearce, whose life's work was the scaffolding for this book.

Contents

Figures and Tables

Figures

Tables

Acknowledgments

This book would not have been possible without the energy and contribution of the countless scholars and practitioners who codeveloped the Coordinated Management of Meaning theory by extending its application beyond the academic world. I would like to extend a special thank you to my colleagues at the *CMM Institute for Personal and Social Evolution* who are working hard to promote healthier patterns of communication in research and in demonstration projects around the world.

Thank you to Kim Pearce for her endless encouragement and support to share this work.

Thank you to Tiffanie Dillard for a patient review of an early draft.

Thank you to the Palgrave Macmillan team, especially my editor, Charlotte Maiorana, and editorial assistant, Leila Campoli, who recognized the potential in this book and worked with me to get it right.

And thank you to my wife, Joy Sostrin, for her unwavering support at every turn along the way.

Preface

Communication is at the heart of our everyday experience at work. Unfortunately for many of us, a day at work can be filled with a variety of unwanted patterns of communication and interaction that make it hard to get our best work done and stay meaningfully engaged in our careers. By exposing the stuff that makes and sustains these unwanted patterns, this book provides a foundation for making something different, something better.

I started working with student leaders in higher education in 1994. The first workshop I delivered was about improving communication with first-year students with the hopes of better welcoming them into the school community and ultimately improving retention for the college. Since then there has not been a single intervention that I have delivered—as a dialogue leader, conflict resolution and mediation specialist, group facilitator, executive coach, organization development consultant, and human resources executive—that has not at least touched on the theme.

Over the years I have continued working with organizations and their leaders across a variety of industries and at varying levels of size; from Fortune 500 companies and large federal agencies, to city and county government agencies and universities, to small businesses, start-ups, and nonprofit organizations. The one single issue that seems to cut across every environment is the challenge of getting communication right. Drawing upon this wide-ranging experience, I wrote this book with two goals: (1) To make the case that what most people have learned about effective communication at work is incomplete and that a new approach is needed; and (2) to provide a set of tools that help people create the patterns of communication and interaction that can align with their values, improve their performance, and lead to a long and successful working life.

In a way, these goals and the origins of this book began long before I started. In the late 1970s two colleagues at the University of Massachusetts at Amherst shook up the academic world of communication when they introduced their earliest version of a new theory of communication, which they eventually called the coordinated management of meaning (CMM). The concepts and potential applications of this new approach to communication provoked strong reactions from the traditional leaders in the field and many difficult battles were fought over the relevance and rightful place of this new theory. If those old lecture halls could talk they would tell stories of passionate arguments by Dr. Barnett Pearce and Dr. Vernon Cronen who codeveloped the work, held fiercely to the urgency and importance it had for them, and patiently nurtured it through the decades.

These two men, now recognized as the fathers of CMM, intentionally brought others along in the collective work of applying CMM in both scholarship and practice. This book could not have been written without the hard-fought contributions they and their many collaborators made over the last 40 years.

I was fortunate to study with Barnett Pearce during my doctoral work at Fielding Graduate University. Through his careful mentoring and eventual friendship I caught a glimpse of the way his career, which was dedicated to understanding communication in all of its complexities and nuances, came down to a simple truth: we make our experience in life through communication.

I needed this clarity and insight because I was at a crossroads professionally. While I loved working with people to help them resolve their workplace challenges, the vast majority of requests for my services were initiated due to some breakdown in "communication." By the time I began working on my dissertation I was convinced that the body of work—training resources, how-to kits, expert advice, and popular books—currently available to managers, human resources professionals, and consulting practitioners was inadequate. I personally had a bloated tool box full of too many methods for "improving communication" that did not get to the heart of the real issues. The result was often short-term improvement, with no long-term change. The more I began to realize that underlying "patterns of communication" were the actual source of the unwanted outcomes my clients so desperately wanted to get rid of, the more I was convinced that we needed a different set of resources and a new approach to addressing issues with communication at work.

Re-Making Communication at Work offers a much-needed reboot of the definition and practice of effective communication at work. The refresh is needed because communication remains a vital source of opportunity to not only spot recurring challenges that hinder performance, but also the intentional choices we have to craft productive relationships that leverage our capacity to work well.

Ultimately this book is the product of my own journey in understanding how communication impacts everyday organizational life and it draws on a variety of theories and practices filtered through my own experience working in the trenches to help resolve conflict, improve individual and team performance, coach emerging leaders for success, and change organizational cultures across a variety of industries. Because of my bias toward offering something useful to managers, consultants, and individual contributors who are interested in using communication to shape a better experience at work, I only summarize the background and context of the theoretical foundations of this work. To accommodate readers who are interested more in the background, I provide thorough notes and resources that acknowledge the key contributions of others, including additional resources.

Re-Making Communication in the Real World of Work...

This book is divided into four parts. The first two introduce the conceptual argument for why we need a new approach to communication and they establish the foundation for re-making communication at work. Parts III and IV are about applying the new approach to communication in your working life, including ways to implement the book's insights and tools at individual, team, and organizational levels. Parts I and II present the "why" and "what," while parts III and IV present the "how" and "when."

I am an impatient reader myself so I can relate to those who may get through part I and say "Alright already, I get the concept, please fast-forward to the part where you describe *how it's done*!" For those quick readers and for anyone else who values the applied focus above detailed explanations of the "why" and "what," I have written alternative summaries for parts I–IV. The purpose of these sections is to get down to the ground level of implementation in order to show a clear picture of what these concepts mean in action. Drawing on years of coaching and consulting experience with organizations and their leaders, I offer plain-language descriptions of re-making communication in the real world of work.

The Flow of the Book

Conversations about manuscripts in progress are always tricky. "Oh, you're writing a book...what's it about?" While this may sound like a straightforward question, in the case of re-making communication at work it is *and* it isn't. It is, of course, a book about communication in the workplace. From the title, you know that it will challenge the status quo mindset about what effective communication is. And you know that it will be full of substance and depth, as well as applicable tips and tools for putting the ideas into practice. However, because of the complexity of communication and its intrinsic place in the spectrum of our organizational endeavors, this only tells part of the story.

In a way this is a book about managing change. It is not instructive about ways to respond to the pace of change, maintain strong work/life balance to withstand the stress of it, or even to anticipate trends better in order to "beat the competition." It is a book about managing change because it offers proven insights for creating the conditions that can "make" the changes you want. At the same time, the book is about leaders and the valuable contributions they can make. It is not a leadership book with tips for charisma and persuasion. It offers no guidelines for ethical judgment or strategies for winning in a changing market and it does not present "five easy steps for effective..." fill-in-the-blank. It is a book about the everyday challenge of leadership because it delivers a game plan for leaders to empower their people to redefine priorities and actively engage in the process of aligning those priorities with the way people work.

Whatever your role is in your organization, the book is about spotting the communication traps and habits that get us stuck when we work with others. It is about learning to resolve obstacles to building high-trust relationships, closing gaps that reduce our own engagement and team collaboration, creating productive routines that lead to improved individual performance, and contributing value that elevate the overall bottom-line outcomes of our organization.

Re-making Communication at Work does not deliver a simple recipe of steps to follow or magic phrases to say that will improve your communication and change the quality of your working life overnight. On the contrary, it is a sophisticated set of insights and practices that match the complexity, contradiction, diversity, and speed of communication and change that characterize the world of work today. Part I dismantles several myths of effective communication at work and suggests a new set of principles to replace them. It shows how communication at work, as broad and difficult as it is to define, has specific implications on some of the most defining factors of individual, team, and organizational success such as: employee engagement, decision-making and problem solving, team development, effective leadership, and the capacity to shape organization culture. And it makes the case that learning the concepts and skills of re-making communication at work can be among the greatest competitive advantages for individuals, teams, and organizations in the world of work.

Part II provides a knowledge guide for re-making communication at work. This includes understanding the basic chemistry of what makes patterns, knowing the physics that holds them together, using the basic design elements that construct them, and learning how to see patterns in your world of work. It introduces a set of sequential processes for deconstructing unwanted patterns and re-making them into something different. And, part II concludes with a look at high-priority patterns, including seven common communication pitfalls and unwanted patterns and seven preferred patterns of communication leaders must get right.

Part III is a practice guide for re-making communication at work. It presents a set of mental models and practical reminders, as well as a variety of single-step practices that can be used alone or in various combinations with others to address a wide range of communication challenges. And it introduces the M-A-I-D sequence that can be used to re-make individual patterns of communication and interaction. This includes information about how and when to use the sequence, as well as four case studies that show what it can do in action. Part IV concludes with suggestions to begin implementing the concepts and tools from the book, including a full chapter of self-guided, interactive exercises that act as virtual coaching for re-making communication at work. It includes a dynamic chapter that marks the correlation between the capacity to re-make communication at work and the effectiveness of leadership and organizational culture change. And it offers tips for sharing the information and ideas in the book with the "hard-to-reach."

Throughout the four parts of the book I may introduce a new topic or theme for the first time with very little elaboration or explanation. At other times you may recognize that a similar thought is being presented again in a new form. The style of writing I chose for this book reflects my own layered experience understanding communication at work. Learning how to "see communication" and actively "make the patterns of communication and interaction" that influence my working life was not easy to grasp. I found it helpful to hook into clear statements that I could understand, and then use those to wade into the more challenging themes. The overall result is a breakthrough resource for understanding how to use communication—in all of its complexity—as a transformational tool to work well.

Blending CMM and Organization Development

Re-Making Communication at Work draws upon CMM and offers a set of practices and tools to recognize the way communication subtly, but powerfully impacts our performance and shapes the quality of our experience at work. When combined with signature research into the everyday challenges of work from an organization development perspective, CMM's concepts and tools can reveal unique insights into how the patterns of communication and interaction at work can be examined and intentionally re-made to reduce unwanted outcomes and align our truer priorities and goals with our experience on the job.

Limitations of this Book

Of course there will always be significant limitations with any effort to say something meaningful about a topic as complex and far-reaching as communication. Was something alluded to in passing that should have been given more attention…was something unimportant inflated with expectations and explained in too great of detail…was something missed entirely and left out of the story about what works with workplace communication…did the emphasis on applying the concepts and tools at work result in oversimplifying the conceptual background?

These and other questions have been carefully considered with the hopes of writing something that would fill a need in the world of work and offer something credible and challenging for readers. It was in the spirit of expressing a new take on old challenges and presenting useful tools that can solve the everyday challenges of work that this book was written, limitations and all.

Audience

This book was written for everyone seeking a better way to respond to the day-to-day communication challenges that show up in their world of work. This includes part-time and full-time, office and field, blue-collar, white-collar, and green-collar workers from every industry that requires interaction with others. The same rules apply across this range and so the book's core concepts and tools can be applied in all of these contexts.

In addition to the benefits for individual contributors who want resources and tools to communicate more effectively with others at work, managers and leaders who need exceptional communication skills to lead their teams effectively will also benefit from the practical applications of proven concepts. And human resources professionals and consultants who need straightforward communication tools to support/coach their clients in their professional development growth can take the book's lessons and frameworks and share them efficiently and effectively with both new and seasoned clients.

This is also a book for students preparing for the official start to their working lives. Maybe they have held internships or part-time seasonal jobs, or maybe they are returning to graduate school after a stint in the world of work to gain further education and set the long-term career trajectory they seek. Whatever the circumstances, this book is essential for undergraduate and graduate students—majoring in organizational communication, business administration, human resources, organization behavior, and industrial psychology to name a few—who need to enhance their knowledge and build their skills for future career success.

BurningQ uestions

Wherever you are on the spectrum of roles and responsibilities in your organization—from an intern, an individual contributor, a new manager, a seasoned leader, or an executive—you likely confront a range of important questions that dictate important outcomes in your future working life:

- How can I progress in my career, stay relevant, and get ahead of the change curve?
- What are the pivotal capabilities and competencies that I must possess to be effective in the changing world of work?

- What new approach could move me beyond the everyday communication and relationship challenges that erode the quality of my working life?
- What specific changes in the way I work could bring my best talent into the foreground when they are so quickly sidelined by reactions to the crisis of the day?
- What can I do to feel better and perform more effectively when I'm strapped with a lousy team, a bad boss, or a disappointing organizational culture?
- If our team is going to be effective with increased competition and rapid changes in our industry, how do we need to work together?

This book offers a way to delve into these and many other vital questions with reasonable hope that the journey will produce positive change. The collective insights and tools presented throughout *Re-Making Communication at Work* can help you transform the often abstract, complex concepts of communication into effective tools for understanding the dynamics of organizational life.

Making Room for Something New

My late mentor, Dr. Barnett Pearce, described the awe and wonder that he often experienced when he saw the depths of richness and complexity in human communication. The first few times I heard him say this I was not moved to consider it in any great detail. I suppose I referenced the phrase "awe and wonder" in relation to the old biblical notions of awe from fear, terror, and dread in the face of gigantic awesome power. Then one day I heard the comments of Jonathon Haidt, a social-psychologist who researches the phenomenon of awe and wonder and I had a change of heart. He describes "awe and wonder" as something so beautiful and vast that our existing mental functions cannot fit it in. This kind of awe and wonder requires the need for accommodation, which is an entire shift in thinking necessary to account for something new.

Now I know what Barnett meant.

In this book I want to challenge your current understanding about what effective communication is. In order to make room for this new approach to communication you will come closer to the richness and complexity of what happens when people spend more time with each other at work than they do at home with their families engaging in endless patterns of communication and interaction. When you are finished reading this book, I hope that something has changed for you.

Introduction: Forget Everything You Learned About Communication at Work

Almost four hundred years ago the seminal philosophers John Locke and David Hume implicitly defined "communication" as a tool for the transmission of pure ideas, meaning ideas themselves are what matter, not the way they are expressed and exchanged. This perspective not only took hold, but it has survived until this day as the dominant way of defining communication. Now known as the transmission model,[1] this approach to communication is the foundation of many academic courses in communication theory and practice, and it is embedded in most business literature and education programs that address subjects related to workplace communication, organization behavior and culture, leadership, conflict resolution, and more.

But what if this accepted model of communication was incomplete? And what if, instead of providing insight for improving the way we communicate at work, its legacy was a distraction from the real story about what works with effective communication at work?

Re-Making Communication at Work argues that the transmission model needs to be replaced by a new approach to communication. The book challenges the status quo by exposing the most common myths that inaccurately define effective communication at work, and it replaces these misperceptions with a set of core principles that deliver a clear mandate for re-making communication at work. By upending these myths, the book not only provides the theoretical foundation for this new approach (derived from the groundbreaking communication theory CMM—coordinated management of meaning),[2] but it uses straightforward models and visually appealing exercises that demonstrate how students, employees, and leaders can powerfully improve the quality and outcomes of their working lives.

It should be noted that while the theoretical progression of new forms of organizational communication has advanced well past the roots of the transmission model—from the classical perspectives, to human relations and resources, to systems theory, to cultural perspectives, and to critical theory—the dissemination of those conceptual changes into the world of work has not occurred at scale. For example, while academic scholars may know that the transmission model, the transactional model, and the conduit model (advances in theory that refer to updated versions of the same basic framework) insufficiently capture the dynamic nature of communication, people in the trenches of everyday working life do not have the updated concepts and flexible tools for addressing their everyday communication challenges. This book fills that critical gap between knowledge and useful application.

Communication Is the Problem, Communication Is the Solution

Exploring issues of effective communication at work is often based on the goal of identifying ways to make it better. In this pursuit, communication can be seen as both the cause of and solution to the same problem. Here are a few stories that illustrate this duality in the words of three leaders who diagnosed their own organizational challenges. These were the messages they shared with their teams and the reasons they gave for requesting consulting services from a workplace communication expert:

> "We are in this mess because we failed to keep the lines of communication open and valuable information was missed. As a result, we made a bad strategic move and now we have to clean up our mess. Moving forward, we will be meeting weekly to ensure effective communication and to make sure this never happens again."
>
> "You two have to find a way to work together; it isn't an option to keep butting heads like this. Your communication styles are like oil and water, but you still have to find a way to talk through it. I need you both on the same page."
>
> "Right now our company is not innovating at the pace that will keep us competitive in the future. I think we have so much more intelligence in these walls, but it is not being communicated well. We have to start sharing what we know and using our new developments to spur innovation across our core divisions."

In these vignettes you can see how various aspects of communication are confirmed as both the problem and the solution to the unmet priorities. In each situation, the identification of the problem was accurate at a basic level (communication was the source of the problem), however, you can also infer that the simple diagnostics that led each leader to ask for solutions such as "more meetings for open communication," "talking through it," and "sharing what we know for better innovation" were decidedly incomplete. For nonroutine, hard-to-define, complex problems, simply stating the need for "more communication" is like responding to a rise in global hunger with the well-meaning, but wholly generic, statement that "we need more food to feed the world." While it may be absolutely true in principle that we need more communication at work, we do not need more of the same superficial approach to communication offered by the transmission model.

Today's emerging and established organizational leaders need proven resources and accessible tools to help them effectively engage people, manage complexity, and lead their teams through disruptive change. The epicenter of the knowledge and skill that define success for today's managers is communication. And, as I said, the problem is that most everything managers have learned about successful communication at work is incomplete. Now that I have your attention with that incredibly sweeping statement, let me unpack it with a bit more nuance.

When you ask people to talk about their everyday challenges at work a short list of barriers directly related to communication will consistently make the top of the list. Despite the fact that communication breakdowns are squarely on the radar of what to watch out for, most attempts to illuminate the challenges of workplace communication result in the same superficial list of prescriptions that do little more than guide people in scripted conversations with strategies that address the presenting conditions, but not the root causes of the problems.

The reason so many of these popular remedies to ineffective communication fall short is that the underlying premise about what successful communication is has been built on a series of myths. *Re-Making Communication at Work* challenges the status quo by exposing the most common myths that inaccurately define successful communication at work. Although the myths and new principles will be discussed in greater detail in chapter 1, here is a quick reference to some of the most prominent myths. Can you see which ones influenced the thinking of those three leaders who diagnosed their issues at work from the perspective of the transmission model?

- Communication is just an exchange of information and ideas. To get it right, you have to listen well and speak clearly.
- You have to know what you want to communicate and have clear messages for every interaction.
- Good communication follows a process, and if you follow the right steps, you'll get good results.
- Once you get the hang of it, you can take the same communication approach into every situation.

Re-Making Communication at Work will show how these and other myths fuel the popular, but terribly incomplete, definition of communication as "a series of isolated conversations that follows a give-and-take process of verbal and nonverbal exchanges with the simple effect of transferring information, interpreting messages, and taking action in response."

It will argue that when efforts to teach productive interpersonal and group communication practices are delivered in the context of these myths that are fostered by the transmission model—no matter how fancy, elaborate, or compelling the presentations may be—they fail to address the underlying causes of ineffective collaboration, unresolved conflict, poor decision-making, misaligned strategic priorities, and the troubled relationships that prompted the need for ideas and resources to "improve communication" in the first place.

The new definition of successful communication at work that can replace the outdated, underperforming transmission model starts with the ability to recognize the *patterns of communication and interaction* where decisions get made, relationships are built, organizational culture is solidified, and the trajectory for ultimate business outcomes are set into motion.

With this new foundation, emerging and established leaders can then develop a combination of insight, skill, and ability that allows them to: examine what they are making, spot the critical moments where something different/better could be made, understand how to create the flexible conditions for change, follow a sequence of steps to re-make unwanted patterns, and learn to avoid everyday pitfalls that can undermine productive patterns of communication and interaction, along with the benefits they bring.

> Referring to challenging communication interactions as "unwanted patterns" is not a judgment about what or who is wrong in the situation; it just indicates the desire for something better. This language can help you approach possibilities for re-making communication at work with less judgment and more curiosity if the unwanted pattern is strongly tied to personalities and feelings.

This updated paradigm of communication has two starting assumptions: (i) communication is substantial and the tangible patterns we engage in represent something meaningful to look at, not just through; and (ii) communication is fluid and the patterns we engage in can be re-made to create and sustain the experiences we want. It stands to reason that if managers can learn how to intentionally shape their patterns of interaction, they gain a powerful tool to meet the challenge of engaging people, managing complexity, and leading their teams through change.

Communication Makes Our Experiences and Outcomes at Work

This book is about the everyday experiences people have at work and how they can make those experiences more satisfying and productive both for themselves and for their organizations. The path toward something better goes through communication. Specifically, if one is to influence the character and quality of their working life and accelerate their positive contributions to the team and organization, they must first see the spectrum of patterns they engage in. Figure I.1 illustrates the way a day at work is no more than a collection of integrated patterns of interaction.

The quality of your working life and the outcomes you experience are a reflection of the patterns of communication and interaction that you engage in throughout the day. If you want to know whether your stress level is rising or falling, check your patterns. If you want to know whether your working relationships are solid or faltering, check your patterns. And if you want to know about your performance and career trajectory, there are clues to both of these in your patterns. Put yourself in the center of the image in figure I.1 and you will see how one single day is filled with diverse, often intersecting communication experiences:

> You are at your desk, planning your day, responding to messages, and wrapping your mind around what you need to be doing... you have casual interactions with coworkers in the hallway, kitchen, and by the water cooler that help you stay connected to what is happening with others... your team meets and relationships are tested and forged, information is shared, decisions are made, and actions are taken... you interface with a variety of coworkers, customers, and partners throughout the day via virtual and face to face connections to get work done... you meet with your manager and get feedback and direction for your work... and you participate in companywide meetings that keep you informed about the strategic and cultural direction the organization is heading... And finally, you bring the cumulative effects of these patterns of communication and interaction home with you to keep processing, interpreting, and deciding which action to take when you go back again.

If your job requires you to interact with other people (as virtually all of them do), then communication is an inevitable aspect of your working life. We could say that "work is communication" and "communication is work." In this way of thinking about the nature of work, the rules are simple: You get what you make. You make it in communication. And if you notice and are intentional about the unwanted patterns you have made, you can re-make them into new patterns that produce better outcomes.

Re-Making Communication at Work introduces a series of thought exercises and practical activities that show you how to intentionally shape the patterns that lead to the results you seek. Before more detailed explanations of the tools and applications can be useful, it is important to describe more about why this is needed. The remainder of this introduction delves into the background theory and provides the full context for understanding the need and relevance of this new approach.

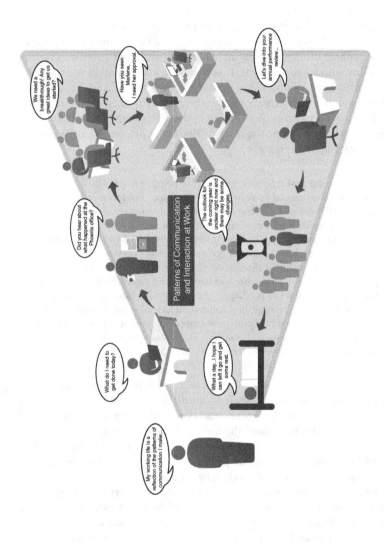

Figure I.1 Our working lives: constant patterns of communication and interaction.

Reversing the Equation

Many of the traditional approaches to workplace and organizational communication focus on communication as it happens within organizations. They attempt to show how communication occurs within the "container" of organizations, including the theories that explain why things happen as they do and what rules and interventions could be applied to improve communication when it falters. As researchers and thought leaders such as Stan Deetz[3] and many others have discovered, however, it is more useful and interesting to look at this in reverse. Rather than searching for ways that organizations impact the communication that takes place within them, I care about finding ways to look at how communication impacts organizational life. This approach, which inverts the more traditional view of organizational communication, could be called the study of organizational life from a communication perspective.

This inverted approach is a departure from the traditional view of organizations, including how organizational communication was originally conceived. Because this change in perspective is the basis for re-making communication at work, it is important to briefly summarize the background theory so you can decide for yourself if this alternative approach portrays a more accurate picture of your world of work.

Providing a condensed summary of the last 75 years of theory is easier said than done in part because organizational communication is just a smaller field in the much larger, fragmented discipline of communication studies. Em Griffin, the author of the bestselling textbook *A First Look at Communication Theory*, covers the breadth of this broad field and surveys more than 90 general theories and approaches (some of which have subtheories and related methodologies) to communication. It literally takes a full textbook to summarize these theories. Re-making communication at work is concerned with practical ways of making organizational life better; therefore, a similar approach to summarizing only the most basic aspects of related theory is sufficient for setting the stage and locating this work within the broader context of the field.

At a macro level, the domains of *organizational communication theory* are generally organized into seven traditions, including: rhetorical (the practical art of discourse); semiotic (intersubjective mediation by signs and symbols); phenomenological (perception and interpretation of individual experience and dialogue); cybernetic (system of information processing, networks, and systems); sociopsychological (interaction and influence from an individual focus to generalizations of trends), sociocultural (people talk, produce, and reproduce social order and culture); and critical (power dynamics that influence communication).[4] Each of these seven traditions is full of related theories and approaches that offer new additions and criticisms to what came before.

The array of *organizational theories* in which these seven categories are embedded can be generally referred to as: classical theory (scientific management, bureaucratic theory, and administrative theory); neoclassical theory (the human relations movement); and modern theory (a systems approach, a sociotechnical approach, contingency theory or a situational approach, etc.). Each of these broader domains is also full of individual, contributing theories and approaches that offer new additions and criticisms to what came before.

Although it may seem straightforward enough to group organizational communication theories into a list of seven traditions, and then compare how those seven traditions influenced, and were influenced by, the three organizational theory domains in which they evolved, it is all quite convoluted. What makes the field of organizational communication difficult—namely, the lack of a unifying theory that reflects relevant application to all of the various elements—is precisely what makes re-making communication at work so useful.

This new approach to communication at work offers a way of considering any aspect of organizational life from a consistent set of principles. It explains aspects of both an *organizational theory* and *organizational communication theory* in complementary, integrated ways. This more coherent approach offers a way of looking at organizational life at the fundamental, root-cause level that makes our organizational structures and cultures, as well as the character, experience, and outcomes of our individual working lives. Although they will be defined and elaborated upon throughout the book, the definitions are introduced here:

> *Organizational communication is made from* the habits of interaction and patterns of communication that people form as they interpret and respond to each other in their ongoing exchanges.
>
> *Organizations are made by* the cumulative patterns of communication and interaction of their people.

Following these definitions, we can further describe "effective communication" as a way to create and sustain the patterns of communication and interaction that produce the meaningful and preferred experiences and desired outcomes of the people who engage in them. To understand how this new set of definitions relates to established views we have to revisit the early days of organizational communication, beginning with the machine metaphor.

The Early Days of Organizational Machines

The roots of organizational behavior and communication theory include the classical approaches such as scientific management, famously pioneered by

Frederick Taylor (arguably the world's first management guru) and administrative management, developed by equally influential and interesting thinkers such as Henri Fayol, Luther Halsey Gulick, and Max Weber. In these frameworks, the organization was seen as a machine and communication was a mechanistic process.

In these early days, the fundamental assumptions about organizations and organizational communication included beliefs that: organizations are mechanical things, and there is one best way to get a task completed. Therefore it is a matter of tuning the machine accordingly. Second, communication is a mechanical process that takes place within the container of the organization. People act rationally within organizations, and therefore communication will follow the structure and rules of the machine.[5]

The first major model for communication that reflected this way of thinking was the Shannon and Weaver model that is now referred to as the transmission model of communication. This model, originally conceived as a mirror to the functioning of radio and telephone technology, involved the sender, channel, and receiver and the free-flowing exchange of information.

In this model communication is defined as information transfer and the subsequent transmission of meaning. This approach imagines communication as a pipeline through which raw information is transferred from person to person.[6] The roles of sender and receiver are distinct and messages are encoded and decoded independently. This is a kind of utilitarian approach that enables people in organizations to manipulate communication as a tool for accomplishing various objectives. Among other challenges with this approach to communication, the obvious limitations include any unexpected element that potentially disrupts the flow of information and the effectiveness of the transmission. These issues include information overload, distortion, and ambiguity to name just a few.

Communication Inside the Machine

The influential communication theorist Robert Craig describes the transmission model and the assumptions about how communication inside the machine took place in a way that is easy to grasp and hard to forget:

> In the simplistic *transmission model* that is so often taken for granted in everyday discourse, communication is conceptualized as a process in which meanings, packaged in symbolic messages like bananas in crates, are transported from sender to receiver. Too often the bananas are bruised or spoiled in transport and so we have the ubiquitous problem of *miscommunication*: The message sent is not the message received; the sender's meaning does not come across. In order to improve communication, according to this model, we need

better packaging and speedier transportation of messages. Good communication is basically a technical problem.[7]

Within this view of communication, problems are simply technical issues that involve some or all of the necessary information failing to be transmitted effectively to the right person in the right way. This informational or transmission view of communication has continued to set the standard for the way communication is perceived and practiced in many of today's organizations. The difference between a "well-oiled machine" and complete chaos comes down to the unobstructed flow of information. Alternatively, "if organizations do not communicate the right information, to the right people, at the right times, and in the right ways—things fall apart."[8]

Organizations Are People

As the march of theory evolved from organizations as machines, the next body of work was labeled the human relations and human resources approach. This included a diverse set of theories and models that sought to overcome the limitations of the classical approaches portrayed in scientific theory and its predominant mechanistic interpretation. Pioneering theorists such as Mary Parker Follett and Chester Barnard represented the transitional shift between the old and the new.

Their work redefined ideas about power, relationships between management and employees, and the variability of individual behavior in organizations. They wrote about organizational life in a way that showed things were not as clean, simple, or predictable as they had been portrayed. Their work brought new concepts and terms into the lexicon that emphasized things like the risks of overmanaging employees, the value and existence of informal processes within organizations, and the importance of skills like "communication." While these are all taken for granted today, they represented significant shifts in thinking in their day.

As others built upon their work this human-centered movement reflected more democratic ideals in the workplace, including everything that went along with that such as: using open communication as a tool to coordinate the contributions of employees, measuring and valuing employee satisfaction, seeing employees as a resource, considering ways to motivate people, measuring the impact of communication on organizational culture, teaching managers to define and pursue organizational goals that reflect (at least in part) individual goals, and developing meaningful participation for employees as a means to increase performance and morale.[9]

This particular domain of theory and the many ways that the ideas ultimately influenced the practice of management and the way we think about organizational life are immense. It is worth reading about in more detail, including the many groundbreaking studies, subtheories, and practical applications it generated.[10]

Organizations Are Systems

The human relations and human resources approach gave way to the systems approach, which introduced concepts related to complexity theory and adaptive systems. Unlike classical theories that portrayed organizations as machines, system theorists viewed organizations as *living ecosystems* and they used systems concepts such as wholeness, hierarchy, openness, and feedback to explain their characteristics.

This paradigm shift put organizational communication in a different role. Rather than the transmission view of communication that takes place "in the container" and simply follows the command and control structure of the organizational machine, communication could be seen as an integral aspect of the linkages, interactions, and feedback processes within the system that actually give form to the organization. The systems view was a way of keeping pace with the increasingly complex demands of organizations that could not rely on simple rules and uniform structures for transmission communication. It provided a broader framework to understand interlocked cycles of communication to manage change and equivocality.[11]

The next major evolution in theory included cultural perspectives and critical perspectives, both of which are still in their developmental stages. Cultural perspectives on organizational communication introduced concepts such as: there is no single objective reality or factual truth in organizations—people negotiate their own meaning of things; communication contributes to making organizational culture and it impacts how work gets done; organizations adapt and change based on their people and environments; and organizational cultures can be classified as "strong" or "effective" based on qualities such as supportive environments, shared vision, and so on.

Critical perspectives on organizational communication include concepts such as: organizations are political and communication produces and maintains systems of power that promote dominant interests; certain groups have access to privileges that others do not; and the structural inequality in organizations often goes unnoticed as it is made to look normal and legitimate.

This cursory review of theoretical perspectives shows how significantly our predominant understanding of organizations and organizational communication has evolved. And yet, despite these additions to the status quo, the everyday challenges of effective communication at work persist. I believe that the key to developing meaningful responses to these challenges begins with seeing organizations as living things that constantly evolve.

Organizations Are Living Things

If you ask the question what is an organization, you can get many different answers. Some point to products or services that bring in revenue. Others point to mission or brand differentiators that give it a unique identity and purpose. Still others may point to physical things such as buildings, logos, balance sheets, or other evidence that it "exists." Notice how each of the typical responses corresponds to stuff. In the alternative view, organizations are the living result of the patterns of communication and interaction among their people. This is not a reference to the ethereal side of organization life; it is actually rooted firmly in the concrete experiences and outcomes of organizational members. Matt Koschmann, professor in the Department of Communication at the University of Colorado Boulder, produced an effective video that describes the view of organizations as communication.[12]

The creative expression of his ideas about organizations *as* communication have modern roots going back several decades. In 1974, the influential organizational theorist Karl Weick said:

> The word, organization, is a noun and it is also a myth. If one looks for an organization one will not find it. What will be found is that there are vents linked together, that transpire within concrete walls and these sequence, their pathways, their timing, are the forms we erroneously make into substance when we talk about an organization.[13]

Organizations themselves do not exist independently in objective reality; rather they are the result of the fundamental process of communication. As people make meaning that shapes their experience and social reality at work, the collection of these meanings becomes the currency of organizational culture and the result over time is an organization. Some refer to this as a constitutive view of communication insofar as it implies that communication is what constitutes or makes our experience. This is a powerful departure from the fixed view of organizations because it frames them not as static institutions that indefinitely exist on their own, but as the natural result of the dynamic communication processes by its members.

This idea that people in organizations do not merely react to an objectively accepted physical environment, but rather they enact and reenact their environment by interpreting and making meaning of their experience aligns with the constitutive view of organizations. When you combine the idea that organizations are living things with the idea that communication is the living thing that makes it, you have the foundation for re-making communication at work.

Communication Is a Living Thing

Without the safety of a machine metaphor that unrealistically projects organizations as predictable, methodical systems, we see that real organizational life is often quite messy and unpredictable. Interactions among people within organizations are anything but mechanistic and people do not follow a set of prescriptive rules when they communicate with each other. Knowing that this is a true picture of work, our way of thinking about workplace communication must match the reality of our messy and unpredictable organizational lives.

Unlike the older models, which misleadingly assume that the essential elements involved in communication are fixed in place when the act of communication takes place, the constitutive model suggests that the various elements of communication are fluid and "constituted" within the unfolding act of communication itself. In this way, communication is now defined as "an ongoing process that symbolically forms and re-forms our personal identities, our social relations, our common world of meaningful objects and events, our ideas and feelings, and our routine ways of expressing these socially constructed realities."[14] No longer merely a technical question of transmission (i.e., how to reduce noise from feedback to get one's meaning across without distortion), the problem of communication has complex personal and social dimensions in a constitutive model.

Why Traditional Approaches to Communication Fail

One of the fundamental reasons why traditional approaches to communication fail is the inability to see communication as living and continuously changing. One reason that communication breakdowns persist and remain at the top of so many "greatest challenges of work" lists is because of the prominence of the transmission model, which casts communication as a mechanistic process with fixed rules, rather than a living thing that is made and re-made every day. One of the fundamental goals of this book is to provide the rational path toward this way of seeing communication as anything but fixed.

One of the reasons we get lulled into believing the transmission model is sufficient is because it is easy to grasp and it does work in some instances. Sending or receiving unambiguous emails, making straightforward plans, delegating clear and noncontroversial tasks, sharing basic information— all of these can be accomplished with relative ease and they can easily follow the trajectory of the transmission model. However, when complexity is elevated due to any number of complicating factors, something different is needed. The traditional approach fails to account for the dynamic movement of people and ideas and it cannot account for the richest aspects of our working lives that do not fit nicely into boxes. These unpredictable, but influencing moments happen every day: An unplanned interaction with a colleague that results in hurt feelings and a breach of trust…a casual comment from a supervisor that causes you to question your value and place in the organization…a frustrating meeting that ends without clear agreements or focused next steps. These are just a few of those everyday interactions that shape our experience and the outcomes we get at work. Anytime we engage in communication we start with the entire context that came before it. And, what we do within an episode of communication creates another context that we act out of. The notion that most of the prior context remains hidden from the people we interact places a high degree of uncertainty and potential confusion on even the most basic exchanges. There is often so much more going on in these situations that we cannot rely on the old method of understanding communication to make sense of how people make meaning and coordinate action.

We Say Communication Matters, But You Would Not Know It

It seems like we have a significant contradiction on our hands. When you ask people about their everyday challenges at work, including the most pressing issues that emerging and established leaders face leading their teams, a short list of barriers directly related to communication will consistently make the top of the list. So, from this fact we can assume that communication is very important. These quotes from prominent scholars and organizational leaders reflect that same level of stated importance:

You cannot not communicate.[15]

Communication is the substance of organizational life.[16]

Developing excellent communication skills is absolutely essential to effective leadership. The leader must be able to share knowledge and ideas to transmit a sense of urgency and enthusiasm to others. If a leader can't get a message across clearly and motivate others to act on it, then having a message doesn't even matter.

—Gilbert Amelio, president and CEO of National Semiconductor Corporation

Regardless of the changes in technology, the market for well-crafted messages will always have an audience.

—Steve Burnett, The Burnett Group

Skill in the art of communication is crucial to a leader's success. They can accomplish nothing unless they can communicate effectively.

—Unknown

The greatest continuing area of weakness in management practice is the human dimension. In good times or bad, there seems to be little real understanding of the relationships between managers, among employees, and interactions between the two. When there are problems, everyone acknowledges that the cause often is a communication problem.[17]

I could fill pages with statements like these, which could reasonably cause one to believe that communication is revered as one of the most critical aspects of organizational life. However, despite the fact that communication break-downs are squarely on the radar of what to watch out for, communication rarely takes center stage in organizational life. The exceptions occur when things have already gone bad and the consultants are brought in to help.

In our lives before formal entry into the workplace most of what we learn about communication is on the fly. If we are lucky enough to have parents, teachers, or other influential adult relationships we may be directly mentored in communication when we violate certain social rules, interact with others in destructive ways, or step out of line with careless words or behaviors that stem from them. You may build on this foundation with classes in high school and more focused study in college, but most of what you learn is in the trenches of everyday life.

Traditional education environments are not conducive to real-world training on how to communicate at work. Excluding those who study communication directly, the closest most people get to learning about communication challenges at work is a class or two that touches on related themes such as ethics, introduction to business, and so on. For business majors who are a little better prepared, they may take general classes on organizational behavior and management skills, as well as technical courses for delivering great presentations, honing pitch skills, winning negotiation strategies, or persuasion techniques to influence others. However, these are so specialized and one-dimensional they often do little more than create false confidence for students. If you do study communication formally, you are equipped with volumes and volumes of interesting theories, rules, prescriptions for various situations, and conflicting strategies for understanding and approaching communication.

By the time you get to your first real job interview, you have a combination of informal and formal education about what effective communication is and what you need to do to be effective around other people. When you look at the standard job description there will likely be two–three direct references to communication. However, these will be among the most unhelpful, unspecific, unrealistic references to communication you will ever see: Must communicate effectively both verbally and in writing...Must demonstrate excellent communication skills with coworkers and supervisors...Effective communication skills with strategic partners, including the ability to negotiate effectively and to resolve conflict as needed.

Job descriptions are written documents that are intended to communicate the essential roles and functions of a given position. Well-written position descriptions should act as screening tools that draw in qualified candidates and position the interview process to more likely find the "right person" for the job. Based upon the perceived importance of communication at work you might assume that communication would grab many of the headlines with regards to experience and skill sets required. However, in a random audit of available positions advertised on job websites at the time of this book's publication, the following details were provided with direct reference to communication. Statements that indirectly referenced communication such as "the ability to mentor others" or "excellent customer service skills" were not included. One of the things that you will notice immediately is that with an average of about 16 bullet points in the required skills/experience sections, most positions averaged fewer than two references to communication. This finding is particularly surprising with positions that one could imagine require extensive communication expertise:

- HR generalist—Ability to effectively present information to management and employees; this position must be able to communicate with all levels of the organization;
- Technical sales manager—Excellent communication skills; bilingual skills (English/Spanish) are an asset;
- Software engineer—None;
- Senior manager, product line management—Communicate the product's integrated value proposition to the sales team, and develop sales tools that support the selling process; excellent written and oral communication skills;
- Education and training instructor—None;
- Business instructor—Develop and maintain communications with representatives of the business community; strong interpersonal communication skills; and
- Administrative manager—Exceptional people and communication skills.

And, just to check a few very specific kinds of examples, I searched available positions with "communications" in the title. Presumably these roles for the people that literally write the books about communication and are the resident experts in their organizations will have a detailed reference to the art and science of effective communication, right?

- Visiting assistant professor of communication—None;
- Copywriter/editor—Communicates and transfers new copy and revisions to other teams; must possess excellent verbal communication skills; and
- Vice president of communications—Develop and implement an integrated strategic communications plan.

One could argue that the position description is simply an introduction to the role and that as a one- to two-page document it cannot possibly lay out the specific demands of the job with regards to things like communication. While this is true, the glaring absence of any substantive treatment of communication skill and experience on most job descriptions sends a very clear message about the contradiction of communication: On one hand we know it is important to the success of individuals and teams, and yet by not referencing it in any meaningful way, we actually show how unimportant it is (or how little we truly understand about it).

So, is communication a critical skill required for success in the workplace? The answer is "yes" if you go by the volumes of books, training programs, and mentions that communication-based themes receive in the expert chatter about work. A search on Google Books, with the key word "communication" as the filter, produced about 120,000,000 results. A similar search with the key words "workplace communication" produced 948,000 results. A keyword search using "communication" on the Harvard Business Review website, which combines podcasts, articles, books, white papers, and articles, produced 5,224 combined references. It is clear that we talk about communication quite a lot.

Yet, when you examine the everyday functional aspects of how work gets done, you see a different reality. For example, you have read the position description for your desired job and now you are ready for the interview. During your interview, the individual or panel of interview committee members will ask you directly about communication. Unfortunately, these questions (even the ones that are behavioral by nature) will likely be quite superficial. Questions and prompts may include: Describe your communication style, and in particular, how do you work with other team members…Provide an example of a time when you had to communicate diplomatically in stressful situations…When was the last time you received performance feedback from a supervisor, and what did you say in response? Satisfactory responses to these basic questions are anything that suggest the candidate has a modicum of common sense and tact. It is rare that the qualifications, and subsequent questions that test knowledge, skills, and abilities in relation to the required competencies of the job, actually determine whether prospective candidates have the capacity to work well with difficult people, are able to translate competing messages within the context of their organizational goals, and so on.

Once you are on the job, nobody teaches you how to communicate at work. While you may be sponsored to attend a communication class (most likely based on the transmission model), you likely won't hear anything about communication, until there is a problem. From the lack of substantive treatments of communication in the recruitment and selection processes, to the lack of educational resources and support available to organizational members, communication is buried in plain sight…until the next organizational issue surfaces.

I believe that what fuels and sustains this contradiction is the fact that the transmission model of communication has failed us. It does not provide any inherent intelligence about effective communication and it has not produced useful tools that help us get communication right. If it was an effective way of structuring communication, would it not have already translated into useful tools to attract and retain great communicators? Wouldn't job descriptions and interview guides be littered with inquiries that target communication (arguably one of the greatest assets a person can bring to a job and to a new organization)? Wouldn't we have a foolproof way—after four hundred years of using the transmission model of communication as the basis for structuring the way we get work done—of spotting bad communicators who could potentially fail in their roles and undermine the team and the organization's success?

In my experience breakdowns in communication are the primary driver of team dysfunctions. However, it is not a breakdown in the communication process; it is a complete breakdown in the approach.

It turns out that the thing we do most at work—talking and interacting with other people—is the very thing we spend the least amount of time considering. It is usually only when communication and performance breakdowns reach a fever pitch that people give pause to consider how things got to the point where they are at. The challenge is that any time and attention given to assessing communication is clouded by emotional stress that often comes along with those breakdowns. This leads to reactions that are crisis-driven in nature, so the result is more like "putting out fires" and trying to get back to "business as usual." A more effective approach would be to consider the causes of the situation and the underlying dynamics that have to be altered to prevent a reoccurrence of the unwanted event.

A New Approach to Communication at Work

Re-Making Communication at Work signals a fundamental change in our questions about the role of communication at work. For example, rather than asking the question "How can we improve our communication to achieve better relationships, increased trust, and higher quality collaboration?" the question becomes "How can we create the patterns of communication and interaction that will produce experiences of better relationships, increased trust, and higher quality collaboration." If we want to have experiences like high-trust relationships that are a foundation for successful collaboration, then we have to make them through communication.

And in the case of addressing existing problems, the question shifts from "How can we increase our communication to reduce our unresolved conflict, lack of information sharing, inefficiencies, and redundancies?" to "What specific patterns of communication and interaction are making the unwanted experience of unresolved conflict, lack of information sharing, inefficiencies, and redundancies?"

If we do not want to experience conflict, insufficient knowledge of what is happening within the organization, and the wasted time, energy, and resources that result, then we will have to find the unwanted patterns that make them and then re-make those into something better. Once any unwanted pattern of communication and interaction is identified, it can be examined and potentially re-made into more satisfying and productive patterns that match the values and goals of the organization and its people.

Conclusion

The established ways of thinking about organizations and organizational communication no longer provide an effective means to understand and respond to the true challenges of communication at work. Based on the transmission model, which views communication as a static transaction of messages between the sender and receiver, the status quo fails to recognize that communication itself is the dynamic process that shapes our everyday experiences at work.

Despite the fact that many organization and organizational communication theories have been slowly updated to reflect this view, to date they have not been broadly translated into useful resources and practical tools. *Re-Making Communication at Work* fills this gap and offers a road map to successfully navigate everyday communication challenges. The book provides the theoretical foundation and application tools for readers to:

- change their organization's culture from within;
- transform troubled relationships;
- develop more resilience in the face of adversity;
- shift conflict effects from closed-damaging to open-building;
- share information to limit assumptions;
- get collaborative decision-making right;
- make sense of complexity and ambiguity;
- integrate creativity, diversity, and innovation in everyday interactions;
- keep people engaged and on the same page during periods of intense change; and
- increase levels of workplace trust and employee engagement from low to high.

Part I exposes the myths of effective communication at work and replaces those with a new set of principles that match the complexity and pace of change in the new world of work. It continues with three chapters that inte-grate the new principles by *taking a communication perspective at work*, see-ing *where communication counts most in the changing world of work*, and recognizing *communication as a competitive advantage* of the twenty-first century. Part I concludes with a brief summary chapter that consolidates the concepts into an applied perspective on the real-world of work.

Partl

A New Approach to
Communication at Work

1

Old Myths and New Principles for Re-Making Communication at Work

The introduction to this book made the case that the epicenter of the knowledge and skill that defines success for today's employees and leaders is communication. The challenge is that most of what we have learned about successful communication at work is incomplete.

Attempts to illuminate the challenges of workplace communication often result in the same superficial list of ground rules that do little more than prepare people for scripted conversations and muddled strategies for negotiating perspectives. The reason so many of these popular remedies to ineffective communication fall short is that the underlying premise about what successful communication is has been built on a series of myths. *Re-Making Communication at Work* challenges the status quo by exposing the most common myths that inaccurately define successful communication at work.

The conventional wisdom of what works with communication at work needs a reboot. The reason for this overdue refresh is based on those misunderstandings about effective communication at work that have dominated popular business literature, education and training programs, and common practice. Beginning with table 1.1, this chapter explains these dominant myths and offers a new set of principles to replace them for a more effective approach to communication at work.

Forgetting Myth #1

Communication is just an exchange of information and ideas. To get it right, you have to listen well and speak clearly...

This first myth is the most significant because it reflects the lineage of thinking that produces many of the other myths. It turns out that

Table 1.1   Old myths and new principles of communication

Myths of Effective Communication	Re-Making Communication at Work
1. Communication is just an exchange of information and ideas. To get it right, you have to listen well and speak clearly.	Communication is made by complex patterns of interaction. To get the results you want, you have to learn the chemistry, physics, and design elements needed to re-make unwanted patterns. It is not about listening and speaking as much as it is about making the communication patterns that shape our working lives.
2. Effective communication is inevitable with well-designed conversations.	Effective patterns of communication and interaction are not the result of a good conversation. They are formed by coordinating episodes of interaction and making desired choices at the critical turns that come together to shape the pattern.
3. You have to know what you want to communicate and have clear messages for every interaction.	How people communicate is not as important as why. It helps to know what you want to say and what messages you need to deliver, but those things alone do not shape our experience or produce the outcomes we get in communication.
4. Communication only occurs when others are present. The active periods of communication take place when people are together (i.e., at meetings, etc.) and it goes dormant when people are not in direct conversation.	Communication is in constant motion at all times and we continuously enact our patterns when we make meaning and coordinate actions with others—before, during, and after face-to-face interactions.
5. The more you know about other people's preferences and types, the better you'll be able to communicate with them.	Assessments that measure style and type explain part of the picture, but can distract from seeing the powerful stories that give structure to our patterns.

6. Good communication follows a process, and if you follow the right steps, you'll get good results.	Communication is unpredictable. Staying present in the moment reduces pressure to perform according to certain rules and process steps, which keeps you open to seeing the communication as the fluid, generative process that makes our everyday experience.
7. Once you get the hang of it, you can take the same communication approach into every situation.	Nothing stands still and every pattern of communication and interaction varies. Principles can hold true, but approaches to seeing and making diverse patterns of communication vary by context and situation.
8. It takes a lot of time to repair dysfunctional communication dynamics and their aftermath.	Patterns of communication and interaction are held together by strong forces that make them easy to sustain, but hard to change. In the right conditions, patterns of communication can be re-made in an instant or they can be sustained for a lifetime.
9. One person can't do much about communication at work because the organization culture dictates what happens.	You get what you make and you make it *in* communication. If you get the pattern of communication right, you can create different experiences. Culture is simply experience over time.
10. Things are so complex and fast-moving; there is no clear starting place for change.	The first skill you need is the ability to spot the critical moments where your patterns of communication are made. If you can spot these moments, you gain leverage to make something better within the turns and episodes that give structure to the larger patterns of communication and interaction that make your experiences and outcome at work.

communication is not just an exchange of information and ideas. And "getting communication right" requires more than simply listening well and speaking clearly.

> Communication is made by complex patterns of interaction. To get the results you want, you have to learn the chemistry, physics, and design elements needed to re-make unwanted patterns. It is not about listening and speaking as much as it is about intentionally making the communication patterns that shape our working lives.

The roots of this myth go back 400 years to the philosophical ideas of John Locke and David Hume. Although our understanding of human communication has evolved considerably over the last 75 years, including recognition of just how dynamic organizational communication is, many present-day communication practices still reflect these old ideas. Despite the theoretical advance of more effective communication concepts and tools, it was this dominant lineage of theory and practice that stuck as the primary driver and influence of how organizational communication is perceived and addressed.

The prevalence of this one-dimensional way of defining communication, referred to as the transmission model, does beg a very serious question: If the transmission model of communication was effective, then, after all of this time, why are damaging communication problems still among the most widely recognized issues in organizational life? Wouldn't those problems have eased a bit with so much awareness, knowledge, and practice of the related recommendations and prescriptions for getting communication at work right? After all, our technology has improved and the means through which we disseminate information across channels has increased dramatically with new software and hardware devices that deliver a 24/7 world of constant communication and information sharing.

It turns out that there is more to communication than meets the eye and to understand it a more dynamic model than *transmission* is required. For example, we know now that different people can interpret the same message differently. And we know that even the same person can interpret the same message differently at different times depending on factors such as context, prior experience, and assumptions. As individuals we hold onto our own private thoughts and feelings, at times we can confuse and mislead others, and we can be ambiguous—even deceptive—in our communication and interactions in certain circumstances.[1] Above all of this, we know that our life experience and the given context in which we communicate have a significant impact on how we make meaning from our communication with others.

Forgetting Myth #2

Effective communication is inevitable with well-designed conversations.

Conversations generally refer to the face-to-face interactions that people have when they intend to communicate with each other about specific topics in the workplace. Over the last 25 years an entire cottage industry has arisen with numerous approaches to the art and practice of having effective conversations, each one subtly emphasizing a different value or aspect of the process. Whether the lead adjective for these conversations is difficult, crucial, fierce, inclusive, or some other important word, these approaches have suggested that well-designed conversations will result in effective communication. The ideas have been written about in books and taught in seminars around the world and much of the conventional wisdom used by today's managers reflects the pivotal importance of these conversations. However, it is a myth.

> Effective patterns of communication and interaction are not the result of a good conversation. They are formed by coordinating episodes of interaction and making desired choices at the critical turns that come together to shape the pattern.

The very structure of a conversation is based on the transmission model of communication, which fails to include the many complexities of communication that make the success of well-designed conversations anything but inevitable. Typical conversations that reflect the transmission model usually include five general stages, including: the opening, feedforward, business, feedback, and closing.[2] The flow of these conversations—from the first greeting that opens the discussion, to the feedforward statement that gives the person a clue regarding what you want to talk about, to the business or substance of the conversation itself, to the feedback where you signal to the other person that you feel the conversation is complete, to the closing where you transition and say goodbye—involves give-and-take where people share turns speaking and listening. This is pure transmission.

Effective patterns of communication and interaction are not the result of a good conversation, although they can help. They are formed by carefully coordinating ongoing episodes of interaction and making desired choices at the critical turns that shape the pattern.

Forgetting Myth #3

You have to know what you want to communicate and have clear goals for every interaction.

This myth, which is securely bound-up in the transmission model's emphasis on the clarity of the message from sender to receiver, is quite often included in most of the generic advice about effective communication at work. Have a clear message that is tailored to your target audience, know your intended outcome and what you want to happen before you start the difficult conversation, use your goals to guide you when things get off track, and so on. Words of wisdom like this that are inspired by this myth are just not consistent with the average workplace experience.

> How people communicate is not as important as why they do so. It helps to know what you want to say and what messages you need to deliver, but those things alone do not shape our experience or produce the outcomes we get in communication.

If you want a specific experience or outcome (i.e., a clear decision by the end of a conversation, a greater degree of confidence in the potential for collaboration with a prospective partner, a helpful exchange of feedback with a supervisor, etc.), then you have to know what kind of pattern of communication and interaction will make that experience. The emphasis on the words that you speak, the messages you send, and the tone you communicate with your nonverbal cues are relevant, but they have far less to do with what is actually achieved as a result of the communication.

Forgetting Myth #4

Communication only occurs when others are present. The active periods of communication take place when people are together (i.e., at meetings, etc.) and it goes dormant when people are not in direct conversation.

Patterns of communication and interaction are ongoing, and while much of the action occurs when people are present with each other at meetings, presentations, or other face-to-face encounters, the process of making meaning and coordinating action does not stop when direct conversation ends.

> Communication is in constant motion at all times and we continuously enact our patterns when we make meaning and coordinate actions with others—before, during, and after face-to-face interactions.

At the end of a long day you find yourself unable to sleep. You are restless because you are replaying a difficult interaction over and over again in your mind. What did your boss mean when she casually said, "Things may need to change around here"—was it a threat about your job security, was it supposed to motivate you to solve some lingering problem, was she just frustrated about the latest financial report? You spend your sleepless night interpreting that exchange, attempting to make meaning from the interaction, and carefully thinking about your next turn in what is now a potentially serious episode of communication. Will you find her in the morning to try to clarify and set your mind at ease? Will you wait to see what she says or does next? The myriad choices about "next steps" you consider in this episode occurs while you are alone, wishing you could sleep.

Forgetting Myth #5

The more you know about other people's preferences and types, the better you'll be able to communicate with them.

Understanding the unique personalities of our colleagues, including their communication tendencies and habits, is helpful at work. Not only does it allow us to notice potential issues to be aware of, but it positions us to work well with people by complementing their weaknesses with our strengths and vice versa. For example, if I know that one of my peers likes to share ideas freely in meetings and switch topics rapidly as the conversation unfolds, then I can use this knowledge to adjust my approach to the interaction. Perhaps I will be more patient, offer more structured comments to retain a consistent train of thought, or perhaps I will share my perspectives more quickly to be sure they are not lost in transition.

> Assessments that measure style and type explain part of the picture, but can distract from seeing the powerful stories that give structure to our patterns.

Some people are sensitive to group dynamics and others are like a bull in a china shop when it comes to etiquette at team meetings. Some people carefully choose their words, while others shoot from the hip and let their opinions rip. One person may actively seek feedback for improvement, at the same time someone else may fear feedback and be disinclined to seek out the opinions of others. Some people are reluctant to confront authority, while others challenge the status quo and question accepted practices openly and often. Whatever the contrast between these kinds of styles, preferences, and behaviors, the usefulness of this kind of information, about ourselves and others, is limited because "how" people communicate is not as important as "why."

Many of the modern assessments that measure style and type are directly descended from the transmission model of communication. They place a significant emphasis on how people send and receive messages, including the ways that distortion and feedback block clear communication across channels. While grouping people into stereotypical categories (i.e., passive, aggressive, passive-aggressive, and assertive) and naming specific attitudes and behaviors that reflect these general "styles of communication" are useful and may explain part of the picture, they can distract from seeing the powerful stories that explain *why* people communicate the way they do.

Re-making communication looks at the "what," including all of the tangible episodes of communication that reveal what was said and done in the communication interaction. However, it is also inclusive of the "why" so that it goes beyond any superficial stereotypes and provides a way of understanding the deeper interpretive process that people use to make meaning and coordinate their actions.

Forgetting Myth #6

Good communication follows a process, and if you follow the right steps, you'll get good results.

This myth was one of the hardest to debunk for me personally because so much of my work as a "process expert" (i.e., mediator, group facilitator, dialogue and deliberation leader, etc.) involved prescriptions for addressing communication challenges with performance improvement processes that followed fixed steps and sequences of action. Whether it was the three steps to resolving a conflict at work, the seven steps for having effective conversations with difficult people, or the four phases of changing dysfunctional team behaviors, I wanted to believe that a good process could lead to good results every time.

> Communication is unpredictable. Staying present and curious in the moment reduces pressure to perform according to certain rules and process steps, which keeps you open to seeing the communication as the fluid and creative process that makes our everyday experience.

Communication, it turns out, is just too unpredictable and rarely flows in a straight line. Understanding the circular nature of communication (i.e., the nonlinear process of making meaning, coordinating action, and enacting episodes of communication with others) requires us to stay present in the moment and avoid the temptation of either predicting or guessing what will happen next. When we are free to stay present and engaged in the moment, without the pressure to perform according certain rules, expectations, and anticipated process steps, we can see communication as the fluid, generative process that makes our everyday experience and follow where that leads.

Forgetting Myth #7

Once you get the hang of it, you can take the same communication approach into every situation.

Communication interactions are dynamic and nothing ever really stands still. Each and every pattern of communication and interaction is in motion, whether it is being reenforced by the episode that just occurred or being potentially reshaped by the ongoing episode. It is virtually impossible to take an identical approach to communication in every situation because each interaction changes us and the other people involved. So, while we may want to repeat a successful approach because we feel it led to a successful outcome or experience, we cannot because no two interactions are ever the same.

> Nothing stands still and every pattern of communication and interaction varies. Principles can hold true, but approaches to seeing and making diverse patterns of communication vary by context and situation.

There is no one-size-fits-all approach to effective communication at work. As convenient as it sounds to take a conversational format, template, or a set of rules into all of the uncharted territory we move through at work, it is just not realistic. What we can do, however, is understand a set of principles that hold up across a wide range of situations and contexts. These principles, which are outlined in the next several chapters of the book, can inform us of ways to apply what we know to be effective in the unfamiliar territory, rapidly changing situations, and complex terrain that the world of work sets up every day.

Forgetting Myth #8

It takes a lot of time to repair dysfunctional communication dynamics and their aftermath.

It is true that our patterns of communication and interaction are held together by strong forces that make them easy to sustain, but hard to change. However, time is not the difficult factor in the change process. In the right conditions, patterns of communication can be re-made in an instant or they can be sustained for a lifetime. What is difficult is the shift in perspective that is required to see our own involvement in the making of these unwanted patterns of communication and interaction.

If we gain this objective vantage point, we can see the specific attitudes, behaviors, and choices that shape the turns we take within the episodes in which we engage. These episodes, including our contributions and those of others, are what give structure and character to our patterns of communication, which ultimately influence our experience and outcomes at work.

> Patterns of communication and interaction are held together by strong forces that make them easy to sustain, but hard to change. In the right conditions, patterns of communication can be re-made in an instant or they can be sustained for a lifetime. Time is a factor, but it matters much less than the intention and tools required to re-make communication.

Time is required to make these shifts and to pay careful attention to what we make. An investment of time and effort is also required to establish new habits that lead to different choices when we want to re-make an unwanted pattern of communication. The fact that some patterns were formed over years of repeated behavior can mean that they will take "time to change" but time to change is relative to the willingness of people engaged in the pattern of communication to re-make it and the skills they possess to accomplish that.

Forgetting Myth #9

One person can't do much about communication at work because the organization culture dictates what happens.

Re-making communication at work redefines organizational culture in a new way. Rather than seeing culture as some fixed identify that an organization has, culture can be understood simply as *the cumulative patterns of communication and interaction people make over time.* This ecosystem of patterns contains the collective behaviors and meaningful actions of all of the people within the organization. While a single person cannot influence all of the patterns of communication and interaction that are reflected in the culture of that organization, they are very influential in their specific patterns. Since it is our own direct engagement in patterns of communication and interaction that give us our unique vantage point on what organizational culture is, we have significant leverage to potentially change it.

> You get what you make and you make it in communication. If you get the pattern of communication right, you can create different experiences. Culture is simply experience over time.

In this way, the power of a single person is greater than it may seem. Organizational culture is made, and re-made continuously. What we do has an impact on our own patterns of communication and interaction, which in turn will influence the larger ecosystem. If we engage deliberately with other people to intentionally make patterns of communication and interaction that result in specific experiences and outcomes, then we are playing an active role in shaping our organization's culture.

For example, if I say that we have an organizational culture based on fear and distrust, but at the same time I act openly and trustworthy toward the people I interact with most, then I not only challenge my own label of the organization's culture (as one based on fear and distrust), but I also use my communication influence in the organization to create moments of openness and trust that are consistent with what I want to make. These efforts, or the lack of these kinds of initiatives, reflect the way we ultimately feel about the organization and our place in it.

Forgetting Myth #10

Things are so complex and fast-moving; there is no clear starting place for change.
The complexity of communication, combined with the immense pressure of work, can make the starting place for positive change elusive. When we see patterns of communication and interaction as completed, final outcomes, it further erodes our confidence and motivation to attempt change. This is one of the reasons that really well-intentioned people can sustain so many unwanted patterns that result in things like troubled relationships, disengagement on the job, poor performance, and more.

> The first skill you need is the ability to spot the critical moments where your patterns of communication are made. If you can spot these moments, you gain leverage to make something better within the turns and episodes that give structure to the larger patterns of communication and interaction that make your experiences and outcome at work.

If you sit down to a five-course meal and examine the table, including all of the splendid dishes made from complex recipes and dynamic ingredients, you may not immediately see what you are really seeing. However, if you ask how a dish was made, and apply that question along with a little focused attention to each dish, you slowly see the actual interpretations of choices, sequence of actions, and coordinated effort that made it. A steaming plate of elegant potatoes au gratin is the choice of potato variety, the technique of peeling and slicing, the selection of cheese, and the degree of preference for creaminess, saltiness, and crispiness. Following this analogy even further, the beautiful pomegranate salad with vibrant colors of green and red is the willingness of the chef to be creative, the unpredictable availability of fresh ingredients, the intention to provide something refreshing to the diner, and the importance of color on the table. Potatoes are so much more than potatoes and salads reveal so much more than nutritious greens.

Like dishes in a five-course meal, our patterns of communication and interaction can be seen as the related episodes that make them. When we ask the key question—how was that made—we can examine each turn within each episode to understand the specific mix of attitudes, choices, and behaviors that influenced the experience it created. The starting place for re-making communication at work is developing the skill to recognize episodes and spot the critical moments within them. If you can learn to see "what you are seeing," you gain leverage to consider, choose, and ultimately make something better.

Old Myths in Disguise

Fixing communication issues with the transmission model is like painting a smiley face on a dead rat. Years ago I heard this poetic phrase from a grizzled military commander who had a unique way of summing up the brutal facts of reality in just a few simple words. While it sounds a bit extreme, the analogy fits. Dressing up the look of a dysfunctional pattern of communication and interaction, without changing the underlying functions that hold it in place, is an exercise in futility. That is why so much time, energy, and money is wasted on transmission-based approaches to addressing communication problems. Teambuilding interventions, communication skills training, anger management courses, and off-site strategy retreats are just the transmission model of communication dressed up in a tuxedo. They may improve the appearance of the situation in the short term, but eventually you're reminded that you still have a rat.

Myths and New Principles in Action

The old myths about effective communication at work focus on the superficial elements and transactional nature of communication. The new approach looks at communication as the driving force that makes the experiences and outcomes we get at work. Consider the following scenarios and notice which of these pivotal turns reflect the old myths or the new approach:

Scenario A

Vice president of R&D: "This is the third time in two months that our teams have gotten signals crossed. We caught it in time—again—but I'm afraid that the next mistake is going to catch the CEO's attention and cause a major problem."

Vice president of sales: "I agree that this is a real concern. We need to figure out what is at the core of these issues."

Vice president of R&D: Okay, so what do you suggest…more meetings to share information, more memos to put timelines and talking points in writing? We have got to get the communication right!"

Vice president of sales' pivotal turn:

1. "I agree: we need to add an additional weekly meeting to make sure information sharing is consistent and effective."
2. "It seems like we have a recurring pattern here. If we do not change something fundamental we will likely just keep repeating it. I think we need to invest some time in looking at the way our groups interact. This could reveal the breakdown and help us craft our next response so that it pushes the trajectory of this pattern of miscommunication in the direction we want to take it."

Scenario B

Manager: "To get our working relationship off to a good start, I'd like you to take this personality and skills assessment. Among other things, it will help me get to know your preferred style of communication."

Employee: "That sounds great. I think it will be a good investment of our time to talk about how to work well together."

Manager: "If there are sensitive conversations we need to have down the road, this will show us the steps to get them right."

Employee's pivotal turn:

1. "Yes, I agree."
2. "I think it is always helpful to learn about styles and preferences. More than any single conversation, I think the habits we develop in our everyday interactions will give us the best chance to work well together. What kinds of daily exchanges do you think will lay the foundation for my solid performance and our good working relationship?"

Scenario C

First colleague: "I'm sick and tired of going round and round in circles! It seems like each week we have new marching orders from corporate."

Second colleague: "I think I have whiplash from changing directions so often."

First colleague: "I'm going to tell Carl that this has got to stop! We're burning through resources on all of these unfinished projects."

Second colleague's pivotal turn:

1. "I'll go with you. I want to let him know that I'm frustrated too."
2. "I agree; he needs to know what's going on. Before we set the meeting, I think it would be helpful if we took a few minutes to map out how this strategic merry-go-round affects the communication, decision-making, and trust within our team. We can show him the specific impact this makes for us when a strategic decision is announced one quarter, then a contradictory announcement is made the next."

If you noticed that the second-level responses in each scenario reflected the new approach, then you are starting to take a communication perspective. In these pivotal turns, there is no unnecessary jargon and no avoidance or postponement of the real issue. Instead, there is an intentional approach to seeing what communication makes and revealing how the next turn in the episode could make something better in the ongoing pattern of communication and interaction.

Communication Matters: We Say It Like We Mean It

Now that you have seen the old myths and new principles defined up close, it might be helpful to see how the old myths commonly show up in the ways that leaders talk about them. Imagine you have been asked to share a few words of wisdom with a new group of recently promoted managers who are about to receive their assignments to lead a variety of teams within a large organization. They are finishing a leadership training program that was designed to "equip them for success on the job" and you have been asked to speak about the importance of effective communication at work, including an honest assessment of what it will take for them to perform well. If you are like most leaders, your talking points about effective communication will likely include many of the well-worn descriptions of what makes good communication and when it should be practiced, including the following:

1. Communication is something you will really want to pay attention to, especially as a leader; your words will count quite a lot.
2. It will be important for you to really know your audience and to be willing to change your approach to get your message across clearly to others with different styles of communication.
3. When things hit a rough patch with someone, ask how they prefer to communicate and then try to accommodate their preferred approach if possible.

4. Your words say a lot, but your nonverbal cues say much more. Remember that your total communication includes your presence, posture, and body language.

5. Try to communicate good content and always get to the point. People are busy and you show them respect when you cut to the chase.

6. Take your time with communication. It shows people that they matter when you spend time in conversation with them.

7. Leaders should listen—I mean really listen to what others think and feel.

8. A great way to listen effectively is to ask people good questions, even when the topic of conversation could be sensitive or difficult to discuss.

9. When people make suggestions or contribute ideas during meetings, try not to say "great idea, but…here's why it won't work." People do not want to hear how great their idea is right before it is shot down.

10. When communication goes wrong a lot of feelings can get hurt. People can have a hard time forgetting, so the more proactive you can be the less damage control you will have to do.

11. So many difficult challenges at work can be traced back to poor communication. Spend time talking openly with your staff about challenges so that they can share concerns clearly; you should have an open-door policy.

12. One thing that will ruin communication every time is when people get unclear information and start to question the integrity of what they hear. All of your efforts to communicate should be honest and consistent.

13. Sometimes it is tempting to say things in a way that people want to hear it, but "communicating just to be liked" always backfires eventually.

14. If you see a conflict you should try to resolve it quickly, but let people work it out on their own if possible. Things can fester and sometimes others will get pulled in as well. If you have to get involved, listen to both sides and really encourage people to be reasonable.

15. Say it once, say it again, and then say it another time! If the message is something really important, tell people at a meeting, put it in an email, then follow up individually if you can.

These descriptions are nice, they are accurate to some degree, and they will undoubtedly serve as useful advice to an eager new group of managers. However, they all reflect the transmission model of communication and reinforce the old myths in some way. The effect of this is a further isolation of communication apart from the rest of work. Communication *is* the work we do. Within each of these words of wisdom, the communication perspective would reveal the complex patterns of communication and interaction that create the outcomes the very same advice cautions against.

Conclusion

The principles of re-making communication at work shatter popular myths about effective communication that view it as nothing more than a process of verbal and nonverbal exchanges where the goal is to transfer information, interpret messages, and act in response. Known as the transmission model of communication, this approach is the basis for many educational programs and popular business books. When efforts to teach workplace communication practices are delivered in these superficial terms—no matter how fancy, elaborate, or compelling—they fail to address the underlying causes of ineffective collaboration, unresolved conflict, poor decision-making, misaligned strategic priorities, and the troubled relationships that prompt the need for "improved communication" in the first place.

The new definition of successful communication at work starts with the ability to recognize the patterns of communication and interaction where decisions get made, relationships are built, organizational culture is solidified, and the trajectory for ultimate business outcomes are set into motion. Applying this new definition in the real world of work requires a communication perspective. Chapter 2 defines what this means in detail and describes a tangible method for doing it.

2

Taking a Communication Perspective at Work

Letting go of the old myths about effective communication is the first step in re-making communication at work. The second step is taking a communication perspective in each area of your working life. Drawing on Pearce and Cronen's development of CMM (coordinated management of meaning) theory, the phrase "communication perspective" has been described in diverse ways and it has come to mean different things. For me, it is just a shorthand way of remembering that: communication actually makes things, and the patterns of communication and interaction that we engage in at work shape our experience, influence our outcomes, and color the quality of our working lives. A communication perspective at work becomes the lens through which you can see the patterns you engage in for what they are and what they can be.

More than just a profound thought to consider, the communication perspective is actually something you do. This is why this chapter's title is subtly worded with the active verb "taking," rather than saying "having a communication perspective." So, if we are serious about re-making communication at work, we need to "take" a communication perspective because it allows us to look at communication (not through it) as the process we participate in to cocreate our organizations.

The word "perspective" implies that we can see communication. When we start to look at communication it brings objective distance, which gives room to step away from the patterns we engage in to glimpse our role and place in the larger process. This vantage point separates us from the strong feelings we sometimes hold about our patterns (e.g., "I know I'm doing the right thing here...even though it feels lousy" or "They dropped the ball and need to change, so I will just keep resisting until they come around"). Without the strong reaction to justify, defend, and advocate, the space gives us the chance to be curious about how things got made in the first place and what may be required if you want to make something different.

Digging deeper, we can see that the call to take a communication perspective is a paradigm shift that signals a new way of approaching the typical way we communicate. Similar to the fixed assumptions embedded in the transmission model of communication, it is based on assumptions and related principles:

1. Communication is substantial and the tangible patterns we engage in represent something meaningful to look at, not just through.
2. Communication is consequential and our patterns create and sustain things.
3. The meaning and results of our experience are not predetermined by external variables but are shaped by the quality and patterns of our interactions with others.
4. We can actually "see" what reality is being made in our interpretive turn-by-turn communication interactions with others.
5. The stories we tell about what we "see" and experience are infused with complexity and have multiple meanings.
6. Our working lives—the cumulative experiences and interactions with events and people—are given meaning by our interpretations of them.
7. With living stories we can reflect on what we made, choose to make something different, and use specific tools and approaches to re-make the patterns of communication and interaction that shape our experience.
8. If we are able to transform our patterns of communication, then we gain powerful leverage for transforming the world of work.

With these assumptions and foundational principles as a starting place, when leaders learn the chemistry, physics, and design rules of communication, including how to intentionally shape their patterns of interaction, they gain a powerful tool to meet the challenge of engaging people, managing complexity, and leading their teams through change.

On the Doorstep of Seeing Communication

Considering the near-universal acceptance of the myths of effective communication at work, the interesting thing is that our everyday language shows how poised we are to re-make communication at work, despite how deeply embedded the transmission model really is. Pay attention to these common phrases:

- "I *see* your point!"
- "Let's *take a look* at it together."
- "I want to be sure we are matching, what is your *picture* of what we need to accomplish?"

- "We will start our session by creating a *vision* of the future we want."
- "Why can't you just *see it* my way for a change?"

These common phrases indicate that our visual capacity for seeing communication is more than present; it is already in use at some level. Taking a communication perspective is the process of sharpening these instincts and using them as a resource to navigate the complexity of communication.

When I teach people to take a communication perspective in their working lives there is a common progression. Each step along the way holds a few moments of insight that together can be transformative. This progression reflects the journey across the major contexts of our interactions, including: intrapersonal (me), to interpersonal (me and a few key people), to group (me and the team), and organizational (all of us). It also reflects the relative position of the individual (you) within each. At each level, there are a few focused questions and related actions that help us take a communication perspective and create the scaffolding to gain an elevated perspective,[1] which increases our capacity to shape patterns at each successive level. Here are the questions, along with sample responses from people in different organizations, that can illustrate how insight-provoking the prompts can be.

Individual

- When I think about the patterns of communication and interaction that shape my working life, what am I making?

  "I experience a lot of stress and never really feel settled. I seem to be making a potential pattern of burn out."

- Can I spot some of the recurring episodes that shape these larger patterns of communication and interaction?

  "My Monday mornings are full of anxiety and I hit the ground running without clearing my mind and focusing on my plan for the week. These are my 'scatter-brain' episodes."

- Is it difficult to notice and name subtle turns within these episodes?

  "Yes, I seem to only notice the stress from the week once it shows up in my kinked neck and short temper...I need to spot the stress-sustaining choices I make sooner."

- Am I able to recognize and call attention to the distinctions among people and the stories they tell about how we are working?

  "Not really, I usually inadvertently just blame the people and circumstances around me for the stress I feel, when I am actually right in the middle of all that."

- Overall, what do I see when I "look at my communication" at work?

"I see a lot of effort, but it often results in me 'spinning my wheels' and wasting a lot of energy. My habits of rushing and always running on empty are also hurting my performance and productivity; this isn't sustainable!"

Team

- When I think about the patterns of communication and interaction that shape my important relationships at work (e.g., my boss, key colleagues, etc.), what are we making?

"I see some nice friendships, easy conversations, and spending time outside of work. With some people I can trust them and collaborate pretty effortlessly with them. I also see a few challenging relationships where I honestly wish I didn't have to work with a few difficult team members. With my boss, there are some subjects we both intentionally avoid because it is just easier."

- Can I spot some of the recurring episodes that shape these larger patterns of communication and interaction? Do the others see them as well?

"Overall I think our team works pretty well together, although we seem to have this habit of coasting a bit. It seems like the accountability comes and goes, which doesn't really challenge people to excel all that much. I think most people who are engaged can see it."

- Can I separate my contributions and the subtle turns I take within these episodes from others?

"Sometimes I think I can tell what I add to the mix. It seems like I will speak up occasionally when things get off track. Honestly though, I often just go with the flow because I wonder what the point is of trying to push others when I'm not the 'big boss.'"

- What kind of hold do the most dominant patterns of communication and interaction seem to have on us?

"This particular pattern, which I'll call 'just cruising along,' seems to have us in a pretty firm grip. Nothing is really great, but nothing is really bad. This allows us to keep the status quo going. I assume that it is what people want in their experience at work."

Organizational

- When I think about the patterns of communication and interaction that our culture reflects, what are we making?

"We are all about solving problems and adding value to our customers. We talk a lot about a workplace culture that rewards people for going above and beyond. Some people just give it lip service because the phrase has been used so much it has kind of lost its meaning. If you look at our competitive position in the market, I'm not sure how consistently we live up to the aspirations of our culture though."

- Can I spot some of the recurring episodes that shape these larger patterns of communication and interaction of leaders, of followers, and the interface between the two?

"I think when we had the last round of layoffs and the salary freeze after the recession, people started thinking less about going above and beyond for the customers and more about survival. Those were tense times and it was a turn for the worse. When we have our all-hands meetings I can still see the remnants of those in the form of skepticism about the future and some mild distrust toward management."

- Overall, can others see these patterns and the affects they have?

"While I don't know how openly it is discussed; people know we struggle with getting everyone on the same page about the future of our company. Sometimes I wonder if everyone is able to connect the dots between our big slump and things like retention and employee engagement."

- If a group of people within the organization wanted to create change of some kind, could they accomplish that in a reasonable way?

"I think an honest acknowledgement of the challenge of change is important. Some days I believe that our more progressive teams can make things happen, but I also doubt because of how slow our executive leadership is to respond. It would have to be the right people, at the right time, to make a big move."

Questions like these facilitate a communication perspective. While the sample responses here reflect general examples, responding to them with your own organizational frame of reference can be a useful exercise. In the following chapters I will introduce a series of practical tools that will allow you to take questions like these down to the level of action.

Where to Direct Your Communication Perspective at Work

Many of the common "breakdowns in communication" that make it hard for us to get our best work done stem from what Kingsley Davis called the "double reality." In essence, there is always a double reality where on the one hand we have a complete system of attitudes and beliefs about "what ought to be," or what should happen in a given circumstance. On the other hand, there is the factual order of "what is." These two realities are not identical, but neither are they ever really separate.[2] The constant tension between our beliefs about what people ought to do and say and how they should behave and act confound us time and again when they simply do not conform. After coaching hundreds of people across a variety of organizations I have come to believe that the gap between our expectations and experience, which sustains this double reality, is the most useful starting place for change.

Taking a communication perspective at work allows us to see how the double reality plays out in the everyday episodes we engage in. When we take a seat in our boss's office for our annual performance appraisal meeting, we walk into the room with a whole lot of expectations about how we think things might, should, could, and ought to go. From the supervisor's vantage point, they also bring some clear expectations about how things should go. Among other things, employees may expect acknowledgment for their valued contributions, praise for their accomplishments, and constructive input on their areas for growth. Employees may feel like they "must advocate" for themselves if what they hear does not match their own opinions or if their supervisor has overlooked some critical accomplishment. Supervisors, on the other hand, may expect a coachable attitude, willingness to hear feedback, and a level of concern for performance and accountability in their work. They may feel like they "must hold their ground" if the employee evades the important feedback and does not show an adequate level of responsibility-taking for the challenge. As anyone who has had their performance evaluated or who has given a performance review can tell you, these expectations are often unmet in both directions.

How we interpret these gaps influences the meaning we make from them and the subsequent actions we take. If we interpret the performance review as *exceeding our expectations*, we may feel that we were being "harder on ourselves" than others, and our boss's demeanor and approach to the meeting was a supportive and pleasant surprise. The experience and result of that *open episode* undoubtedly shapes the likelihood of the next one to follow a similar course. It would be easy to image the next episode as one of "increased pride, focus, and engagement in your work" or "confidence to take on new challenges" or "leverage to ask for a promotion in the near future."

If, however, the review goes poorly and the feedback does not match our own expectations about what we thought we should hear, then we may feel like we are misunderstood, undervalued, or even retaliated against. The likelihood that this *closed episode* will influence the next one accordingly is high. Episodes that we might call "doing the bare minimum," "tuning up the resume and planning the escape," or "sulking to show how wrong s/he was" would not be uncommon following a difficult performance appraisal like this.

This performance evaluation example is just one of the many recurring episodes that shape our ongoing patterns at work. As you can see from the example, taking a communication perspective potentially changes how you think about your work, talk about your work, and act into your work with others. It becomes the basis for moves that close or open something in ourselves and others. These openings become the scaffolding for something better when the presence of an unwanted pattern threatens the quality of our working lives and our individual, team, and organizational performance.

Once we have awareness of and take ownership for the conditions that make patterns, we become active builders in our world of work. This is a key differentiator in talent today and at the end of part I, I will elaborate on the ways re-making communication at work can give you a significant competitive advantage in your ongoing challenge of standing out, getting ahead of the change curve, and staying relevant at work.

Listening for Stories

When training groups to begin taking a communication perspective in their work, I often describe that old anecdote about a chance encounter between canines. Two dogs meet on the street and one says to the other: "Hi, my name is NO! NO! STOP THAT! BAD DOG! What's yours?" How did that dog come to know its name? What stories were told about the dog that solidified its identity?

The communication perspective at work sharpens our ability to hear the labels, names, and stories that explain our own experiences and those of others. Stories help us make sense of our interactions and find meaning within them, which makes our stories our teachers. One fundamental way of thinking about change is to think about altering our stories of what was, what is, and what might be. Taking a communication perspective makes it easier to re-cast the stories people tell at work and to see how those subtle shifts can alter their ongoing patterns of communication and interaction.

Stories are much more than hypothetical. They are tangible clues about the attitudes, feelings, and behaviors that people may not directly express. For example, bumping into a colleague in the hallway and catching an earful about their opinion on the newly hired regional manager could be an unproductive situation to get away from as soon as possible. Alternatively, it could be a chance to listen to a potentially important story that reflects how one person at work is making sense of the latest leadership transition. The story they tell undoubtedly exposes the way they feel about the change, including clues about their willingness to support the change and "be on board" with what results.

This is an example from the personal level, but stories are relevant to the highest macro level as well, organization structure and culture. If you ever want to understand complex organizational processes such as change management, you can look to the stories to understand them. The renowned coach and thought leader, Peter Bregman, described the power of stories this way: "You change a culture with stories… If you want to change the culture, you have to change the stories."[3]

New Perspective, New Questions

When you take a communication perspective, the traditional ways of talking about communication at work change. When communication is understood as one of the primary processes through which work gets done, we recognize it everywhere. This changes the way we ask questions about what we have and what we want:

- "How can I be a better communicator?" turns into "How can I use my patterns of communication and interaction to achieve outcomes that match my priorities?"
- "We need to improve our communication around here!" becomes "We need to develop a clear picture of the preferred patterns of communication that will ease these headaches and create the closer collaboration that we need!"
- "We have a communication problem on our team" shifts to "We need to look at what our communication is making and pinpoint the blocks that reduce our team's effectiveness."
- "S/he is a horrible communicator!" becomes "I don't value the patterns of communication s/he makes because they do not meet my needs."

One unfortunate side effect of communication breakdowns is that when they get ugly, we have a tendency to villainize the other people involved. In over 15 years of conflict mediation I have rarely seen evidence of purposeful intentions to hurt others. Much of the typical frustration and pain from unresolved conflict and broken communication is due mostly to unspoken and unmet expectations and accidental oversights that festered. Taking a communication perspective allows us to ask the question: How can a group of talented people with good intentions make such unwanted experiences and outcomes at work? Questions like these can restore the objective curiosity needed to explore how things were made, rather than the spirit of advocacy to prove who was in the right and who was in the wrong.

The old quip that *National Geographic doesn't publish excuses, just pictures* rings true here. People experience behavior, not intentions. Our visible communication behaviors are the raw material from which others interpret, make meaning, and take their own next action. The communication perspective helps us see these and as a result we do far less guessing about ambiguous intentions, what was meant versus what was said and heard, and so on.

The Communication Perspective Is Improvisational

The world of improvisation can also teach us important aspects of communication. A great teambuilding exercise to do with a group is to create a few

prompts, or have people suggest them on the fly, and invite different configurations of the team to take the theme and run with it. It is amazing how
people, within just a few minutes, are able to create vignettes and scenes that
reflect the patterns of communication and interaction of everyday working
life. These can be hilarious, but also real in the sense that they can evoke a
range of emotions and responses to the action. What this suggests is that
people know how patterns are made, how they are enacted, and how they play
a role in making sense of what we see.

The interesting thing about improv is that it is not random. There are
some suggested rules that players can follow and these rules are catalysts for
the next turn in the action when things could potentially stall out or move
in directions that break the continuity of the story being told. I like the way
Tina Fey summarized her rules for improv in her book *Bossypants*, which are
highlighted here:

> The first rule of improvisation is AGREE. Always agree and SAY YES... The
> second rule of improvisation is not only to say yes, but YES, AND. You are sup-
> posed to agree and then add something of your own... The next rule is MAKE
> STATEMENTS. This is a positive way of saying "Don't just sit around and ask
> questions all the time" [and]... The best rule: THERE ARE NO MISTAKES,
> only opportunities... and beautiful happy accidents.[4]

Here is an example of how I use these ideas to take a communication perspective in the real world of work. I coached the CEO of a small technology firm who hired me in to help re-make the culture of the organization.
In his words things "had turned toxic" during the last few difficult years.
That tumultuous period had produced layoffs and several difficult leadership
transitions. Prior to my arrival, this leader had spent thousands of dollars
on "team building" facilitation and "communication skills training" experts
to address the issues, but those proved too superficial to get at the underlying problems. He was just desperate enough to try a different approach,
and after learning about my way of working he agreed to work together. The
project began with a session for all managers in the company and I designed
an improv activity so I could get a read on the flexibility of how people interacted with each other (and have a bit of fun).

Following the activity, I discussed the ways we make our experience at
work from the same kinds of patterns of communication and interaction that
we just "whipped up" during the improv activity. Rather than random themes
like "a goose crosses the road" or "crying babies at the movie theatre," we act
out scenes, tell stories, and make patterns that we could call "the wasted staff
meeting" and "what nobody says, but everybody thinks." Delving into the
depths of these real examples challenged the group and several people opened
up in ways that led us down a few very productive avenues of discussion. This
was also a great opportunity to highlight the fact that, in addition to many of

the difficult and dysfunctional patterns that made their organizational culture feel "toxic" to so many people, there were helpful patterns that revealed strong relationships and character-affirming strengths to build upon.

During a break, I remember the leader who sponsored the engagement approaching me at the coffee station with a gleam in his eye, and saying, "This was so much easier when all we had to remember to communicate well was to make good eye contact and let one person speak at a time."

The Subject-Object Shift

Another way of talking about this new communication perspective at work is to reference what Robert Kegan called the subject-object shift. He describes a key to any transformational learning as the shift from the "subject," which includes unquestioned assumptions, values, theories, and the related attitudes and behaviors that we take for granted, to the "object." Things that are object can be seen objectively and evaluated with a degree of independent-mindedness. When something is subject, we take it for granted (believing it is true, useful, or simply a fact of life) and as a result are unable to reflect, consider, and assess its validity and value to us.[5]

The subject perspective is pervasive in the most common complaints about people in communication, for example:

"He is such a jerk! Why can't he listen to other people's ideas?"
"They just don't get it."
"She means well, but she just can't track the conversation."

Re-making communication at work is the evolution from subject, to object. Making communication visible and giving people tangible patterns of interaction to look at opens up a world of potential reflection and learning. Dislodging our subjective vantage point and moving toward a more objective treatment of communication is hard. After all, the taken-for-granted approach to seeing our role in communication events is deeply embedded for most of us. However difficult it may be, the shift is an important step for embracing the increasing levels of complexity that are actually involved in communication. The short-cuts, quick assumptions, and fixed beliefs (that all require no effort to challenge) afforded by the subject perspective make little room for complexity. The object perspective does. Here is what the shift looks like:

"He is such a jerk! Why can't he listen to other people's ideas?" = He is holding persistently to a belief that his views are right. How did he come to feel that way and what does he want me to know or do about it?

"They just don't get it." = The people that have to be on board with this idea either do not like it (and refuse to say so) or perhaps they have no reference points to understand the way it is being described.

"She means well, but she just can't track the conversation." = The intentions behind her words seem genuine; however, I'm disappointed because I don't think she understands the potential within my ideas.

The capacity to be neutral toward our own contributions to communication—especially when what we do not like about a pattern is us—allows us to refrain from judging ourselves and making hard assumptions that slip us back into subject mode. If there was ever a time where the old adage "easier said than done" was true, it is with this shift. To conclude this chapter and continue offering insights to support the application of these concepts, here are three final notes about taking a communication perspective at work that may help to clarify any remaining points of confusion.

Stay Calm, Just Act Unnaturally

Taking a communication perspective at work can result in unnatural acts, which is a good thing! It requires new muscles and new movements, which may feel foreign until new muscle memories are made. "When we assume that 'acting naturally' is what brings us to any situation that we perceive as needing to be changed, the one sure recipe for preserving that which we want to change is to continue to act naturally."[6] Acting unnaturally, including whatever uncomfortable feelings it may bring, reminds us that we are in the realm of movement toward potential change.

Talk Is Action

I vividly remember one of the first times I led a group of senior leaders through a "re-making communication at work" program. One of the pivotal leaders in the room interrupted me after the fifty-seventh time I used the word "communication," and said: "This is all well and good, but talk is cheap. We need to take action and *do* things to turn our situation around." I could feel the room slipping away from me as others nodded their heads in quiet agreement. He made an important point—action is usually felt in changed attitudes, behaviors, and outcomes, not in the words we hear.

In nervous response, I explained that our meeting—at this very moment— was accomplishing multiple objectives simultaneously. Yes, we were talking, but we were also exchanging constructive ideas, learning about information that was previously unknown, and creating a habit of open engagement that was sorely missing. Thankfully, the CEO stepped in at that moment to say, "In the last three years I don't think we have spent this much time in one room, with the full leadership team present, talking about what matters to us. This is precisely the kind of action I expected."

Communicating as a Way of Being

Peter Vaill, the organization development pioneer, established the concept of "learning as a way of being."[7] He meant that learning is not something you do in one specific context (i.e., training program, seminar, etc.) and then stop. It is something that goes on continuously and extends into all aspects of life. His metaphor convinced me that we need to consider communication in much the same way: communicating as a way of being. Here is the logic model: If to be human is to interpret our experience and take action based on the meaning we make from it...and if communication is the process of making meaning and coordinating action...then to be human is to be in communication. Communication is a way of being human...*communicating as a way of being.*

Conclusion

Taking a "communication perspective at work" is a way of remembering that: communication actually makes things, and the patterns of communication and interaction that we engage in at work shape our experience, influence our outcomes, and color the quality of our working lives. A communication perspective at work is the lens through which you can see the patterns of communication and interaction you engage in for what they are and what they can be once they are re-made in ways that align with your highest values and aspirations.

Taking a communication perspective at work increases the capacity to look at everyday patterns of communication and interaction objectively, without the need to justify and defend the stories we tell and the reasons we give for the things we say and do. This subject-object shift allows you to see the hidden side of communication, including the origins of the deeply held attitudes, beliefs, prior experiences, and untold aspirations they influence. Once the communication perspective is your focus, new questions, possibilities, and pursuits open up in ways that reveal the full spectrum of communication challenges and opportunities. Chapter 3 describes where communication counts most in the changing world of work, which helps to focus the communication perspective.

3

Where Communication Counts Most in the Changing World of Work

In the chapters that follow you will learn about the subtle and powerful ways in which our everyday patterns of communication and interaction with people at work influence the major aspects of our performance on the job. You will also see that these patterns not only impact our performance and shape the quality of our working lives, but they mark the character of our teams, give our organizations their structure, and reflect the identity of their cultures.

The implication of this within organizations is that we can re-make the undesired ones in ways that improve achievement levels of individual and team performance goals, organizational development initiatives, and culture change efforts. To translate this from concept to action, part II presents a complete knowledge guide for re-making communication at work and part III offers a practice guide to deconstructing unwanted patterns and re-making new ones.

In order to get the running start you need for these later chapters, the purpose of this chapter is to identify specific examples where organizational communication counts most in the changing world of work, including the many reasons why re-making communication is a vital resource for anyone with a stake in their individual, team, and organizational success at work.

Where Doesn't Communication Count?

It is perhaps more fitting to ask the leading question of this chapter in reverse: where doesn't communication count in the changing world of work? The introduction of this book presented a perspective of communication at work that is all-encompassing and showed how it pervades every meaningful aspect of our organizational lives. It follows that the specific answer to the question "where does organizational communication count most in the changing world of work" is "everywhere, all the time." Although this wide-sweeping response is accurate, it is not particularly helpful when you need to understand the specific intersections of people and work where communication can go right and result in important outcomes, or go wrong and significantly reduce performance. One of the most effective ways to summarize these interfaces is by referring to the collection of these intersections as the "communication bundle."

The Communication Bundle

Organizational life includes a spectrum of activities that vary depending on the specific role and function we perform in our organization. Within each of

Table 3.1   The communication bundle

What we do at work	What we really do (When we are doing what we do at work)
• Planning and coordinating our tasks and responsibilities	• Figuring out what we can do that will add the most value to the team and organization
• Interacting with other people formally and informally	• Avoiding people who will waste our time and seeking people out who can help us work better
• Setting individual and team goals and priorities	• Interpreting company goals in relation to our own responsibilities
• Attending training and on-the-job learning	• Staying relevant by increasing our learning and performance
• Building rapport and trust with colleagues during meetings	• Building great relationships with allies who can help us succeed and get ahead
• Sharing information, making decisions, and responding to change	• Trying to stay one step ahead of the latest change in order to avoid getting blindsided by potentially challenging situations
• Identifying issues and resolving conflicts	• Picking battles and figuring out when to stand up, or step aside
• Developing strategic plans and long-term goals	• Looking for ways to influence the future, rather than reacting to circumstances
• Completing compliance and procedural checks	• Doing what is needed to avoid mistakes
• Addressing unexpected situations as they arise	• Living in the whitespace of the organization chart where people and responsibilities are often ambiguous*

*Whitespace refers to the often unexpected interactions between people and functions that are not formally noted in things like organizational charts. Rummler and Brache wrote about the subject and are credited with popularizing the concept. Geary Rummler and Alan Brache, *Improving Performance: How to Manage the White Space in the Organization Chart* (San Francisco, CA: Jossey Bass Business and Management Series, 1995).

these categories of activity, there are many subtle initiatives that we take before, during, and after to ensure their success. I call the wide range of these interfaces the "communication bundle" because collectively they reflect the major interactions that make patterns of communication. The most common, value-added endeavors that I see targeted in organizations are included in table 3.1.

With a communication perspective, you can use the communication bundle to quickly locate yourself in the environment. Each domain listed here includes a series of related endeavors and activities, each with their own communication patterns that play out in the course of everyday interactions of people at work. Looking at the way you work will help you see more than just the tasks and activities that reflect the patterns we make. For example, "managing change" is included in the communication bundle and there are many common patterns of communication and interaction that show up with relation to change management efforts (several are outlined later in this book). Managing change then is no longer just about the process of identifying external and internal trends, assessing their potential impact, scenario planning adaptive responses to the potentially new conditions, and then proactively implementing a change plan to meet the challenges or take advantage of the opportunities. It is also the exploration of the very concrete patterns of interaction that facilitate adoption or resistance to changing conditions.

Great Communication at Work

According to the well-respected Great Place to Work® Institute, which has spent the last quarter century refining a research-based model to determine the best places to work, the three factors that signal an employee's belief that they work for a great organization include: trust in the people they work for; pride in what they do; and enjoying the people they work with.[1] These three factors are nuanced and the full version of their model assesses the level of credibility, fairness, and respect within employee-leader relationships, the sense of camaraderie within employee-employee relationships, and the degree of pride that individuals hold regarding their own contribution to their organization.

When I analyze these factors, including the statements on their full culture audit, I can see that there are many aspects of communication within each of them. For example, communication at work can directly increase levels of trust in leaders as a result of transparency in issue identification, creating choice through participation, and the empowerment that comes with peer-to-peer contribution to problem solving. Pride in work is elevated when the quality of working life is considered and specific patterns are created that give people a direct avenue to contribute their best work to the highest priorities. And camaraderie is enriched among colleagues when there is an authentic and respectful exchange of perspectives and ideas.

Surveys that measure individual perceptions about factors like this are great. They are especially useful when they point us toward the more meaningful aspects of peoples' experience, which can be explored in more detail. The challenge with surveys is that they are often reduced to the search for a killer app, the secret sauce, the magic formula, or essential tool kit for great communication, which is just distracting. Rather than looking at the effects of communication, as most surveys do, looking *at communication* as the source of our experience is the more effective starting place. Drawing upon conventional wisdom, including elements of the Great Place to Work culture audit, I look at where communication counts with this perspective:

For Me

- I believe this is a friendly and safe place to work;
- I have the necessary resources to do my job effectively;
- I receive recognition for a job well done;
- I have opportunities to learn and advance in my career; and
- I receive competitive compensation and opportunities for growth.

For Us

- People work hard to get the job done;
- people are trusted to perform well;
- people are informed about potential changes and important issues when they are known;
- people look forward to coming to work and there is a sense of purpose beyond "having a job"; and
- people regard each other with respect.

For Them

- Leaders understand the true experience of people, including accurate assessments of workloads and demands of the job;
- leaders encourage mistakes through trial and error because innovation is important;
- leaders are approachable and there are venues for honest conversations about challenges;
- leaders are open to feedback and suggestions for improvement; and
- leaders focus on effective results, not playing favorites with people.

Behind each of these statements, which reflect the presenting conditions of one's experience, there is a rich system of patterns of communication and interaction that make them. When I say that "in our organization, leaders are open to feedback and suggestions for improvement," I make the statement by drawing on past interactions where colleagues told the truth about their honest assessment of things to managers and they were heard, listened to, and their quality feedback was acted upon. If I say that "in our organization, leaders are not open to feedback and suggestions for improvement," I may draw on past patterns where honest perspectives were suppressed or feedback was shared and then ignored by those with authority.

Thinking about these statements in this way begins to form a picture of where communication counts most in organizational life. To further make the case, here is a brief description of various aspects of the changing world of work, which illustrates the increasing necessity of taking a communication perspective.

The Changing World of Work

In the next chapter I make the case that re-making communication at work is one of the competitive advantages of the twenty-first century. This claim is plausible when you consider the intrinsic importance of communication and the potential one gains when they learn to leverage their individual, team, and organizational performance by re-making unwanted patterns of communication into something closely aligned with team priorities and organizational objectives. In order to see where communication counts most in the world of work and to establish the background for this statement more fully, a more accurate picture of the pressures of work in the twenty-first century is necessary. The following trends summarize several of the most compelling examples of the changing world of work that drive the mandate for re-making communication.

Work Is Undefined

There was a time when your title, job description, and business card said all there was to know about who you were and what you did at work. Those times are gone. Today, work is largely undefined. In our knowledge-driven service economy most people are responsible for inventing much of their own work with the purpose of finding new ways to add increasing value to their organizations.

In my book *Beyond the Job Description* I write extensively about that fact that we are all working two jobs. The position detailed in our standard job description summarizes the various tasks and activities we are responsible for completing, but this is only part of the picture. There is often a "job-within-the-job" that requires additional skills and poses many challenges to getting our best work done. I argue that people who succeed over the course of their working lives will be the ones that understand this "hidden curriculum of work"* and learn how to transform their everyday challenges into opportunities for continuous learning and performance.

Another reason work is so much less predictable is the pace of change and the inverse equation of accomplishing more with fewer resources. As organizations are squeezed by these pressures their people must draw upon a range of knowledge, skills, and abilities that were previously not required or valued in the same way. While some may refer to this as the soft skills revolution, there is nothing soft about it. Among other things, today's workers are required to process vast amounts of information, think critically about priorities, make decisions, understand how to relate to and work effectively with diverse people, manage their time and motivation in a climate of cutbacks, and stay ahead of the competition in one of the most job-insecure economies in memory.

While it may be easier to grasp these changes when you think about traditional roles that directly require creativity, innovation, and strategic insight (i.e., brand manager at a marketing firm, regional sales manager at an insurance company, etc.), even positions with core repetitive functions (i.e., entry-level sales associates, call center operators, technicians, etc.) are confronted by a diverse array of challenges that require flexibility in thinking to address them. While they may not get the credit they deserve, people who succeed in these roles contribute much more than their job descriptions suggest.

Exceptions to this undefined work include more traditional manufacturing environments where skilled labor and production are guided by strict processes that intentionally reduce variability and increase quality outputs. In these environments mental flexibility, out-of-the-box thinking, and evolving roles are not always needed on the front lines. That said, it only takes a quick review of the product evolution in your favorite brands to realize there is a whole army of people behind the scenes who are imagining the next homerun product, predicting how their customer needs will change, and designing more innovative ways of combining people and technology to achieve greater levels of efficiency.

Work Is Virtual

Work moves at lightning speeds due in large part to the technology capabilities that have expanded our capacity for real-time communication and interactivity. As things have evolved from brick and mortar offices, physical presence at the desk and face-to-face interactions are not required to coordinate work. We are now in a much more virtual world of work where people have 24/7 access to each other and to information that is no longer bound by the four walls of the office.

Work Is Connected

At the same time that work is increasingly virtual, it is also more connected. We can report to a boss halfway around the globe, respond to client needs on the other side of the country, or collaborate with colleagues on a team project from a favorite coffee shop or in pajamas from the living room. Despite the physical distance, our work is more connected than ever. For example, vendor and customer needs influence production in real time; sales and marketing strategies influence information technology training, implementation, and acquisition; and recruitment and selection processes executed by human resource departments impact company finance.

What these connections mean is that when parts of the system are not operating effectively, there can be significant disruption to the rest of the system. Whereas in the past, it was much easier to hide issues of underperformance or missed opportunities, things are so connected that even small breakdowns can become game changers.

Work Is Survival

Continuous learning and performance is one of the key success drivers for both individual contributors and leaders. This means acknowledging that past performance is not enough to withstand increasing competition and turbulent business environments. Rather, people must adopt methods and practices of continuous learning that not only include upgrading their own skills, but developing new ways of identifying opportunities and challenges, planning innovative strategies to capitalize on them, and managing ongoing change effectively.

For organizations, the capacity to shape patterns of communication and interaction is the catalyst for proactively responding to the changing environment in ways that capitalize on the greatest opportunities and maximize the productivity and effectiveness of its people. At an individual level, continuous learning is a critical factor in the pursuit to stay relevant at work and ahead of the change curve. What better way is there to become indispensible to an organization than to become proficient in the process of engineering the patterns that materialize the value-added changes an organization can benefit from directly?

Communication and the Changing World of Work

So what do these changes in the world of work have to do with communication? The fact that our roles evolve in virtual but connected systems requires us to meet a constantly changing set of circumstances and priorities. The capacity to create alignment among individuals and teams in this difficult environment, including clear and precise descriptions of goals, responsibilities, intentions for action, and clear expectations for collaboration, becomes one of the paramount demands of working well. Rather than a static concept of communication that reflects the old way of working (i.e., brick and mortar offices, physical presence at the desk, fixed roles, face-to-face meetings to coordinate work, etc.), dynamic forms of communication that are flexible enough to keep pace with change and consistent enough to be relied upon across a vast array of contexts are required.

In the new world of work employees are increasingly waking up to the need to be self-reliant and change-minded at all times. Driven by our shift to a service-driven economy, this self-reliance requires the need for customized solutions to meet a wide range of evolving customer demands, a matrix of communication tools that empower individuals to solve problems and communicate independently from anywhere in the world, and a move toward project-based initiatives accomplished by small teams.[2] There is no more effective route toward self-reliance than to establish the skill set, confidence, and experience necessary to shape the patterns that produce the results you need to succeed at work

Meeting the Communication Challenge

The communication challenges in today's world of work are endless. Whether it is at the individual, team, or organizational level, the quality of the patterns we make and sustain matter significantly to our overall effectiveness. Regardless of the circumstances or situation, here are a few of the essential skills required to meet these challenges:

1. Flexibility with change and understanding when to pivot or hold steady
2. Thinking critically to challenge potentially faulty assumptions
3. Persuading people and creating support for ideas
4. Building rapport and strong relationships for collaborating effectively
5. Gaining agreement during decision-making processes
6. Leveraging disagreement for diversity and innovation
7. Making sense of different viewpoints to enhance meaning
8. Motivating self and others

Developing the skills to meet these challenges can lead to "communication competence"[3] It is widely understood that communication competence, or the ability to select and perform a communication behavior that is appropriate for a given situation and effective for the desired outcome, is among the most important skills for group members. However, this is where an obvious insight breaks down in the transition to application.

The conventional wisdom of what we learned about effective communication with others at work—choose your words more carefully and consider the listener as you craft the message, remember the six keys to great listening, don't forget about the power of nonverbal cues, build trust through empathy and validation of others' experience, set aside your own emotions to hear the speaker's message when your temper flares, build better rapport for the time when things get tough, be more assertive with people, be persuasive with difficult people and manage conflict effectively, mind your ps and qs and remember the etiquette of communicating with leaders, and so on—only helps us navigate the various relational and situational rules. It does not help us to alter the underlying patterns of communication and interaction among group members that can fundamentally shift the dynamics and change the final outcomes.

Conclusion

Communication matters in virtually all aspects of organizational life. The most common activities in our working lives can be organized into a communication bundle, which reveals the countless patterns of communication and interaction behind the everyday challenges of getting good work done. As work continues to evolve—becoming more undefined, connected, and virtual—these trends extend the communication bundle and place increasing pressure on people to develop the necessary communication skills to deal with intensifying change and uncertainty. Chapter 4 describes the way the concepts and tools of re-making communication at work can be leveraged as the competitive advantage of the twenty-first century.

4

Re-Making Communication: The Competitive Advantage of the Twenty-First Century

The term "competitive advantage" refers to any factor(s) that can be leveraged to stand out, get ahead, and win in a given pursuit. In business, competitive advantage matters significantly when you are operating in a climate of hypercompetition with ever-increasing costs of doing business. Knowing and using your competitive advantage wisely in the marketplace can make the difference between innovation and growth, or decline. When it comes to identifying competitive advantage, leaders often ask questions that set them apart from their peers such as: what do we know how to do, that they do not; what resources or technologies do we have, that they do not; what do we understand about the market, that they do not; and what do our customers love about us, that they cannot find anywhere else? We can refer to questions like these as the search for competitive advantage in the form of things.

These are important questions. However, notice how none of them focuses directly on the greatest asset that every organization possesses—the collective potential of people and their performance contributions. When I work with leaders and their teams on their strategic planning, issues of competitive advantage invariably surface. When the theme arises, I surprise them with this question: If you had no industry intelligence, no breakthrough technology, no innovative production or service delivery model, no singular resource, and no brand loyalty that could push you ahead in the market—*who* would you rely on for your competitive advantage? This hypothetical question wipes the slate clean and temporarily redirects people away from the obvious competitive advantages they may consider (e.g., goods, services, technology, etc.). We can refer to this question and others like it as the search for competitive advantage in the form of people.

Now, at this point reactions are often positive and many people affirm the intent of the question with statements like these: Yes, of course, people are our most valuable asset; We absolutely need to win in the talent war; we have to hire the best in order get all of that potential innovation and next-generation potential through our doors—and keep it away from our challengers, and so on. While statements like these may ring true, if you ask people what they need in their talent, there is very little consensus on what would truly deliver a competitive advantage.

Some people will restate many of the tried and true leadership dimensions that have survived the test of time. They may say that we need people who are honest, committed, focused on our mission, on board with the team, willing to do the little things, and committed to the hard work that it will take to succeed. Still others may refer to the more popular, recent assessments of skills for the new millennium by saying we need our people to be change-minded, capable of synthesizing complex ideas, right-brain thinkers with a penchant for innovation, self-starters who can identify challenges and opportunities without being told, tech-savvy individuals who can leverage new technology channels for virtual work, outstanding contributors with capabilities that can be adapted in flexible ways as our needs change, and so on. Both of these lists are useful and I would agree that all of these qualities matter in some way. But if everybody knows they matter and recruits accordingly, there really is no competitive advantage in them.

A New Kind of Advantage

I believe that one of the most significant competitive advantages for organizations in the twenty-first century is a workforce that has the capacity to identify unwanted individual, team, and organizational patterns of communication and interaction and re-make them to better align with their true values, priorities, and desired performance outcomes. To help people grasp this new definition of competitive advantage, I introduce a scenario that provokes more specific discussion about the power of what people do when they truly are an organization's competitive advantage:

> Imagine that you have to re-build this organization or team from scratch. You do not have any of the typical competitive advantages you relied on in the past (no stuff) and for the time being you can only work with the people you have right now. In this scenario, how would people need to communicate and interact with each other in order to create the necessary conditions of success?

This question, hypothetical as it may seem, is critical because it forces you to think not about people and things at the surface level, but about what people do—specifically, what habitual patterns of interaction must exist at the foundation of the enterprise's success. I facilitated a discussion like this with two merging nonprofit leadership teams. The executive directors and pivotal board members from both organizations were present, and the question was relevant because the merger would (at some level) rebuild a new organization from the best of both existing agencies.

As they moved through the discussion, they were able to pinpoint critical themes within their responses to the prompt. The group heard comments such as: "People will need to communicate without fear of being seen as part of the old guard. While there should be some pressure to let go of old ways, many of the old ways worked," and "The interactions of leaders need to be focused on the common goals that prompted the merger in the first place. If there are clear roles, then those interactions should work together to accomplish more." As the session progressed, these kinds of concrete statements that named qualities of the patterns of communication and interaction provided sufficient resources to draw upon to help them re-make communication at work. One of the most interesting things about their responses was the fact that the people in the room proactively started dealing with two of the greatest potential merger challenges—blending cultures and establishing a unifying purpose—without being prompted.

This entire book is dedicated to showing people how to spot unwanted patterns of communication and interaction that produce negative outcomes and experiences that reduce individual, team, and organizational performance. And with that simple ability, another way of describing this competitive advantage is "the capacity to literally re-make unwanted patterns into coordinated efforts that align people with priorities, bring out the best in people's talent and motivation, and boost learning and performance by closing the inevitable gaps that form when things go bad."

If this competitive advantage is put fully into practice it can have dramatic effects at the individual, team, and organization levels. For individuals, they will be able to stand out and stay ahead of the change curve in an environment of high job insecurity, meet the various challenges of the changing world of work, and craft a working life full of meaningful experiences and outcomes they want. For teams, they will transform conflict and collaboration breakdowns by re-making them into growth opportunities, boost team performance with greater efficiency and alignment, and create more high-impact results in response to the challenges and opportunities they face. For organizations, they can leverage their viable business models with people to carry out their plans efficiently, get out of their own way by increasing the alignment of people and activity that are consistent with priorities, and sustain optimal recruitment and retention of high performers who thrive in the kind of cultures that emerge when you re-make communication at work.

Make no mistake about it, every competitive advantage should be captured and leveraged to its fullest. If there are technology breakthroughs, innovations in production, marketing strategies, recruitment and selection improvements, or any other people/things that can help the organization succeed, they should be put in play. That said, any discussion about these perceived competitive advantages will be more effective if it includes the third domain described earlier: a commitment to intentionally making the patterns of communication and interaction that must exist at the foundation of individual, team, and organizational success. Just as the old saying "behind every great man, there stands a great woman" challenges traditional notions of power, success, and gender, I think it is important to challenge the traditional notions of competitive advantage by stating that behind every competitive advantage an organization possesses, there are patterns of communication and interaction among its people that give it value.

Conclusion

One of the most significant competitive advantages for organizations in the twenty-first century is a workforce that has the capacity to identify unwanted individual, team, and organizational patterns of communication and interaction and re-make them into something that better aligns with their true values, priorities, and desired performance outcomes. Implementing the concepts and tools of re-making communication at work can accelerate this competitive advantage, which marks a shift from relying on "technical resources" and "people" to a focus on the ways people intentionally develop patterns of communication that create the conditions for achieving the organization's greatest goals. Chapter 5 summarizes the first four chapters of part I with a focus on applying the insights in the real world of work.

5

Applying Part I to the Real World of Work

Communication is an intrinsic aspect of our working lives. There is not a single collaborative initiative we could pursue that does not require some form of communication with others. And there is not a day that goes by where the interactions we have with other people do not in some way "influence" the quality of our day and the work we produce. In a world of work that is more undefined, virtual, and hypercompetitive than ever, getting communication right is increasingly important. Unfortunately, most of what we learned about effective communication at work was incomplete.

The conventional wisdom about what works with communication at work focuses on what people say and how they listen to each other. In other words, the sender of the message must choose his/her words carefully and the receiver of the message must listen well to decode the message in order to understand what it means. If one or both people are distracted, or if there is too much going on around them, the message cannot be accurately transmitted. With this sender-receiver transaction at the core, popular explanations about communication at work were built on a series of myths, including misperceptions such as those listed below:

- Communication is just an exchange of information and ideas. To get it right, you have to listen well and speak clearly.
- Good communication follows a process, and if you follow the right steps, you'll get good results.
- Once you get the hang of it, you can take the same communication approach into every situation.
- Communication only occurs when others are present and face-to-face, and it goes dormant when people are not in direct conversation.

These and other myths, widely accepted as true and continuously taught in leading education and business contexts around the world, must be challenged. How we talk and listen to each other does matter, but effective communication at work requires much more than that. This old model needs to be replaced by a new approach to communication, which requires a "communication perspective."

Taking a communication perspective at work is just a shorthand way of remembering that "communication actually makes things and the patterns of communication and interaction that we engage in at work shape our experience, influence our outcomes, and affect the quality of our working lives." A communication perspective at work becomes the lens through which you can see the patterns of communication and interaction you engage in for what they are and what they can be. This is so much more than "sending and receiving messages."

While it may seem simpler to rely on the conventional wisdom of effective communication at work—"Choose your words more carefully, consider the listener as you craft the message, actively listen until they are done speaking, don't forget about the power of non-verbal cues, build trust through empathy and validation of others' experience, set aside your own emotions in order to hear the speaker's message when things get tense, build rapport so you can rely on that during difficult conversations, communicate assertively by advocating for your own ideas without shutting others down, and be persuasive by mirroring other people's style of communication"—these simple prescriptions, which are all based on the transmission model of communication and a superficial understanding of organizational dynamics, are just not enough to thoroughly address the difficult challenges of communication.

In order to match the dynamic, complex nature of the challenge of communication at work, an equally dynamic and flexible process is needed to address them in the real world of work. The new definition of "successful communication" at work starts with the ability to recognize the patterns of communication and interaction where decisions get made, relationships are built, organizational culture is solidified, and the trajectory for ultimate business outcomes are set into motion.

With this new foundation, emerging and established leaders can then develop a combination of insight, skill, and ability that allows them to: examine what they are making, spot the critical moments where something different/better could be made, understand how to create the flexible conditions for change, follow a sequence of steps to re-make unwanted patterns of communication and interaction, and learn to avoid everyday pitfalls that can undermine these new patterns and the benefits they bring.

Applying this new definition of successful communication at work can be a significant source of competitive advantage because it can give individual contributors and leaders the capacity to literally re-make unwanted patterns into coordinated efforts that align people with priorities, bring out the best in people's talent and motivation, and boost learning and performance by closing the inevitable gaps that form when communication goes bad. Fully applying the principles and tools of re-making communication at work can have dramatic effects on individuals, teams, and organizations, for example:

Two business partners are locked in a battle of wills, both feeling supremely confident that their strategy and approach to leading the business is sound. Believing that their partner's ideas are flawed, their persistent disagreement reduces the trust between them and the partnership dissolves as the business erodes in a wash of unmade decisions and acrimonious discussions...

The Board of Directors in a once-inspiring nonprofit uses their quarterly meetings to play out a turf war with lines drawn around the founder and former executive director and the new executive director's management team. With good intentions and right on every side, both camps fail to effectively lead the organization and, over time, they compromise the relevance of the mission and the organization's financial stability...

A new manager responds to a surprise promotion with passion and motivation for making her mark. Several of her newly assigned direct reports had been friends as they all came up together in the organization. In the transition to "boss," she is unable to adapt an equitable and consistent way of working across the team. With sagging credibility and frustration all around, her aspiring leadership fades as undermining activities reduce collaboration and morale...

Some people could read these three scenarios and cynically say, "That's just how it goes in the real world of work." While it may be true that these kinds of unwanted, destructive patterns of communication and interaction can be part of our everyday working lives, taking a communication perspective at work reminds us that nothing is fixed. Even the most challenging patterns can be re-made.

...After a seemingly intractable conflict, two business partners find common ground in the love for what they do. As they work through their differences, they deepen their respect for each other's unique values and principled way of working. Over time, the business thrives as they balance their roles and let organizational decisions, not personalities, lead the way.

...After a fractious time made worse by difficult economic circumstances, a nonprofit Board of Directors suffers a series of community relations issues as their in-fighting spilled over into the community. Facing the possibility of closing the doors, they choose to put personal convictions aside and form a new vision that preserves the tradition of the past and captures the excitement of the future. With their full support behind the staff and a commitment to more constructive ways of discussing future concerns, the mission thrives once again.

...After a rough six months on the job, a new manager develops a versatile approach to leading her blended team. Working through challenging relationships and a few skeptical personalities, she learns to make hard decisions by establishing consistent accountabilities and shared responsibilities. As her confidence grows, so does the respect and commitment she maintains from her team.[1]

In hallways, boardrooms, at water coolers, around cubicles, and in corner offices people are living with what they have made at work. The very fabric of organizational culture is a reflection of these deep and enduring patterns of communication and interaction.

Part II

Knowledge Guide for Re-Making Patterns of Communication at Work

6

Communication Chemistry: What Makes Patterns

R e-making communication at work requires a communication perspective, which in turn requires you to look at the basic building blocks that make patterns of communication and interaction. Getting down to the basic level of *elements* lends itself to using a "chemistry metaphor." Understanding what makes patterns requires knowledge of the composition, properties, and behavior of communication matter. The goal of this chapter is to describe basic communication matter, including the distinctions among key elements and common ways they interact with each other.

As communicators engage in a continuous process of making meaning and coordinating their actions, the interactions are an exchange of the basic building blocks of communication. While the dynamic combinations of what can be made from them are immense, the basic elements are straightforward and consistent across the workplace. The sources include the following:

1. Primary Elements
   - Raw Sensory Data
   - Perceptive Filters
   - Retained Content
2. Bonding Elements
   - Interpretive Context and Meaning Making
   - Speech Acts
   - Inertia from Critical Moments
3. Background Elements
   - Master Contracts
   - Working Life Scripts
   - Preexisting Patterns

Primary Elements

Our working lives inundate us with vast amounts of "raw sensory data." These are the collective inputs to our five senses, especially eyes and ears, and they include all of the visual and auditory stimuli we will ultimately select from to interpret and then act upon as we move through our interactions with others. Which email you pay attention to more than others in an overflowing inbox, which voice mail you return when there are multiple people waiting for your attention, which side conversation you choose to join in with as people wait for the meeting to begin, which aspect of the quarterly report you chose to pay close attention to and study for clues about the health of the organization, which subtle facial expression catches your attention; which key phrase during your boss's two-minute monologue you hear and reflect on...these are all examples of the sorting that takes place among an avalanche of raw sensory data.

To sort effectively, we rely on our "perceptive filters," which are the mental models we use to ignore, delete, select, organize, modify, and distort raw sensory data in an effort to filter it down to the essentials for quick and effective interpretation. These filters include the conscious and unconscious values, assumptions, and beliefs previously filtered and accepted as "right" by our prior experience.

What is left when all the selection and filtering stops is the "retained content." These are the interpreted stimuli that got past our filter, including all of the symbols, words, and nonverbal cues understood within the context we referenced them in. This is where chemistry and biology meet: the experiences we make through our patterns flow directly from this retained content and action we take based on those specific interpretations.

In the last few paragraphs I summarized a very complex set of ideas. While the summary is sufficient for the purpose of this chapter, I encourage you to delve more deeply into the rich and intriguing details of this topic. There are many articles and books that describe the filtering process in great detail and they can be quite useful in understanding both the helpful side of this kind of rapid selection, as well as the unhelpful side that distorts information, takes wrong-turn shortcuts based on faulty assumptions, and leads to repeated patterns of behavior that no longer provide positive experiences to us.[1]

Bonding Elements

Bonding elements are like glue; they hold things together over time. One of the strongest bonding elements in the chemistry of communication is the "context" we draw upon to interpret the interactions we have with people. While I alluded to the perceptive filters earlier, including their function in the process of selecting and organizing the raw data that we use for conscious and unconscious interpretation, meaning making is somewhat separate from this.

We learn about communication unconsciously in childhood through socialization and continue developing our culturally reflective perspectives and approaches through our working lives. As we make meaning we give our experience coherence through both our perception and cognition. Meaning making happens consciously and unconsciously all of the time. We take action on what we interpret intentionally and unintentionally. From our meaning perspectives we derive a set of habitual expectations that inform, limit, and distort how we think, believe, feel, and act now and in the future.[2]

For example, imagine that you work in the Operations Department of your company and you strongly believe it is not worth the time and effort to bring potential issues to the Research & Development Department (R&D) for their review and input. If that is your belief then it is very likely that you act on it accordingly. But how do you know that is true and where did the belief come from in the first place? It is likely that the conclusion about the ineffectiveness of R&D was established after a particularly challenging episode or pattern of communication where issues were misunderstood, things took longer than necessary, and the outcome was unsatisfactory at best. Despite the fact that the pattern is not ongoing (i.e., you have not been interacting with the R&D because of the perceived ineffectiveness), you still draw upon that prior experience, or context, to make real-time decisions. Seeing the interpretive context as a bonding element is a useful way to understand why we do (or do not do) certain things.

Another key bonding element in the chemistry of communication includes "speech acts" that anchor people in their response-patterns. A speech act can be described as "action that you perform by speaking...they include compliments, insults, promises, threats, assertions, and questions."[3] Beyond this technical definition, in the world of work we may recognize speech acts as inviting participation in a meeting, rewarding performance with formal and informal incentives, recognizing valuable contributions through acknowledgment, promising opportunities in the form of promotion, ordering compliance in the form of new policy, challenging allegiances through consensus building, and more.

A third bonding element includes "critical moments," which are specific interactions that can change our working lives. The collective critical moments of people working together within an organization ultimately shape the culture of that organization and establish the parameters of what is possible with its performance. Sometimes we recognize and give names to these important turning points—my annual performance review, the choice to confront a colleague about a growing concern, a key hiring decision for the team, the big divisional sales meeting, the quarterly offsite executive strategy session, a new CEO's vision for the company, and so on—and at other times these moments surface and pass without our awareness of their potential to impact the fundamental aspects of our working world. They often carry a certain level of inertia with them due to the logical forces and both constitutive and regulative rules that produce the knee-jerk reactions informed by past experience and expectations.[4] As a bonding element, these strong but unseen forces hold some of the greatest challenges and opportunities for re-making communication at work.

There is a strong connection between "context," "speech acts," and "critical moments" that get triggered by these rules and sometimes cause us to act out of step with our true intentions. For example, imagine somebody challenges you on a decision during a meeting. Rather than responding to their challenge in a reasonable way, you avoid the discussion by simply calling upon your authority with a statement like "As the director, I'm saying this is the right thing to do." This speech act references your power on the organization chart and suggests that the topic is not up for discussion because the decision is right and has been irrevocably made. This is likely a "critical moment," or turning point, for people because it signals that open discussion is not welcomed (at least on this topic). It also is a strong *context* that people will draw upon in the future as they interpret situations and choose their actions. In practical terms, it may lead people to think twice before they raise a concern in the future.

Background Elements

In the chemistry of communication there are several background elements that powerfully influence communication in unseen ways. These background elements were previously made, but are then carried over from prior situations and experiences to influence the current pattern of communication and interaction. In a way, they are like the back-story that explains the often contradictory ways in which people interact with others.

Master Contracts

"Master contracts" refer to the previously defined relationships among the communicating participants, or what each believes they can expect of the other in a specific episode or ongoing pattern.[5] These unwritten rules are often quite complex and they are tested tentatively until the pattern becomes solid and more predictable. At that point there is an inherent assumption that the performance of future communication acts will follow certain rules that will predictably shape the turn(s) each person takes.

One of the most common master contracts in the world of work is one of support and allegiance. In these situations people make supportive comments of each other's ideas and they tread carefully when there are potential disagreements in order to project a unified front and unwavering backing for each other. The opposite can be true as well, as some master contracts are implicit expectations for disagreement or antagonism. Regardless of the latest idea or suggestion, these people will not support each other's efforts or show public agreement.

While master contracts are played out face-to-face between the people involved, it is usually assumed that they will also be carried out during interactions where one of the parties is not present. In the case of the supportive relationship, one could expect that the same level of allegiance would be modeled whether the person was in the room or not. In instances where there is a breach of a master contract (e.g., a colleague disparagingly describes the contribution of someone else, etc.), the integrity of the agreement is called into question along with the potential trust of the relationship.

Working Life Scripts

"Working life scripts" are the combination of anticipated episodes a person expects they will participate in during the course of their time at work. My concept of a working life script comes from the notion that each of us also has a personal life script that reflects the stories we believe and tell about our working lives. These stories begin early in life and they reflect the perceptions we hold of ourselves and the world around us. The stories powerfully shape the narrative about what we can and will do throughout our lives.[6] A working life script is the relevant part of the story you tell about who you are and how you show up at work.

The deep, often unseen effects of these stories shape the overall image we have of our potential contributions and limitations, including the choices we feel we should make in the circumstances we encounter. A life script is said to be influenced by our family of origin and other major life events, which is to say that our own stories are often a reflection of our family's history and the early formative experiences we endure.

Drawing on this concept, a working life script is the professional narrative we believe and tell about our anticipated career potential and experience trajectory at work. Will I get that promotion? Will I get passed over time and again because people around me just don't see my potential? Will I enjoy working for my boss and with my colleagues? Will I detest my boss and loathe the fact that I have to work with others who don't have a clue? The anticipated answers to these and other questions reside in our working life scripts.

The prior relationships we have had with past supervisors are a significant contributing factor to the script and it often shapes our anticipation of the manager-employee relationship moving forward. If we had a "great boss" we are optimistic that things like mentoring and support are possible and likely in our future. If we have had "bad bosses" then we may be cautious and expect that low-trust, arm's-length relationships are the best way to protect ourselves from managers who are incompetent or who we assume do not have our best interests in mind. Overall, the quality and outcomes of

prior patterns of communication and interaction from our previous organizations—including any major events such as damaging conflict, surprise
promotions, difficult layoffs, and so on—have the most powerful effect on
"what we expect work to be" in the future. Unless we examine them and challenge the assumptions they hold, our experience at work often follows the
story arc we already believe and tell.

A new manager who takes over an existing team must quickly learn the
working life scripts of the staff because they do not end or magically reset when
personnel changes. They are deeply embedded in the way we think and act
about work matters and the clues to them are often only revealed when we
make unwarranted attributions (e.g., "You're just like my old boss..."), give
sharp demands (e.g., "You have to..."), make subtle hints (e.g., "Don't you
think it would be better if we..."), or model attitudes and behaviors that are
inconsistent with context (e.g., When a person is triggered to heightened emotion or urgency because of a what appears to be a relatively small matter, etc.).[7]

With a communication perspective at work, a mindful individual and/or
a skilled leader can elicit elements of people's working life scripts by engaging
in thoughtful conversation to get to know people. The following questions
can be used for just such a discovery process: "Could you tell me a little bit
about what you care most about at work? Where and how did you develop
these values? What are some of the things you believe about how work is versus how work should be? What would you say are some of the assumptions
you have about work that your first few jobs taught you? What are some of
your underlying mottos that reflect the truisms of work?"

Preexisting Patterns

"Preexisting patterns" are the cumulative, premade interpersonal patterns,
team patterns, and organization-based patterns that influence and, in some
cases, dictate acceptable communication at work. Unless a person happens
to be the founder and first employee in an organization, there are always
preexisting patterns encountered when you join a new company. In many
instances people simply refer to these as "the culture of the organization" but
they are much more than that generalization implies.

The normative features of preexisting patterns have a direct impact on
how people talk and act, including what is permissible in many of the most
important settings where work gets done. Direct manager-employee relationship cues, indirect leader-follower relationship cues, team meeting etiquette, and the venues for and expectations of team-to-team interaction are
all features influenced by preexisting patterns. In some cases people are specifically recruited because of the assumption/hope that they will be able to
"change unwanted patterns" (e.g., we need fresh and innovative thinking to
breakthrough, etc.) and in other cases people are selected because of their

perceived potential to "maintain desired patterns" (e.g., s/he would fit in well with our culture and keep the tradition of excellence alive, etc.) that are the presumed causes of organizational success.

Seeing the Chemistry in Communication at Work

This chapter introduced a variety of terms that explain the fundamental building blocks of communication at work. Some may question the need for all of this by asking, "Is communication really that complicated?" Here are two examples that demonstrate the complexity of communication and the need to integrate these basic elements in order to understand how the chemistry of communication affects every aspect of our experience at work.

A white elephant is a rare white or light-gray Asian elephant that is revered in parts of Southeast Asia and India. In Siam (present-day Thailand) there are stories about the ancient practice whereby kings gave white elephants as gifts to members of the royal court.

When a king wanted to reward a loyal subject and elevate their status in the kingdom he would provide a gift of a white elephant. Because they were sacred, white elephants could not be used as draft animals and the owner incurred a significant expense to care for them with little tangible benefit in return. For these favored subjects, the king would not only give them the white elephant, but he would also provide the means to feed and care for the animal.

It is said that if the king wanted to destroy a member of his own court who had fallen out of favor for one reason or another, he would also present that person with a white elephant. However in this case, the gift would not come with a land grant or financial support to cover the costs of caring for the animal. Because they could not reject the gift, the overwhelming burden to the recipient would likely ruin them financially and in so doing, indirectly exact the king's wish.

Has your boss or a colleague ever given you a white elephant? When is an assignment just an assignment? When is a gesture just a gesture? When are words just words? When does a speech act mean one thing in a certain context and yet something quite different in another? Understanding the chemistry of communication provides a key to answering these questions. For example, take these words, spoken by one colleague to another: "We need to talk? I have a few things I want to discuss."

Are these just words? Is this a simple, odorless, and colorless transaction of information intended to set up a meeting? Both colleagues may indeed perceive it in these simple terms. However, considering the rich chemistry of communication it is likely that more than an invitation gets *made* by this interaction.

Any preexisting patterns of communication and interaction between these two people will color the way the words are perceived across the range of possible interpretations, from innocent invitation to distress-causing speech act.

Depending upon what has already happened in the relationship, maybe this is a critical moment. Does the person want to talk about an exciting opportunity, a major concern, or just a passing idea to share? For the colleague who has just been invited to meet, a lot of guesses about "the meaning" of the invitation will be drawn from their interpretive context, or prior experience. The perceptive filters that we use to take in information, select what to focus on, and process the meaning are all based on our existing assumptions and beliefs and these are the background context that will be used to understand the invitation.

Depending upon the context, the phrase "we need to talk" may be seen as a speech act that announces "something is wrong." If so, this interpretation will likely sound the alarm and increase the apprehension or defensiveness in the next turn. If the same phrase is interpreted as an "urgent, exciting opportunity to speak face-to-face," then it will inspire an entirely different next turn in the episode.

If there is a master contract or some kind of repetitive pattern already in play, then the phrase "I have a few things I want to discuss" could be interpreted as: "Here we go again; they are not happy with me, my performance, etc." If the master contract is one of mentoring and unconditional support, then the invitation could be interpreted as "another exciting opportunity to potentially learn and grow." Or, if the master contract between the two people is one of "I'll leave you alone if you leave me alone," then this could be a breach that announces, "I am no longer able to avoid these sensitive discussions—we need to talk."

If there is a working life script in play whose story is "Whenever somebody wants to talk, something is about to go really wrong," then the perception of the invitation will be skewed by that story and any prior, negative experiences of being blindsided by threatening, surprise information that validates it. Alternatively, if the working life script tells a story about the value of face-to-face communication, then the invitation could be a welcomed next step to positively build on the working relationship.

In this example you can see that an exchange between two colleagues—"We need to talk? I have a few things I want to discuss"—can amount to a critical turn in an important episode. Or, in some cases it could just be a few simple words that coordinate one of the commonplace activities of work. When you are personally at the center of things—receiving your own "invitation" to a meeting—taking a communication perspective at work will help you look at the chemistry of communication and all of these influential elements that otherwise are hidden in plain sight.

Communication DNA

Fifteen years is not long if you look at the timeline of our human history on earth. However, that is precisely how long it took to complete one of the most ambitious scientific undertakings in history. Beginning in 1990, a collaborative effort to map the entire human genome began. Although it was originally supposed to take longer, a series of technological advances accelerated the project and it was finally completed in 2003. For the first time the 20,000—25,000 genes in human DNA were identified, the sequences of the three billion chemical base pairs were determined, and the information was stored in electronic databases for analysis, study, and transfer to the private sector.[8] The implications of this project on industries like health care and biotechnology are staggering. Not only does it provide important clues to understand human biology, the specific application about the effects of DNA variations may lead to new ways of diagnosing, treating, and even preventing many of the deadliest illnesses that affect people.

Some have referred to DNA as nature's complete genetic blueprint for building a human being. In a similar way, I consider communication as the DNA of organizational life. The patterns of communication and interaction that people engage in at work are the blueprint for their individual experience and they shape the structure and culture of the organization.

Think back to your high school biology class and you may remember that DNA is a molecule that encodes the genetic instructions used in the development and functioning of all known living organisms on the planet. What something is is a reflection of the unique and specific sequence of DNA of its genome. In a similar way, communication is an intrinsic element of work that is the force that makes our experience through the patterns of interaction we engage in. In the same way that science has advanced with tools to study and understand the 25,000 genes that comprise human DNA, re-making communication at work provides a way of understanding the "chemical sequences" of interactions that form our patterns of communication and interaction, which in turn influence the constitution of our experience.

Conclusion

Understanding what makes patterns of communication and interaction requires knowledge of the composition, properties, and behavior of basic communication elements. The chemistry of communication includes a variety of primary, bonding, and background elements that combine to make the various patterns of interaction we engage in. Dissecting common communication exchanges can reveal the subtle ways those elemental building blocks of communication mix together to create complex and unique outcomes. Chapter 7 builds upon the chemistry of communication and describes the physics that hold patterns of communication and interaction in place.

7

Communication Physics: What Holds Patterns Together

In the same way that there is a basic chemistry of communication, there are rules that influence how these interactions take place. These rules are the physics of communication and they act as the invisible forces of energy that mix and hold the various elements of communication together. If the science of physics is concerned with the study of interactions between matter and energy, the physics of communication focuses on the interactive forces that influence people in communication.

Like gravity and the laws of motion, there are no pockets of the organizational ecosystem where the physics of communication do not apply. They pervade our day-to-day experience at work at every level of the organization chart. "In any situation, unseen, unspoken connections among people influence everything that happens. Leaders are typically not aware of these connections, and they can't be, unless the right conceptual lens is available."[1] Re-making communication at work provides one such lens that allows you to see the silent forces and "connections" in action, which ultimately influence the patterns of communication and interaction you make.

The purpose of this chapter is to define what some of these forces are, including the various ways in which rules, logical forces, and hierarchies of context influence the ways we make meaning and take action during communication events. Building upon the previous chapter about the basic chemistry of communication, understanding the physics will provide the foundation for knowing how patterns get made in the first place, including how they can be re-made into something better when the same basic chemistry and physics are applied with a different intent.

Rules That Influence Our Patterns of
Communication and Interaction

The essence of CMM (coordinated management of meaning) theory begins with the assumption that two individuals engaged in an interaction are simultaneously constructing their own meaning and taking coordinated action based on those interpretations. The perceptive filters—identified earlier as part of the basic chemistry of communication—that people use to make sense of their experience provide the parameters for their conclusions and the inherent sense of rules give structure to the actions that they take.

The respected author and educator Stephen Littlejohn summarized these rules succinctly when he said that "individuals within any social situation first want to understand what is going on and apply rules to figure things out."[2] Two different types of rules that individuals can apply in any communicative situation are: (1) constitutive rules, which communicators use to interpret or understand an event or message; and (2) regulative rules, which determine how to respond or act based on a given interpretation.

A good example of these rules in action can be observed in the hypothetical situation where a person is talking with the boss and the supervisor asks the subordinate if s/he can take on an additional task. Based on the constitutive rules the employee may interpret the request as "something they have no choice about" or "a chance to show what they are capable of." The regulative rules that influence how the employee responds in action likely reflect the hierarchical relationship that exists and the sense of how one should behave with a superior. If the employee plays by the rules, then a likely response may be to say "yes, absolutely" with no hesitation. Or, it could be a more sophisticated negotiation such as "I would be happy to do that; could you help me think through where this fits with the existing priorities on my plate?"

In another scenario where the relationship dynamics are horizontal, such as two friends covolunteering on a project, a similar request to take on an additional task could produce drastically different meanings and responses based on the change in rules. For example, if I am asked to take on extra work, I may wonder "is my co-volunteer shirking their duty," and "is the right thing for me to do to say no in order to avoid over-committing?" "Is my partner reaching out for help because they need me," and "this is my chance to respond in a supportive way?" Whatever the response, it is often instantaneous and influenced by these constitutive and regulative rules that depend on each person's existing beliefs (refined from prior experience) within a given context and how they might be applied to the current situation.

For the most part these rules can help us. They guide us through situations that do not require much special attention and they keep us in line when acting outside of the rules could offend or harm people unnecessarily. However, these rules also get us into trouble when they cause us to jump to actions that we actually do not want to take. And when the meaning we make and the actions we take lead us to outcomes that we do not want, we have to challenge these rules. In order to do that we must first expose them.

Without exposing our rules and questioning their service to us, we simply end up carrying the best available combination of old rules along with us. Carrying old rules around with us—the ones that were formed and refined in different contexts with different people—and bringing those old rules into new communication interactions often produce the same patterns with different names.

For example, in the world of work many people carry an old constitutive rule with them about receiving feedback. I know this from my experience coaching many first-time managers through their insecurities and concerns about giving effective feedback to their team members. The rule varies, but in a general sense the conflicted meaning we make in these communication acts goes something like this: The first reaction to oncoming feedback is fear (i.e., we could be under attack, get ready to defend yourself, raise the walls and don't let anything get in that could harm us, etc.); the second, slightly more reasonable trigger then pushes back (i.e., I need to stay calm, maybe there is something I can learn. Either way, it will be over soon). The regulative rule structure of receiving feedback (especially when it is from a superior) reflects the hierarchical context and most interactions lead to conformity (i.e., sitting politely across the desk or table, listening without saying much, and signing on the line that says you received the feedback).

The results from most feedback sessions are really poor and that is why it is such an important topic for managers. However, so much of that exchange is governed by the rules the employee follows regardless of what a manager does to change their approach. The reason that many changes to the format and features of performance review processes do not improve the outcomes is because they deal with cosmetic issues (e.g., changing the frequency of feedback, renaming categories and rating scales, having different people complete them, etc.) and fail to address the powerful rules that foster such closed reactions.

A more ideal set of rules would lead us to enter the room clear-minded, with an open attention toward our performance. The meaning making cues we take would be based on our actual experience this time, not from baggage of prior feedback meetings that went wrong and left us feeling berated, unappreciated, and inaccurately assessed. Anticipating an honest, but supportive environment we could even potentially look forward to the experience as a source for valuable professional development and an indicator of our potential career advancement.

The Power of "Should" and Other Logical Forces

Related to the constitutive and regulative rules that influence us, logical forces are another key aspect of the physics of communication. Logical forces are the subtle, but powerful urges that hold cycles of reaction and behavior in place. Sometimes our response in a turn seems to be on autopilot and it "leads us." When this happens, whether we recognize it or not, the inertia of the pattern makes it very difficult to change course. It pushes us toward the perception of what we "ought" to do and all the shoulds, musts, mays, and cannots that go with it. Exploring logical force gives us a vocabulary and visual framework to depict influential webs of "ought-ness" or "should-ness" that subtly but powerfully influence communication and shape relationships.

We can expose the presenting aspects of these logical forces by asking questions about various situations at work. For example, when a group of people join together to collaborate on a project, what do you think each person should be responsible for? How would you describe the two or three most important things that all leaders must do? When someone at work bullies or threatens a colleague, what should the response be? When a candidate arrives for an interview, what do you think they ought to be able to show to the selection committee? Answering questions with specific wording like these reveals the often hidden expectations, and expectations are tethered to logical forces.

In the scenario where the potential new hire shows up at the interview and they did not even do basic research on the company or prepare their resume accordingly, your definitions of and expectations for a "prepared candidate" are unmet and the logical force of that situation will likely move you to reject their candidacy out of hand. When a team member fails to pull their weight on the group project, that sense of "should" may compel you to confront them about their lack of involvement, or take silent action by avoiding them in the future. Even in these simple examples you can see the way in which the strong sense of should moves us to action (whether we can or do openly discuss the reasons why or not).

Especially in our working relationships we tend to develop a strong sense of what we think we "should do" in a specific context and then we carry that over into others. Over time, whenever that familiar context presents itself, the same limited set of choices emerge and the behavior we choose naturally follows the same well-worn experience of the past. Rather than stopping to evaluate what we want out of a given situation, we effortlessly replay a similar pattern of words, nonverbal communication cues, and attitudes that embody this sense of what we ought to be doing and the invisible forces that pull them in a specific direction or pattern of communication.

Hierarchy of Influence on Patterns

In addition to rules that influence meaning and action-taking, another way of thinking about the factors that influence the physics of communication is a structure of hierarchies. The hierarchy includes a number of contexts that are drawn upon simultaneously during a communication event. They are not all equal, however, and drawing out the hierarchy of influence allows you to see which are the most influential in the current pattern of communication.[3]

The concept of hierarchies has proven invaluable to my own understanding of patterns of communication and it is a useful concept to share when helping others re-make communication at work. When I work with individuals and teams I often share my updated version of the hierarchy that is specific to an organizational context. In this updated hierarchy, these four factors influence what makes communication and help us to pay particular attention to the forces and functions of the stuff that generates our patterns:

- Organization—The written and unwritten rules of what is permissible, impermissible, and desired within an organization; the influence of its culture and values
- Relationship—Mutual expectations among the people interacting with each other
- Self-concept—An individual's definition of self, including self-efficacy and believed limitations
- Episode—The specific combination of coordinated turns that shape part or all of a larger pattern of communication and interaction
- Turns—Communication actions that involve a rapid process of interpreting the previous turn and taking action based on its meaning

Thinking about a hierarchy of meaning as a series of interconnected levels presents a model of seeing what is most important to us in a given moment and how that can vary by context and situation. For example, when you make a decision at work what is the highest context that influences your ultimate choice? That will likely vary by situation, so there is no universal answer. Sometimes you may make a decision based upon an organizational value or priority. In another situation, you may make a decision using the context of relationship as the highest value. Regardless of the specific circumstance, exposing the presence and sequence of your hierarchy allows you to sort through the subtle and powerful stories that are used to interpret and take action on what is happening around you.

Learning the physics of communication, including how to evaluate your interpretations, subsequent belief systems, and action-taking drivers is a critical skill required for re-making communication at work. It is essential for managing effectively in the complex, constantly changing world of work where faulty assumptions and unexamined belief systems exist. Despite the often veiled nature of the physics of communication, evidence can be seen through unwanted patterns of communication if we follow the frustration that they often produce.

Evidence of the Physics of Communication:
Unwanted Repetitive Patterns

When Newton's apple came down, he had evidence that the invisible force of gravity existed and had real consequence to all matter (especially the apple and its interaction with his head). In the same way we can identify evidence of the physics of communication when we experience unwanted repetitive patterns. This phrase, likely coined by the fathers of CMM theory, Barnett Pearce and Vernon Cronen, refers to behavioral patterns, influenced by logical forces, that we do not want because they no longer serve a useful purpose for us. Let me say this again, we experience something repeatedly that we know we do not want, yet we continue participating in the same undesired experience. What else would explain this kind of maddening contradiction than the presence of invisible forces that hold unwanted patterns in place?

A colleague pushes your buttons again during a meeting. You immediately catch a glimpse of the high road and consider letting the offense go without a response…but, in that same moment, the urge to react with the full force and measure of what you feel is deserved takes over. After the uncomfortable exchange you feel bad, they feel bad, and nothing productive comes of it. Why did you react when you knew there was a better way to handle the situation?

After the umpteenth time you get triggered into a pattern of anger and frustration that leaves everyone feeling beaten up, it hits you over the head like an apple falling from a tree: "I don't have to react this way just because I feel that I should. I have a measure of influence and control through the alternative choices I could make." Once we see these unwanted repetitive patterns for what they are, and learn how to recognize the physics of communication, we can handle moments of choice more effectively in our quest to see alternative paths that lead to something better.

The Culminating Moment of Right Now

The final element of physics that is worth mentioning is time. Time is a fundamental dimension in which events can be ordered linearly from the past through the present and on into the future. Many physicists are interested in time because it poses some really big questions going back to Einstein and his efforts to explain space-time and the ways we measure it with clocks. For example, one of today's preeminent physicists Sean Carroll from Caltech, states, "I'm interested in the arrow of time: the fact that the past is different from the future. We remember the past but we don't remember the future. There are irreversible processes. There are things that happen, like you turn an egg into an omelet, but you can't turn an omelet into an egg."[4]

If you take a communication perspective at work and consider time in relation to the past, present, and future, you can see that the simple linear definition does not hold up. And, like a curious physicist, you may be interested in things like omelets that become eggs, or explanations about where the egg came from in the first place. I would argue that communication unfolds at the culminating moment of right now. This means that all of our prior episodes and previously made patterns are compressed into the context of the present moment, which unfolds in a way that simultaneously draws up the plan for the future moment it will make.

At the critical moment of interaction where communication occurs, we are between stories ended and stories just beginning. The next turn we take is at the top of stacks and stacks of previous turns that have already been taken and whose effects have influenced the episodes that became the patterns that shaped our experiences and outcomes. The inertia from right now is part of the physics of communication that pushes against what is possible in each communication event. Everything is old, everything is new. Everything is set, nothing is set. The story is already written, the story is yet to be written.

Conclusion

There are communication rules—the physics of communication—that act as the invisible forces of energy that mix and hold patterns of communication and interaction together. Two different types of rules people apply in any communicative situation are: (1) constitutive rules, which communicators use to interpret or understand an event or message; and (2) regulative rules, which determine how to respond or act based on a given interpretation. Within these rules there are logical forces, the subtle but powerful urges that hold cycles of reaction and behavior in place. Without awareness and focused attention on the rules and forces that influence our communication choices, they can potentially re-produce unwanted patterns of communication and interaction. Chapter 8 describes the precise way that the chemistry and physics of communication follow design principles to make patterns of communication.

8

Communication Design: Deconstructing and Re-MakingP atterns

With an understanding of the basic chemistry and physics of communication we can now focus on basic design, or what gets made when the building blocks of communication and the rules that influence their interactions combine. Knowing some of the basic design principles will help you understand how to deconstruct existing patterns and construct new ones. If you are starting to ask yourself if all of this is really worth the effort, remember that it is not really a true up or down choice to participate or not participate. You cannot sit back and consider whether or not you want to invest in making communication at work because you are *already* doing it.

The question here is whether you are willing to invest energy and time into bringing a greater focus and determination to what gets made. If you are, the starting place is to see the basic design of patterns, episodes, and turns that constitute communication at work. In theory it may seem logical to introduce these three themes in the sequence of macro to micro—patterns, episodes, and then turns—but in practice it is more helpful to go from small to large, so we begin with turns.

Structure of a Turn

Turns are the transitional exchanges within an episode where what happened in the prior turn, and what could happen in the next one, can be shaped by the precise enactment of the present choice within the communication. Turns are the most basic of all the communication design elements. The following continuum shows how the current turn is possible because of the last turn, and the way it is poised to influence the next turn:

Last Turn// .... **Current Turn**// .... \\Next Turn

Here is a simple example of a three-turn sequence that shows the action, reaction, action of a workplace conversation between two colleagues. It is an example of a rapidly escalating exchange that shows the powerful impact turns have on what gets made with communication:

> Last Turn…"I wish I could trust people to do what they say they will." .... \\
> **Current Turn…** "I wish we had competent leadership and clear direction." ..... \\
> Next Turn…"I know where the door is and I can certainly help you find it!"

Turns are not always in consecutive order, though in this case the entire sequence was under 30 seconds. A frustrated manager was trying to express his concern about the state of things, but the blame-oriented language in his turn only triggered more blame from the most seasoned team member (who seemed to feel the need to stand up for others and indirectly call-out her manager for a lack of leadership). The response in the final turn was a speech act in the form of a threat. Three turns, two potential career-altering regrets, one very avoidable situation. In an exchange of turns that is comprised of a passive-aggressive criticism and a staunch ultimatum, what gets made?

Here is a second example of how a progression of turns played out in a reflexive sequence that gave structure to the episodes they formed over a period of time. From both examples you can see how a few turns, punctuated with a beginning and an end point, become an episode that can be named:

> Last Turn// .... At a recent staff meeting, the team's leader excitedly announced a new plan that everyone "must be onboard with and work together to make happen." The big, new initiative fizzled out shortly thereafter and the time and energy spent preparing for it was wasted. When one employee approached the manager to find out what happened in the failed effort, the explanation was all of two words: "things change."\\ ....
>
> **Current Turn//** .... The same manager and employee are discussing the status of the database used by the company for its customer relationship management. Looking for direction, the employee asks the manager what the next step should be to address their concerns. The manager asks for an exhaustive report regarding options, as well as a plan of action to prepare for a major software changeover. The employee asks if this is the best course of action knowing that "things might change" and the manager responds by saying the employee just needs to "just get on board."\\ ....
>
> \\Next Turn .... During the next week's staff meeting, the employee announces that "progress is being made and that things are moving forward with the report and action plan." In reality, however, the employee has disengaged from the project and is biding their time waiting until a new goal is announced by the manager. The opportunity for valued contribution and

substantive conversation around priorities is significantly diminished by this three-turn sequence.

Structure of an Episode

Episodes are a structured set of turns, punctuated by a beginning and end point held together by a common theme. They are what happen when people in communication literally make part or all of an ongoing pattern of communication.

You may not be familiar with the term "episode" as a way of understanding a day-in-the-life at work, but if you take a look at some of the most common episodes listed here, you will likely see your experience reflected. More will be said later in this book about the permeable boundaries of episodes, including the ways in which we can punctuate and name them in diverse ways. I have simply named them in a way that most closely matches the general vocabulary of most workplaces. Some of the most common everyday episodes—both open and closed—at work include the following:

- The difficult conversation
- The left-handed compliment
- The failed delegation
- The annual performance appraisal
- The ambiguous email
- The job interview
- The wasted staff meeting
- The watercooler gossip

The continuum that follows shows how the current episode is possible because of the last episode, which is then poised to influence the next one:

Last Episode//............... **Current Episode**//............... \\Next Episode

If we look back to that rapidly escalating three-turn exchange from that meeting ("I wish I could trust people to do what they say they will."… "I wish we had competent leadership and clear direction."… "I know where the door is and I can certainly help you find it!") we can see how that first passive-aggressive public fight was only one in a series of episodes. From that first blow-up, which I will call "The Threat," this is how that situation progressed:

Last Episode//............... **Current Episode**//............... \\Next Episode
"The Threat"**"Reprimand in the CEO's Office"**// \\"Stronger through Adversity"

Immediately following the "The Threat" the CEO called both people to his office to find out what was going on. He believed in the manager and was planning to stick by him, but he also respected the perspective of the longtime staff member. Based on "The Threat" you might guess that things were pretty bad and unlikely to turn around. However, it was the pivotal middle episode where the leadership of the CEO provided a venue for both of these gifted contributors to work through their differences in an honest way. This episode made it possible for them to create the next episode, "Stronger through Adversity," which included several turns that deescalated the tension, used humor to make both people more human to each other, and improved their working relationship enough to truly present a unified front to the rest of the team.

One of the things I like about this example is that it actually worked out and the final episode resulted in a better working relationship. Had that forum (along with the accountability for their bad behavior) not been given, it is likely that the last episode would have been named "Gather Your Things, This Is Your Last Day."

Structure of a Pattern

Our patterns of communication and interaction get their structure from the specific episodes that link together to form a coherent, recognizable experience and/or outcome. We have a pattern when we can look at a series of episodes, distinguish that cluster from others by punctuating it with a beginning and end point, and give it a name that tells the story of our experience and the result of living through it. With a few thousand pages I could describe many of the most unwanted and preferred patterns that show up in the world of work, but I believe it is more important to know how to spot them, than to have an exhaustive inventory of them.

The Architecture of Patterns of Communication

It is hard to write about basic design and not carry the analogy further into the world of architecture. After all, architecture is the combined process and product of planning, designing, and building and this is what we do when we re-make communication at work.

Although many of us do not consider the planning and designing portion with great reflection, we all know what those rocky communication interactions are like. When we experience our working lives as "prebuilt" we do not consider that we are partners in the planning, designing, and building of the patterns we engage in—but, we are. We may not always have a prominent role, but we can influence the form of our patterns to reflect functional, personal, and social aesthetic values we care about.

It is not uncommon to focus on the negative and consider all of the things we do not like about work—from the way information is shared and decisions get made, to the impacts that they have on the culture of the organization. When these faults cause hardship it can be tempting to simply look at senior management, point a finger, and say, "They did this!" It is another thing to take responsibility as a contributor—in whatever role you play—who takes turns, engages in episodes, and builds some of the most influential patterns of communication that affect your working life.

In architecture, cost estimating is the honest assessment of what will be required to construct something well. This is a useful concept when you take stock in your available energy and time for re-making communication at work. Candidate patterns for re-making are everywhere. However, being selective about which ones we pay particular attention to can lead to a better use of our time and energy available for making them better.

The Roman architect Vitruvius said a good building should satisfy the three principles of *firmitas*, *utilitas*, and *venustas*. With regards to our constructed patterns of communication I think they should follow those three truths as well: durability (the preferred pattern will last); utility (the preferred pattern will produce desired outcomes); and beauty (the preferred pattern will improve the quality of my working life).[1]

Making Is Easier than Re-Making

Nobody likes to pay for prevention, but when the pain comes you do not hesitate to pay up quickly to alleviate it. In part this is why an army of consultants spread around the world are more or less standing by on the ready for the next blunder at work that causes a chain reaction of bad choices and harmful consequences. When enough of the right people's days are ruined, the cavalry is called and the situation is "fixed" through some kind of intervention. This entire process is inefficient and unnecessary.

Right now, if you thoughtfully scanned your working life for challenges, you could probably find plenty of "small pains" in the form of: less-than-perfect outcomes, missed performance opportunities, learning gaps, unsteady relationships, and waning motivation. Wouldn't it be worth an ounce of prevention to focus a little effort and energy into fine tuning existing patterns before things got bad?

Using Design Principles in Everyday Communication at Work

It is only when we see the turns within episodes and the episodes within patterns that we gain a vantage point greater than our current thinking. Current thinking habits are so closely tied with the mental models that prompt our shortcuts that we are often unable to accurately assess existing patterns, judge their results, or explore ways to re-make them.

For example, imagine you are in a recurring pattern of communication and interaction where no fresh ideas emerge and creativity has been replaced with stagnation. As a participant in this you are likely too close to the situation to do anything beyond recognizing the nagging voice in your mind that says "must innovate and be creative." However, if you step back and just look at the way the pattern is built, you may recognize how inflexible attitudes lead to turns that close creativity. And likewise, you may see how an episode of curious and honest questions can expose new ways of thinking and inspire a competitive spirit among team members. The clues to re-making unwanted patterns into the experiences and outcomes we want are right in front of us, if we can see them.

Conclusion

Patterns of communication are simply structured, ongoing interactions. When two colleagues work together over a period of time, they establish habits in the way they communicate and interact; these habits form their patterns. Patterns—unwanted or preferred—are made from specific episodes and the turns that give them their structure.

Turns—fragmented or aligned—are the transitional exchanges within an episode where what happened in the prior turn, and what could happen in the next one, can be shaped by the precise enactment of the present choice in communication (e.g., you said this, then I say that, you did this, so I did that, etc.). Turns are the most basic of all the communication design elements.

Episodes—closed or open—are a structured set of turns, punctuated by a beginning and end point held together by a common theme (e.g., the difficult conversation, the left-handed compliment, the failed delegation, and the annual performance appraisal, etc.). They are what happen when people in communication literally make part or all of an ongoing pattern of communication.

Re-making patterns of communication requires an understanding of the chemistry, physics, and design elements of turns and episodes. Once these are understood, you can see the ways in which everyday patterns are made and re-made. Chapter 9 presents a practical guide for learning to see patterns, episodes, and turns in communication.

9

Learning to See Patterns, Episodes, and Turns in Communication

With the three foundational chapters on the basic chemistry, physics, and design of communication, you now have the essentials to see your patterns, episodes, and turns in communication at work. This chapter provides a simple framework that allows you to take a snapshot of your current working life and then to sift through it to identify potential patterns, episodes, and turns to re-make. The things that are working well for you and producing the kinds of experiences and outcomes you seek can be validated and left alone. The ones that are producing inconsistent outcomes or unwanted experiences are candidates for re-making. This straightforward process will help you identify those with the most potential for transformation. We begin with patterns, then proceed down to the levels of episode and the turns within them, but first, a metaphor to help you learn how to see communication.

Seeing Communication with Maps

Taking a communication perspective at work requires seeing the ecosystems of patterns of communication and interaction that constitute the organization. The analogy I prefer to use when "learning to see" is that of a map. Jerry Brotton, the renowned professor of Renaissance studies, describes maps as abstractions of the world around us.[1] Maps are visual representations of how we make meaning of the physical space around us. Mapping our patterns of communication creates the physical representation of what we have made and this provides a guide to interpret, make meaning, and take action from our experiences with others. With any map, the lines and symbols on the page give order and ways of understanding the messiness of the world. This order brings us confidence and perspective to engage and manage what's out there. In a world of work that at times can seem vast, complex, and indecipherable, a good map shrinks the enormity of the terrain it reflects.

The power and authority to make the map should not be the same as it is in the traditionally hierarchical realm of management. Each person is entitled to make their own map, including the interpretations they generate from it. This is one of the quiet, democratizing aspects of re-making communication at work. It is no longer the exclusive role of formal leaders to identify and name the state of things. On the contrary it is everyone's right and responsibility to understand what *is* in relation to their priorities, problems, goals, and expectations. The writer of the map creates an image from what they see, which is constrained by what they filter out, cannot see, or choose to integrate into their full picture. The viewer of the map—whether it is their own or somebody else's—gains power for interpreting the imagery, arrangement, and depth of the visual depiction.

Of course, making a map is an egocentric process that flows from the perspective of the cartographer. In this case, that perceived bias is not as much of a problem as you would think. The imaginative process of putting yourself at the center of your map is good. You locate your experience across the patterns you engage in. In some cases you are perhaps the lead contributor, and in others you may be more of a passive participant or bystander. Themes like accuracy and objectivity gain importance when we compare our maps to those of others, but to begin with the subjective eye of the maker is unavoidable. And, for the purposes of re-making communication at work, this is desirable. The goal is to surrender the search for the one single right map that accurately reflects the truth of what is. This is an unnecessary and impossible task, which also happens to be true in the discipline of geographic cartography where the subjective interpretations and choices of the map maker can produce endless variations in maps that cover the same terrain.

With regards to our communication patterns, we want our maps to be full of useful information, but too much irrelevant information distracts with clutter. To strike this balance we build them from the three basic elements of communication: turns, episodes, and then patterns. Over time you will learn to tune your eye to see the specific areas of interest that can really help to clarify your vital interactions and your place within them.

The interesting thing is that maps are never finished because the world of work continuously evolves. They are important markers of our evolution through organizational life and because of this, I consider them snapshots in time that are useful in ways that are limited to the time and circumstances in which they are created. For that time, however, maps can get people to look at communication, talk to each other about what they see, and clarify distinctions among their perspectives. In my experience on the job I have seen no other way of working through communication challenges at work that can produce the powerful results that good maps can make.

Setting the Pattern Continuum

Looking at communication is about seeing the nuance and complexity of the stuff that makes it. When learning to see and map patterns of communication and interaction it can be overwhelming to begin with the full picture, so I often start with polarities that allow for a quick sort of what we observe, recognize, feel, and experience. The way in which I begin to make meaning of the patterns, episodes, and turns of communication and interaction I observe starts with a continuum approach, where the space between the two ends of the spectrum acts as a useful scale to subtly measure the degree to which something is "more of this," or "more of that."

The irony of this approach is that everything I have written thus far has promoted a more open understanding of communication, which has been a move away from the either/or and right/wrong way of how many people consider communication. However, when you look deeper at the two ends of the spectrum, you see that these polarities reflect the equally opposing forces that we struggle with. While we may never be at one end, our movement along the continuum can produce significant learning from the way in which we hold the tension of both ends together.

At a fundamental level, the most basic polarities can be framed as *unwanted* and *preferred*. Therefore, I organize the most common patterns in these two groups. Unwanted patterns go by many names and descriptive adjectives. They are unhealthy, unproductive, limited, stuck, destructive, confusing, repetitive, tired, and out of sync with priorities and goals. Preferred patterns also go by many names and descriptions. They are useful, desired, productive, healthy, flowing, forward-moving, successful, engaging, aligned, and more. Preferred patterns are meaningful. They reflect back what is important to us, and although they may be difficult, they are worth the effort to make and sustain because they allow us to contribute and receive something important. Unwanted patterns take the important things we want from our experiences. They drain our time, energy, happiness, focus, and motivation. They are just plain difficult and ultimately they prevent us from contributing and receiving the things we value.

When we look for patterns to map, we can follow clues that reflect people's experience. The stories that they tell about their everyday working lives are like a trail of breadcrumbs that leads back to the pivotal patterns they engage in. Another one of the reasons that I use the continuum approach and sort patterns by the two categories, unwanted and preferred, is because most people naturally sort their own stories in a similar way. This is important because "how people think and talk about their work and how they feel about the relationships they maintain at work and the company itself all have a significant impact on their behavior choices and, ultimately, on the performance of the organization."[2]

Table 9.1 shows a quick set of pattern examples that are organized according to the two polarities. I have intentionally described each of them in a manner that reveals the presence of patterns within typical organizational

Table 9.1 Sample pattern continuum

Unwanted patterns	Preferred patterns
• Compensation matches status + *relationships*—ineffective people are promoted	• Compensation matches talent + *performance*—the most effective people are promoted
• Directors across divisions operate independently—information gaps produce redundancies and missed opportunities	• Directors across divisions take time to compare notes—information gaps are avoided
• Top leaders do not recognize the individual contributions of people at different levels in the company—employee morale is stagnant	• Top leaders validate the individual contributions of people at every level of the organization—employee morale is elevated
• Employees avoid spending extra time and energy on improving the customer experience—the customer experience is lackluster	• Employees invest significant energy and attention to make their customers' experience memorable—customer loyalty is strong
• Ongoing learning and performance improvement initiatives and career advancement opportunities are not supported—employees do not commit long-term to the company	• Ongoing learning and performance improvement initiatives and career advancement opportunities are supported by the organization—employees commit to the company

dynamics. Each pattern produces many aftereffects, or *pattern echoes*, but the two primary root interactions can be seen in the table.

Even from this basic list you can see that if we were to zoom in on one of these examples we would see an entire web of episodes that combine to make that pattern. Let's take the preferred pattern where employees invest significant energy and attention to make their customers' experience memorable. It is quite likely that there are very consistent episodes before, during, and after those customer service exchanges where managers encourage, expect, and reward this ongoing investment of energy and attention in customer service. If leaders did not value the extra effort, or on the contrary if they prevented it by placing greater importance on things like call-time efficiency and number of trouble tickets "solved," then the pattern would shift into something else. And, because consistent customer experiences do not happen without training, there are likely a variety of episodes where new employees receive careful training and mentoring, as well as ongoing monitoring and evaluation to ensure that they understand what great service is in that company.

The pattern echo here of course reverberates outside of the organization to the customer experience. When employees invest significant energy and attention to make their customers' experiences memorable we can imagine episodes where customers choose to stay loyal to the brand, they rank the customer service high on feedback scores, they tell their friends and colleagues about the great service, and do many other positive things in response to a positive interaction with a strong brand.

In a similar way we could choose any of the patterns on either side of the continuum and expose the same potential episodes that influence the structure and outcomes of the pattern. An important thing to keep in mind right now is that there is no need to be tricked into absolute black/white thinking about the polarities. Is it likely that in the example given earlier regarding excellent customer service there are occasional lapses where people drop the ball and really disappoint the customers? And on the other side is it also likely that amid a culture where the customer experience is not valued as highly as other priorities, great moments of service happen and people go above and beyond to surprise and delight their customers? When I begin to plot patterns on the continuum I will often ask, "Is it a little more of this, or a little more of that." This specific language implies the mixed nature of patterns and the way they naturally slide across, but never rest on one extreme.

Setting the Episode Continuum

Similar to the aforementioned pattern continuum, I organize the most frequent episodes into two categories: *closed* and *open*. Closed episodes are difficult to experience, they sustain the status quo and make new possibilities less likely, they block productivity, they frustrate people, they cause hurt feelings, they erode motivation and engagement, and more. Open episodes are useful experiences that open new possibilities, remove blocks to productivity, decrease frustration and hurt feelings, increase motivation and engagement, and more. In order to establish a clear conceptual link between patterns and episodes, I will continue building upon the list of patterns given earlier with this inventory of common episodes that would likely show up amid those patterns, which are displayed in table 9.2.

Even from this basic list of episodes you can see that if we were to zoom in on one of these examples we would see an entire web of turns that combine to shape that episode. Let's take the open episode where during a visit to a branch office, top leaders hosted a lunch and recognized five front-line staff members who helped turn the fate of the office around. It is quite likely that the manager(s) at the branch office who coordinated the visit likely advocated for their staff to be recognized. A turn in this whole episode could have gone something like this phone call:

Branch manager: "Hi Sarah, it's Chuck. I hope you are doing well. Listen, we are excited about your visit next week. In preparation we have arranged to get some lunch brought in. I don't think our group needs any kind of formal program, but if you were looking to mention a few names, I'll email you five people that really were instrumental in turn-ing things around last year."

Senior vice president: "Thanks Chuck, lunch sounds good. And yeah, send me those names. I would love to mention them and just let people know that the home office sees the good things that are happening."

I am intentionally keeping this dialogue simple to illustrate the main point. This episode of "Top Leaders Visiting the Local Branch" did not just occur. There were likely a series of turns before, and of course there are turns during and after that all combine to shape the experience and outcomes pro-duced by that episode. In the positive sense, when open episodes like this one occur frequently enough, we could say that the company has a preferred pattern of staff recognition. The pattern echo of this is immense and we can imagine potentially high levels of employee engagement, strong retention of staff, and various bottom-line impacts driven by these two factors.

Alternatively, imagine that Chuck was so busy he did not take the time to call his senior vice president, Sarah. Or consider the possibility that Sarah was in town only for the afternoon and declined lunch in order to spend time with Chuck and the other two managers on the financial projections for the next year. These two potential turns would completely close the episode and set a trajectory for a very different experience.

Table 9.2   Sample episode continuum

Closed episodes	Open episodes
• A high-potential young staff member is told by a manager not to bother thinking about that promotion because the vice president "has her favorites"	• A high-potential young staff member is offered a promotion for their effort, contribution, and potential
• The director of operations and the director of sales conduct their annual strategy meetings with no participation across the groups	• Following the first session of an annual planning meeting, directors across divisions share their draft strategic plans to check for interdependencies
• Top leaders visit a branch of the company that was hard hit by the recession and have no direct interaction with front-line staff	• During a visit to a branch office, top leaders hosted a lunch and recognized five front-line staff members who helped turn the fate of the office around
• A customer service call focuses on fixing the initial problem, with no effort to understand the customer's additional needs	• After the presenting issue was solved, the customer service representative carefully asked the customer, "How are you liking our product and do you have any other questions about it?"
• The budget for leadership development education was pulled and no career development alternatives were offered	• The budget for leadership development education was pulled, so managers created an informal course by using internal talent as guest presenters

Setting the Turn Continuum

As I do with patterns and episodes, I think of the most impactful turns in two domains: *fragmented* and *aligned*. Fragmented turns follow rules (i.e., "shoulds" and "oughts") whether they are helpful or not, they trigger escalated responses, they create defensiveness, and they lead to closed episodes. Aligned turns are clear, invitational, empathetic, assertive, balanced, focused, and they open up new possibilities to shift or awaken something in ourselves and others. Fragmented turns can look like, feel like, and sound like demands and mandates, attacks and criticisms, harsh questions and interrogation, doubts and fears, and confusion. Aligned turns can look like, feel like, and sound like apology and reconciliation, inquiry and reflection, empathy and concern, and clarity.

Using the same flow as the last two sections, table 9.3 shows an inventory of the most likely turns that could unfold within the patterns and episodes described earlier.

If you put the entire picture together you can see the way episodes shape patterns, and the turns within those episodes can change the entire character of what gets made. Considering this set of threaded examples, reflect on

Table 9.3   Sample turn continuum

Fragmented turns	Aligned turns
• A high-potential young staff member polishes his resume and puts feelers out, feeling like his chances to grow are limited by company politics	• A bright person without the right college degree decides to share more of their great ideas knowing that they have a shot at being promoted
• The CEO of the company demands to know why two different divisions independently spent significant resources on virtually the same project	• With the CEO's mandate for increased collaboration, two directors put aside their apprehensions and invite key members of their teams to give input on their strategic plans
• A busy manager does not make a planning phone call and a disorganized visit from corporate leaders leaves people doubting that their efforts matter	• A manager advocates for his staff and makes the extra phone call to ensure that the branch visit from corporate is valuable
• At the morning meeting, the customer service manager berates a representative for spending too much call time with customers	• At the morning meeting, the customer service manager reminds people that a customer for life is the most valuable outcome of their work
• A new manager who was promised the opportunity to get training feels betrayed	• A senior director speaks individually to a new manager who was promised a training opportunity and works together on an alternative plan to make good on the pledge

these questions and then read below as each pattern becomes the inevitable product of the turns and episodes that made it.

What is made when a turn takes shape? What is made when a few turns form an episode? What is made when episodes link together with others? What experiences and outcomes do people get from the overall patterns of communication and interaction they make? How do the patterns impact the individual's quality of working life, the team's potential for success, and the organization's overall health and performance?

Employees avoid spending extra time and energy on improving the customer experience—the customer experience is uninspiring! At the morning meeting, the customer service manager berates a representative for spending too much call time with customers...the next customer service call focuses only on fixing the initial problem, with no effort to understand the customer's additional needs. Employees avoid spending extra time and energy on improving the customer experience—the customer experience is uninspiring!

Employees invest significant energy and attention to make their customers' experience memorable—customer loyalty is strong! At the morning meeting, the customer service manager reminds people that a customer for life is the most valuable outcome of their work...the next customer service call addresses the presenting issue, then the customer service representative carefully asks the customer additional questions, such as: "How are you liking our product and do you have any other questions about it?" Employees invest significant energy and attention to make their customers' experience memorable—customer loyalty is strong!

Compensation matches status + relationships—ineffective people are promoted! A high-potential young staff member is told by a manager not to bother thinking about that promotion because the vice president "has her favorites"...then that same high-potential young staff member polishes his resume and puts feelers out for a new job, feeling like his chances to grow are limited by company politics. Compensation matches status + relationships—ineffective people are promoted!

Compensation matches talent + performance—the most effective people are promoted! A high-potential young staff member is offered a promotion for her effort, contribution, and potential...then another bright person in the company, without the right college degree, decides to engage more deeply by contributing more of her great ideas knowing that they have a shot at being promoted. Compensation matches talent + performance—the most effective people are promoted!

Pattern Echoes

Most workplace culture audits begin with individual meetings or small focus groups where two simple questions are asked: "What do you like about working here?" and "What don't you like about working here?" The responses that people give are the *pattern echoes* that reflect the everyday experiences and outcomes they live through at work. If people had the language for it, they might describe various turns and episodes that more comprehensively answer the two questions. In fact, one of the goals of this book is to help people find a better way to talk about communication at work that does more than just recast the presenting effects of what has already been made.

To make this point, imagine that you are wading out into the ocean for a relaxing swim when an unexpected wave crashes into you and knocks you off of your feet. When you get your head above water you curse the wave. Every story you tell about that day's adventure will go back to that large, unforeseen wave. However, waves are like our experiences at work; they are just the presenting effects of things that have already been made. You definitely felt the wave, but it was no more than the turns and episodes of swell, water temperature, depth, wind speed and direction, and tides. These things are what created the conditions for the wave to knock you off of your feet.

We are now getting further and further away from the ten myths of effective communication at work, going from concept closer to hands-on action. The new principles, the communication perspective at work, and the basic chemistry, physics, and design of communication have come together to help you learn how to see patterns, episodes, and turns in communication. This is the basis for re-making communication at work. The practical aspects of learning to see communication can be assisted by three exercises, including: the "pattern finder," "episode mapper," and "turn selector." There are complete examples of each of these tools in chapter 14; to introduce the exercises, here are the bones of the processes.

Pattern Finder

The pattern finder exercise will help you to scan your world of work in six questions. The result of the process will be a clearer map of the unwanted and preferred patterns that you experience. As you read each question, simply write what comes to mind in whatever format is useful. Using the sequence of questions will help you spot patterns that matter.

1. What recurring experiences or outcomes do I have at work?

2. What makes these experiences and outcomes real?

I say, think, feel, and act...	Others say, think, feel, and act...

3. When and where do the interactions that produce these experiences and outcomes take place?

4. If I connect the dots, what story does all of this tell and how would I name it?

5. Where does this story or pattern sit on the continuum?

    Unwanted..Preferred
    -3 -2 -1 0 $+1$ $+2$ $+3$

6. Does it need to be re-made in some way?
    • If the pattern is in the (+) range, that's good!
    • Does it create the kinds of experiences and outcomes you want from work?
    • If it is in the (−) range, or if it is not producing the quality of working life you need, would you consider re-making it?
        i.   If no...stop right now and move on.
        ii. If yes...go to the episode mapping exercise.

Episode Mapper

Now that you have a pattern, another six-question sequence can help you break it down to see the episode(s) that shape the pattern.

1. Who are the players?
    • Who is involved? Who seems to matter most?

2. When/where does it begin and when/where does it end?

3. Frequency and impact checklist:
    • Does it repeat? How often?
    • Does it have a minor, moderate, or major impact on my day when it happens?

4. When the episode plays out, the results are more:

    Closed..Open
    -3 -2 -1 0 $+1$ $+2$ $+3$

5. What name would I give the episode?

6. Does it need to be "opened" in some way to contribute to a better pattern?
    • If no...stop right now and move on.
    • If yes...go to the turn selector exercise.

Turn Selector

Now that you have a pattern and the name of a key episode that is worth exploring, you can take notice of the specific turns that can shift the quality of the episode in the way you want to alter it.

    1. What are the three pivotal turns?

Starts with me...	Starts with them...
• I say, think, feel, do... • They say, think, feel, do... • Then I say, think, feel, do...	• They say, think, feel, do... • I say, think, feel, do... • Then they say, think, feel, do...

    2. Is there a specific speech act that frames one of the turns, which sets a tone and direction for where things go from there?

    3. What rules seem to prompt our responses within each turn?

Me	Them
How I interpret what they say...	How they interpret what I say...
How I act based on that interpretation...	How they act based on that interpretation...
The logical forces or sense of "should" that compels me to respond in a certain way...	The logical forces or sense of "should" that compels them to respond in a certain way...

    4. These turns are:

Fragmented...Aligned

          -3 -2 -1 0 $+1$ $+2$ $+3$

    • Do the turns make it hard to stay in communication?
    • Is different communication required to make better experiences and outcomes?

    5. What pivot in my next turn, or in their next turn, could lead to more alignment?

    6. When will I take the next turn to create that shift?

Conclusion

Three simple frameworks—the pattern finder, episode mapper, and turn selector—allow you to take a snapshot of your current working life and sift through it to identify potential patterns, episodes, and turns to re-make. These three building blocks can be mapped on a continuum, which reveals the specific way in which they impact your working life. The ones that produce preferred experiences and outcomes can be validated and left alone, while those that produce unwanted experiences and results can be re-made. Chapter 10 introduces a variety of high-priority patterns that commonly affect individuals and teams in the world of work.

10

Identifying High-Priority Patterns

This chapter presents two groups of common patterns that play out in organizational life. The Seven Communication Pitfalls and Unwanted Patterns produce challenging outcomes with closed episodes and fragmented turns. The Seven Preferred Patterns of Communication and Interaction produce preferred patterns with open episodes and aligned turns. These specific patterns are unique because they are like systems of patterns or super patterns. When you read the descriptions of each one you will likely be able to imagine that within each of these super patterns, there are micro patterns—along with all of the related episodes and turns—unfolding in the experiences of the people involved in them.

One of the benefits of presenting this list is that it demonstrates the terrain you will likely cross when you begin taking a communication perspective at work and looking at some of the most common organizational challenges. You may recognize these patterns from other traditions of describing them (i.e., leadership and organization development terminology, behavioral psychology frameworks, etc.), so I encourage you to focus less about semantics and more on substance.

Seven Communication Pitfalls and Unwanted Repetitive Patterns

The majority of my research and consulting work with organizations and their leaders has focused on identifying the most common barriers to learning and performance that affect individual, team, and organizational success. I created the most exhaustive inventory of barriers to workplace learning and performance available[1] and my recent book, *Beyond the Job Description*, shows how these barriers form a hidden curriculum of work* that everyone must confront. In that book I provide a system for revealing these hidden challenges, as well as a process for fully resolving them.[2]

For this summary chapter I simply isolated seven pitfalls and unwanted patterns that consistently prevent individuals and teams from doing their best work, erode the quality of people's working lives, and reduce the overall impact of individual, team, and organizational performance. Following the list, each is explained in sufficient detail to help you identify whether that pattern is relevant to your current working life.

1. Gridlock from egos and emotions
2. Surrendering creativity for consensus
3. Priority whitewashing
4. Overcollaboration
5. Sticking with a failing solution (because we've always done it this way)
6. Elephants and ghosts that haunt the future
7. Taking the stuff of trust

Gridlock from Egos and Emotions

This is a pattern where things get bogged down and stuck because of a combination of ego and emotion that entrench people in their assumptions, beliefs, and actions. With no objective distance to step back and gain a wider perspective, the impasse and gridlock prevent movement and progress and the likely side effects include physical and emotional stress, a decrease in engagement, increase in unproductive conflict, and an inability to respond quickly to new challenges and opportunities.

Surrendering Creativity for Consensus

At first glance this is a pattern that can seem "positive." However, when people prematurely surrender a perspective in the pursuit of consensus or collegial agreement they often miss out on the potential for creativity and innovation. The creative dissent that emerges from disagreements handled professionally is the stuff of positive change. When these clunky, but necessary conversations are ended prematurely and are then wrapped up in an artificial bow of perceived agreement, it can be one of the most silently dysfunctional patterns that a team can experience.

Priority Whitewashing

This pattern occurs when all goals, priorities, and outcomes are treated the same. And when everything is important, nothing is. The concept of whitewashing recalls a hillside in a Greek village where all the houses are whitewashed with lime and indistinguishable from the others. The rudderless effect of priority whitewashing results in unproductive experiences (e.g., endless meetings where nothing important seems to happen, teams drifting among half-hearted objectives and uninspired initiatives, and managers unable to hold people accountable for achieving the organization's top priorities).[3]

Overcollaboration

This pattern occurs as a result of excessive teamwork and collaborative action that serves no performance-based rationale. We should only engage in leveraged collaboration, which is the intentional choice to partner with others when the combination of skill, ability, and available resources can create a more effective outcome than is possible alone. In situations where the outcome matters less than the process, leveraged collaboration can also be used when relationship building is a priority. When people overcollaborate they increase the risk of dysfunctional patterns that can emerge in the space between something important getting done and the unnecessary collaboration that slows or prevents it.

Sticking with a Failing Solution (Because We've Always Done It This Way)

This is a familiar pattern for anyone who has ever envisioned a change and subsequently hit the brick wall of resistance when trying to implement it. Relying on past success and aligning the identity of the team/organization with that past success often results in a reduced incentive to take risks and make change happen. The rationale is often given in simple terms that reflect the inertia of what came before it. Saying that we do things around here because that is how we've always done them is the equivalent of parents explaining a decision to a child with the very unsatisfying "because I said so" explanation.

Elephants and Ghosts That Haunt the Future

This pattern involves the scars, memories, and fears of previous experience. While people in organizations come and go and things eventually change, real dysfunctional patterns can leave an afterlife that becomes a separate pattern by itself. This pattern is shaped by the proverbial elephant in the room, or the issue that is taboo and is believed to be undiscussable. It is amplified by the ghost of some personality or perspective that is either sacred or feared and the visceral impact of their legacy remains, despite the fact that the prior circumstances have shifted and influential people may have already gone.

Eroding Trust

This pattern involves a general erosion of trust among people interacting in situations that require at least a moderate level of willingness and ability to act trustworthy toward each other in the pursuit of their common commitments. Often the pattern forms over time when there is a perceived imbalance of contribution or clash of unmet expectations among people. Whether there is a recognizable moment where a breach of trust occurred, or whether it is a slow and steady decline of respect and belief in the other's ability to follow through on the things they say matter, patterns of distrust can be the most difficult to re-make, and yet the most powerful when changed.

Learning from Pitfalls and Unwanted Patterns

One of the interesting qualities about these seven common pitfalls and unwanted patterns is that they often show up in clusters. Very rarely have I consulted with a team or an organization and seen just one. While there might be a single pattern that gains the lion's share of attention due to its greater visibility, there are often several, interchangeable patterns present at one time. Winding your way into these gaps and learning about the various ways they hold us within contradiction presents many opportunities for re-making communication at work

When we find ourselves in the middle of an unwanted experience it usually boils down two important questions: "How did we end up at the place we're at?" and "How do we get to the places we want to be?" These questions serve as the opening step to start moving toward something better. This is the ultimate definition of change from the inside. Change from the outside fits with the mindset of using communication skills to attack the presenting issues of the breakdown in communication. Change from the inside is about shifting the patterns of communication and interaction that made the breakdown.

Seven Patterns of Communication Leaders Must Get Right

In the same way that there are consistent pitfalls and unwanted patterns that reflect our held-in-common experience at work, there are also patterns that leaders must get right because of the positive, multiplier effects. Even if you have not experienced one of the seven unwanted patterns directly, you likely have had an intuitive feel reading their descriptions because you have seen them show up in the experiences of others. In the same way, there are innumerable healthy micro patterns of communication and interaction that typically lead to positive experiences and outcomes (i.e., "patterns of acknowledgment for a job well done," "patterns of accountability and shared responsibility for accomplishing priorities," etc.). However, these do not have the same effect as large-scale defining patterns that are comprised by these micro patterns.

While I have already said that every episode affects its pattern, and every pattern has an afterlife that affects other patterns, there truly are some significant organizational endeavors that drive expanded change more than others. To really leverage the potential for re-making communication at work it is important to look at a few of these super patterns that have a cascading effect. These include the following:

1. Patterns of shared investment
2. Patterns of willing examination
3. Patterns of honest context
4. Patterns of diverse purposes
5. Patterns of leveraged collaboration
6. Patterns of simplicity within complexity
7. Patterns of integrated learning

Patterns of Shared Investment

When patterns of shared investment are present, individuals take ownership for the experience and outcomes they get at work. There are no victim-minded attitudes that blame others for unwanted outcomes if they surface. When mistakes are made and unmet expectations are realized, teams practice a process of understanding what went sideways, and then they re-make something better.

While levels of knowledge, experience, and interest in shared investment vary from person to person and ebb and flow with the circumstances of life, there is a consistent level of engagement in this process of co-owning responsibility for team and organizational outcomes. People are held accountable for this approach, and they are rewarded for following through with it.

Patterns of shared investment lead to other micro patterns of proactive problem-solving, enhanced collaboration, and empowered teams.

These patterns reflect an organization's commitment to the inclusion of diverse viewpoints and the recognition that great ideas can come from any level of the organization. Shared investment can lead to a decentralization of the traditional control structures that own the defining parameters of problems and solutions (i.e., it is not just management's job to know what the problems are and how to fix them). The flip side of this can be heard in the language of pragmatic invitations from managers to individual contributors: "We created this mess; we need to get ourselves out of it...If we want to achieve that goal, then we will need to build the patterns that will make it" Rather than alienating people, reducing morale, and gaining limited buy-in and support for these efforts, organizational members become challenged and empowered to join in the effort and reward.

Cynical, indifferent, or resistant attitudes toward important organizational activities are reduced when people take ownership over the outcomes they will experience. So, rather than indifference to everyday challenges at work (the big and the small), there is interest and engagement. Many of the negative behavior cycles that surface when people are alienated and disempowered—deflecting criticism, scapegoating, blaming other people or events, avoiding tasks, or behaving in ways that shift responsibility to others—are reduced or eliminated within patterns of shared investment

Patterns of Willing Examination

When patterns of willing examination are present, there are no sacred cows or taboo topics that are off the table. Even sensitive subjects that directly relate to individual and team performance are discussible. There are shared and agreed upon expectations that enhance the constructive way in which ideas, relationships, decisions, and outcomes are examined and it is rare that people get bruised and battered by these honest exchanges. With a greater emphasis on curiosity than correctness, people explore their everyday experience at work with a communication perspective. Small groups and teams use various questioning paradigms and process frameworks that are systemic and pattern-focused. As a result, they help people see their own roles in making communication at work and increase their collective willingness/capacity to examine the patterns that make team dynamics and organizational culture in a transparent and consistent way.

Patterns of willing examination lead to micro patterns of credibility for leaders, healthy conversation cycles about necessary change, and more productive uses of resources for individual and team development.

The interactions that occur within these patterns cultivate the ability and willingness of people to successfully adapt to fast changing, complex, and uncertain conditions. Rather than settling for known solutions that fit with a more superficial assessment of how things are now, or have worked in the past, a more rigorous examination of current circumstances and possibilities produces openings for novel, innovative approaches to getting great work done.

That old bad habit that many teams have, suppressing failures and ignoring mistakes, can be reduced or eliminated with a willingness to carefully examine what they are making at work. This "warts and all" approach turns blemishes into interesting avenues to pursue, rather than objects of blame to project on others. Careful examination can help us solve the right problems quickly and effectively by avoiding cursory diagnoses of situations. People would rather be helpful than right, so petty differences are set aside and higher priorities gain more attention than chatter.

When an organization's culture and system of structuring the way work gets done fail to create forums for willing examination, they constrain these useful interactions and, by default, make the more complex and important patterns of communication off-limits to explore. Investing resources to establish and sustain these forums will allow you to take the time to examine challenging patterns and sniff out issues like: the presence of quiet but damaging unresolved conflict; subtle, but game changing innovation roadblocks; and slowly emerging gaps in strategy that impact the bottom line.

Patterns of Honest Context

When patterns of honest context are present, the stuff of organizational life can be dealt with simply and effectively. The "hard to hear" facts of reality are not only tolerated, but they are welcomed because of their potential to show a path through the challenges they bring.

Jim Collins described these as "the brutal facts of reality,"[4] which is a catchy phrase that leaves no doubt about its meaning. Because there can be so many versions of "facts," I find it more useful to think of it more as a set of demanding questions: "Who are we right now?" "What is really happening around us?" "With our present course, where are we really heading?" When people possess a willingness to see the current circumstances in the clear light of day, no matter how challenging, they gain a relevant context to interpret their current experience and outcomes. This unfiltered context allows them to then pinpoint the specific patterns that contributed to making the situation and/or that must be present if something different is going to exist. In this way, getting to a more desired future experience or set of outcomes is not possible without an honest context of what is happening in the present.

Patterns of honest context lead to micro-patterns of well-defined problems and needs, authentic discussions that build trust through transparency, and solutions that address root-cause issues.

Rather than clinging to a fixed, positive organizational identity from the past at the expense of current and accurate organizational assessments, people who engage in open exchanges about the true state of things operate from a current reality that will not move under the pressure of changing attitudes and trends that do not reflect their highest priorities. This firmer starting place prevents lapses into the double-reality gaps between *what we expect and think we should get* and *what we actually have.*

In addition, people are not pressured to think and act in the same way, which usually results in groupthink and produces a lack of innovative, critically tested ideas. This honest context replaces complacency with a sufficient level of urgency to make necessary changes based on the critical importance of what is happening. Honest context also enables an accurate assessment of available margin. Insufficient margin, or the lack of resources to meet available demands, is often the cause of failed change efforts and large-scale initiatives that require extra everything from everyone involved.

Patterns of Diverse Purposes

When patterns of diverse purposes are present, people do not cling to single-minded approaches or the kind of black-and-white thinking that precedes it. They define issues and challenges in multidimensional forms and respect the diverse ways in which those problems can be defined and resolved. When patterns must be re-made people do not assume that it is feasible, or even desired, to develop one single shared "solution" or purpose for what the new pattern will be.

The shared recognition that individuals are driven by their own unique ambitions and desires for specific experiences and outcomes at work prevents generic goal-setting exercises that result in half-commitments and waning motivation of the people who are responsible for carrying them out. These efforts flow from the understanding that working life is complex, fast moving, ambiguous, and constantly changing. The reality of this enhances the value of diversity inside teams and organizations and it signals intrinsic value in each person's uniquely defined and expressed priorities and desired purposes.

Patterns of diverse purpose lead to micro patterns like active commitments to seeing diverse possibilities, empowering people to engage more deeply in their work, avoiding the myth of one mission, and embracing diverse purposes that have overlapping commitments.

Healthy and productive patterns invariably require the alignment of priorities, resources, and people. Successfully taking on new initiatives often requires a common purpose and sense of direction. However, alignment does not mean uniformity. There can be alignment within a diverse range of individual purposes, which is where the most important synergy happens. Working toward a common goal that actually means different things to different people provides a great opportunity for shared investment. It requires the investment of time to explore what people's definitions of purpose are, including the ways they contrast and compare to others.

When diverse purpose are compared outside of a zero-sum game mindset (i.e., meaning that if you achieve your purpose and goal, it means I must fail to achieve mine and vice versa), then compatible efforts to achieve complementary purposes can be established. The effective integration of diversity disarms people from the tendency to only look for what reinforces their own existing beliefs and to advocate during the times they feel their interests are threatened. When you are intentional about seeing other possibilities, priorities, and values then you will see them. Of course there are times when diverse purposes are incompatible and traditional compromise is needed. However, these times may not be as common as one would think.

Patterns of Leveraged Collaboration

When patterns of leveraged collaboration are present people work alone as much as they work directly together. They recognize that collaboration includes the face-to-face time on task, but it is also punctuated by necessary periods of individual reflection and action that make the shared time more valuable. Not all collaboration is created equally. The most effective collaboration occurs when you deliberately seek out leveraged collaboration that serves a specific purpose and matches the needs of the moment. This kind of intentional partnering that equally meets a strategic goal simultaneously breaks the overinflated value of "collaboration at all costs."

While the value of collaboration pervades the organizational culture at all times, people work together only when needed, they act alone when that is most helpful, and they use the intersections of face-time wisely. There are no more "meeting cultures" that sustain the myth that work only gets done at meetings. Instead there are high-touch interactions that focus on the patterns that must exist to get important work.

> Patterns of leveraged collaboration lead to micro patterns of longer productivity cycles, value-added face-to-face meetings, and greater initiative taking among individual contributors.

As time marches on and organizations mature, they often accumulate lots of "stuff." The creation and forced use of "organizational stuff" such as policies, procedures, and structural practices that can at times be overly formal and bureaucratic reduce the capacity of people to respond to challenges and opportunities in real time. Routine collaboration is an example of an ongoing practice in organizations with "stuff." People have checks and balances that require sharing information, gaining approvals, seeking input, and sharing in the responsibility to implement new things. Generically speaking, these things are good; however, they are only good when they improve the quality of the experience and/or finished product in a measurable way.

When collaboration happens without an evaluation of whether it is necessary and useful to getting a good outcome, it can simply waste time and energy. On the flip side, when there are informal and decentralized initiatives to get great work done either independently or in collaboration with people that need to be engaged, it supports the balance of formality/informality that is most useful to the situation. Rather than collaboration and planned consensus decisions (that can often be at odds with intelligent, effective decisions) that create bottlenecks on progress and delay decision-making, leveraged collaboration works. As a result, people do not get bogged down with collaboration fatigue, group think, or analysis paralysis that can all result from mindless partnering.

Patterns of Simplicity within Complexity

When patterns of simplicity within complexity are present, people break things down to the smallest level possible in order to understand and take action on their meaningful priorities. Despite the rapid increases in complexity (i.e., the speed of change, uncertainty in the marketplace, etc.) people gain insight into the culture and performance of their organizations by focusing on the patterns that make them.

By focusing on specific episodes, people can find simplicity within complexity. Asking straightforward questions such as "What actually happened?" "How was this made?" "Do we need to make something different here if we expect better outcomes," and so on can help us identify unknown factors that impact performance in complex patterns.

> Patterns of simplicity within complexity lead to micro patterns of fearless approaches to managing change, consistent follow-through on difficult priorities, and greater influence on factors that can be controlled.

Re-making communication at work is about stripping away the layers of our experience on the job and focusing on the specific patterns that—at a fundamental level—create the experience and outcomes we make at work. The search for these basic elements requires simple thinking. The objectivity that often emerges in the search for simplicity can reduce the emotional, confrontational, reactive, and personality-driven attitudes and behaviors that accompany complex and confusing patterns of interpersonal communication and interaction. And, the systemic approach to finding patterns and mapping episodes allows you to map the complexities of the world around you in ways that produce meaningful interpretations that are consistent with your capacity to create the conditions for optimal response.

Patterns of Integrated Learning

When patterns of integrated learning are present, unwanted episodes of communication and interaction are not repeated. People live with unwanted patterns and the painful episodes that make them long enough. When a decision is made to deconstruct a pattern of communication and re-make it into something else, the practice of integrated learning ensures that the experiences of the past remain visible enough to influence the present change.

Patterns are never set in stone and so ongoing reflection and learning about what works, what is desired, and what is ultimately inconsistent with values and aspirations is also an ongoing practice. This allows for patterns to be "re-made on the fly" or fine-tuned, rather than significantly overhauled after their damage has been done.

Patterns of integrated learning lead to micro patterns of breaking silos that divide communication and learning, reducing unwanted repetitive patterns, and decreasing frustration and burnout from the cost of recurring, damaging patterns of communication and interaction.

These patterns start with and lead to flexible attitudes and practices within an organizational culture that encourage innovation and the acceptance of useful mistakes. Rather than making the one big mistake, the emphasis on reflection and learning from measured risks and small mistakes leads to greater potential for innovation and breakthrough. It is only this kind of integrated learning that allows you to change the underlying mental models and belief structures that drive patterns of communication and interaction.

What's Possible with These Patterns?

Part III of this book introduces a variety of practices to re-make communication at work. If one or more of these seven preferred patterns is not present in your organization or team, you can use these practices to begin making them. If several of the unwanted patterns are present, you can re-make them into something better. Overall, one of the best things you can do with these patterns is notice their unique combination of power, influence, and stickiness. The stuff of our organizational lives is reflected in these patterns. If we want to know what our individual, team, and organizational experiences and outcomes produce at work we need to look no further than the patterns that create the conditions for them to be present.

Conclusion

There are two groups of common patterns that play out in organizational life. The Seven Communication Pitfalls and Unwanted Patterns produce challenging outcomes with closed episodes and fragmented turns. The Seven Preferred Patterns of Communication and Interaction produce preferred patterns with open episodes and aligned turns. These specific patterns are unique because they are like systems of patterns or superpatterns. This means that they are often comprised by a set of micro patterns that combine to form the larger superpattern. For example, an unwanted pattern of gridlock from egos and emotions likely includes smaller, related patterns such as hypercompetition, silo-thinking, and ineffective collaboration. The implications of this include: the importance of identifying core challenges (rather than presenting issues); the need to see patterns of communication as part of a larger system; and the predictability that certain challenges will likely be accompanied by other, related issues. Chapter 11 provides a practical summary of how these kinds of patterns and the capacity to take a communication perspective can be applied to the real world of work.

II

Applying Part II to the Real World of Work

When we try to pick out anything by itself, we find it hitched to everything else in the universe.

—John Muir

Communication is action, reaction, action, reaction—picking out one thing with the hope of saying "see, this is it" is impossible. Everything is connected to everything else. To unpack this vast subject I have separated the stuff that makes communication by showing the relationship between turns, episodes, and patterns. However, in the end these are all interconnected, virtually seamless parts of the whole. This is not to say that they are predictable, it is just to say that the moving parts of communication are connected and in constant motion. At the end of the day, it doesn't matter if something was technically a turn, an episode, or a pattern—what matters is that you see the actions and reactions that make the experiences and outcomes you get. Figure 11.1 illustrates a picture of the way communication is made.

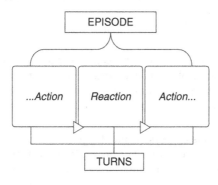

Figure 11.1 Communication is made one episode at a time.

In plain language, here is a breakdown of re-making communication at work:

- When you say or do something before, during, or after an interaction with a colleague it is a turn. Turns can be fragmented or aligned.
- When you exchange a few turns that have noticeable starting/ending points, you have an episode. Episodes can be open or closed.
- If you string a few episodes together that can be described by a common theme or story then you have a pattern. Patterns can be preferred or unwanted.
- The quality of our working lives is a reflection of our patterns of communication and interaction.
- If you want to transform an unwanted pattern to something preferred, you have to get down to the level of turn in order to shift the episode's trajectory.
- Overall, if we want a better working life, we have to make preferred patterns that reflect our values, aspirations, and motivation to make them.

By re-making communication at work you can create the conditions you need for the results you want. To do this you have to reflect at every turn, hold expectations in every episode, and have a purpose for every pattern. If you are concerned about what you get, you have to care, engage, and stay active in what you make. All of this begins with seeing the action, reaction, action, and reaction. These are some common action-reaction cycles in the real world of work:

- When you respond too impulsively, I question your judgment.
- When I have too many ideas and take no action, you hesitate to commit.
- When you are aloof and cold, I withdraw.
- When I overanalyze things and get caught in the weeds, you get frustrated and tune out.
- When you jump to action without a consistent strategy, I do not support the effort.
- When I fail to see the likely implications of a decision, you get blindsided.
- When you are unable to bounce back from adversity, I cannot rely on you.
- When I do something different from what I said, you do not trust my integrity.

There is a chemistry, physics, and design of communication that reveals the way communication is made from basic elements. Our desire to label things as good and bad or unwanted and preferred has no effect on what gets made:

- When you take the time to say what you mean in helpful ways, I appreciate that effort.
- When I act in ways that are fair and consistent, you trust me to watch out for your interests.
- When you respond with empathy and make an effort to connect, I do the same to you.
- When I give you specific information and make an extra effort to give you the full context of the situation, you operate with a clearer picture of what is important.
- When you are optimistic about the future and realistic about the challenges we face, I have a confident belief in our likely success.
- When I take ownership and responsibility for things that go wrong, you value my transparency and take accountability in your own way.
- When you are reliable and follow through on your commitments, I rely on you more.
- When I look past petty issues and personality quirks, you take the same high road.

Re-making communication at work provides an opportunity to interrupt this cycle of action, reaction, and action at the precise moment where *your* next response will shape the one that comes after that. For example, rather than: When you are aloof and cold...I withdraw. You can follow this sequence of prompts in table 11.1 to reflect on and subsequently choose to make something different.

Table 11.1   Re-making communication at work starts with reflection and choice

When you are aloof...	REFLECT	CHOOSE	...I ignore it and give you space to be you
	• I have a choice in how I respond	• I could withdraw and expect a cool tone and some cold shoulders	
	• Each choice will make something different	• I could speak with you directly about how the aloofness makes me feel	
	• My natural tendency is to withdraw, but I have options	• I could let the anger pass and try to find out if something is wrong	
	• What do I want most out of this interaction and the ones that come after it?	• I could ignore it and give you space to be you	
	• Which option aligns with my hopes and is realistic for me to implement?		

From Concept to Implementation

In the following pages you will learn from the real, everyday experiences of three people who learned to see the patterns, episodes, and turns in their communication with people at work. This allowed them to begin the process of confronting their unwanted patterns of communication and to re-make them into something better. With an unvarnished view of the way communication actually makes the experiences and outcomes we get, you will see how they applied the concepts from part II in the real world of work.

Julianne's Story

Meet Julianne, she is 46 years old, reliable, conscientious, loyal, invested in her career, and genuinely wants to help the company to succeed.

- People tiptoe around her because they say she is "rough around the edges."
- People just agree with her because they say "it isn't worth the battle."
- People avoid her when disagreements arise because they say "you don't want to get on her bad side."

These are actual comments gathered from Julianne's 360-degree feedback assessment. These and other sentiments were shared by the seven colleagues that work most closely with her. How could someone who is reliable, conscientious, invested in her career, and genuinely wants to help the company succeed make so many unwanted patterns of communication and interaction?

The answer to this question can be found in the everyday interactions Julianne has with her colleagues. Each turn played a part in creating the episodes, which made the patterns, which produced the experiences and outcomes she got. The clues to how all of that was made come from two directions: (1) the frustration Julianne felt from what she was not getting; and (2) the frustration Julianne felt from what she was getting (described in the statements from her colleagues given earlier).

The frustration that Julianne felt about what she was not getting in her experience at work was described in her own words during my initial conversation with her. She said: "I feel like I have all of this value to contribute, yet people do not come to me for advice or mentoring. My perspectives do not seem valued by other managers...and I notice that others get together informally to work on things, yet they do not include me in those meetings. I know I can have a short fuse sometimes. And, I can feel the people in the room tense up anytime I get passionate and focused on an issue." This is part of what Julianne was making at work.

Now, consider the frustration Julianne felt from what she was getting as reflected in the statements from her colleagues. As you reread them, imagine what small interactions unfolded over time that led people to perceive, feel, and believe in these things: She is "rough around the edges." Challenging her perspective is just "not worth the battle." And, avoid her when trouble starts because "you do not want to get on her bad side." This is the other part of what Julianne was making at work. Thankfully for Julianne, she was ready to take a communication perspective at work in order to re-make these unwanted patterns of communication and interaction.

Julianne's Breakthrough

Following her introduction to the concepts and principles of re-making communication at work that occurred after her 360-degree feedback coaching, Julianne made a few simple observations and insights that led to her breakthrough. She went on to use the methods and tools outlined in part III of this book, but the most useful shifts occurred when she began to *see* her communication. Keep in mind, Julianne was not any more open or self-aware than the average manager. She was just ready for something different. These are the words she used to describe the process of coming to terms with what she was making in her patterns of communication and interaction at work:

- "It seems like I have this story that says 'if I don't step up and take charge, things will just fall apart.' This is clearly not true. In fact, if I keep running over people then things may indeed fall apart. For whatever reason, I just keep doing it even though I know it's not effective."
- "I have been kind of rigid in my approach to solving problems, including over-structuring and controlling others' work. When I just launch into my prescription for how we'll tackle this issue and that problem, I think I'm being helpful. What I'm doing is shutting down the quieter voices and that limits the discussion and ownership people take."
- "I am pretty impatient with anything that takes time. When a team member proposes a solution, if it will take a bit of time and be one of those slow-building changes, I immediately shut them down and look for a quicker way. It is no wonder that people tend to just go along with me because they know I will push back if their ideas do not match my own."
- "I know that if I want to prioritize others' contributions and share the credit for team accomplishments, I have to sit back and let things happen. This means staying present—which I am not good at, and avoiding the need for a clearly defined goal in every situation."
- "If I am going to make an environment where people's individual strengths and skills are featured, then I have to speak less and listen more. Realistic expectations about what we focus on and accomplish as a team have to be made in collaboration with others; I can't just decide what they are in a vacuum and expect everyone to line up."

- "When I say that I am just 'rough around the edges,' that has been my excuse for avoiding the necessary change. I can see that adjusting my approach will make a positive change for me and likely my team."

Dale's Story

Meet Dale, he is 52 years old, talented, charismatic, versatile, and hard-working.

- People smile and nod because they say he "can't have real conversations about the facts."
- People try not to collaborate with him because they say he "wants to control things, but is unwilling to follow through."
- People do not share honest feedback because they say he "deflects responsibility and avoids owning the issues."

These are the actual reflections from Dale's team members who shared their perspectives and concerns during confidential interviews. How could someone so talented, charismatic, versatile, and hard-working make so many unwanted patterns of communication and interaction? Like Julianne, Dale's answer to this question was found in both the preferred experiences he was not getting and the unwanted experiences and outcomes that he was getting.

From Dale's point of view, the missing preferred patterns of communication and interaction sounded like this: "Here I am, one of the senior leaders in the company and I'm not having the influence I want to have. I can mentor people, I can give direction—but none of this has an effect when people don't come to me for help. I have said that I have an 'open door policy' but that doesn't seem to change anything. I know there is a lot that could be better but those discussions are not taking place."

Dale's initial blind spots aside, if you contrast his perspective with the comments of his colleagues—"can't have real conversations about the facts...wants to control things, but is unwilling to follow through...deflects responsibility and avoids owning the issues"—you can easily see how the mix of unwanted outcomes he got was an obvious contradiction to the preferred experience he wanted. The tension between these two opposites was the starting place for Dale to re-make communication at work.

Dale's Breakthrough

Following his overview of re-making communication at work, Dale wrote down a few of his insights. It took a real concerted effort on his part (e.g., each Monday Dale spent about 20 minutes in the morning reflecting on his performance), but ultimately it led to his breakthrough. Once he made a few mental shifts, Dale was able to use the M-A-I-D sequence outlined in part III of this book to really accelerate the change. Like Julianne, Dale really was not unusual with regards to his professional development. He had some bad habits and blind spots, but he too was ready for something better. These are the words he used to describe his fresh thinking about unwanted patterns of communication and interaction at work:

- "I have always thought that one of my best attributes was my sense of humor. I can really see how staying in social mode too long is another way of avoiding touchy subjects. I guess I'm the last to know on this one because it seems my team already figured this out about me."
- "There is a really strong 'should' that pops up for me every time somebody else steps up to lead. I realize that I lock them out of my thinking until the very end so that I can play a central role in the situation and gain more control of the outcome."
- "Whenever I have some kind of strong reaction, people end up walking around on egg shells. I can see how this pattern prevents us from getting into the heart of the issues."
- "If I look at all the different things I value, I guess the one I put above all the others is 'being seen as an expert.' This focus has led me to believe that no one else can do things, which is just wrong."
- "There is a repetitive pattern when it comes to getting stuff done. The buck stops with me because ultimately, I'm responsible. But when things sit on my desk for too long people are stuck in a holding pattern. Because I am not in the habit of delegating and trusting others, I just hold onto things. I know now how frustrating this is for people."

Lena's Story

Meet Lena, she is 28 years old, dynamic, intelligent, willing to take initiative, persistent, and committed.

- People do not challenge her decisions because they say it is "disagree at your own risk."
- People burn themselves out trying to keep pace with every new idea because they say "her constant search for the next-best-thing is the only option."
- People keep busy—even if they are unproductive—because they say "discussing issues and carefully considering alternatives is just a waste of time."

These are the actual issues that were identified during a meeting with Lena's team. The goal of the meeting was to honestly explore the real challenges facing the group and nothing was held back in the discussion. How could someone so dynamic, intelligent, willing to take initiative, persistent, and committed make so many unwanted patterns of communication and interaction?

Just like Dale and Julianne, Lena's working life was simply the cumulative effect of her everyday patterns of communication and interaction. She, along with everyone else on her team, made these experiences. She was ready to take ownership for her role and she admitted that her "hard-charging approach" was a major source of the issues she faced. When she addressed the group, her transparency and willingness to be honest was the catalysts for change.

She said: "I know that there is a lot of talent in this room and that my leadership style and approach has made it hard for some of you to share your ideas and bring your best contributions to the table. I want to change that and I know that if we all try, we can do it." This accountability and the earnest desire for something better proved to be the starting place for Lena and her team to re-make communication at work.

Lena's Breakthrough

Lena's breakthrough happened quickly the instant she realized that she was managing her team in the same way her old boss did. He was a strong influence on her, for better and for worse. As a new manager and young professional, Lena only had a few role models and her thinking was boxed into those experiences. The flash of insight came when she realized that she had a choice in how she interpreted the role of a leader. After a review of the concepts of re-making communication at work, Lena latched onto the idea that leaders are pivotal in their role as "architects of patterns of communication and interaction" that shape team and organizational culture. With new thinking and momentum, Lena was ready to make something different. Here is what she said after her first-round effort to re-make communication at work:

- "When I don't see the value in other people's ideas, it shuts them down. Worse, when I appear to be threatened by their contributions, it is detrimental to an honest exchange of the merits. This is why we've been moving forward with subpar solutions."
- "My refusal to give up on problems is a signal to people that they need to just 'go along with me' until I lose steam."
- "My competitive nature makes a win/loose environment. I understand why people feel like they have to 'disagree at their own risk.'"
- "I feel a strong sense of 'should' any time things get messy and feel like they are getting off track. I leap into fix-it mode, but my cavalier response to others' concerns leads people to feel I cannot be trusted to listen and understand more deeply."

In their own ways, Julianne, Dale, and Lena took ideas about re-making communication at work and put them into practice. The simple insights eventually led them to breakthrough thinking, which combined with the methods and practices presented in the following chapters, set their working lives on a new trajectory. Rather than the unwanted patterns of communication and interaction they were getting, they chose to make something better.

Part III

Practice Guide for Re-Making Patterns of Communication at Work

12

Introduction to the Practice of Re-Making Communication at Work

Part III of the book presents a practice guide to re-making communication at work. While several activities and processes will be introduced—all of which can be used to improve the quality and outcomes of communication at work—I try not to present things in a prescriptive formula or sequence of steps. This is because re-making communication at work focuses less on the finished product of what is made and more on the process or practice of making it.

In the three chapters that follow you will see a two-part progression in practice alternatives. It begins with a versatile range of single-step processes and then moves to the M-A-I-D sequence, which is a useful set of reminders for re-making individual patterns. To effectively set you up to begin using these practice tools immediately, the remainder of this introduction provides additional concepts and ways of thinking about re-making communication at work.

Learn to Live with Construction

Have you heard the urban myth about home remodels leading to frequent divorce? I have heard people say that the divorce rate among couples who take on major home improvement renovations is as high as 90 percent. Until all 50 states add a new box on divorce filing paperwork (something to check-off right beside "irreconcilably differences" called "failure to agree on tile or hardwood"), it is unlikely we will know. According to Ojai-based contractor Bill Gordon, the emotional toll remodeling can take on homeowners is significant. Gordon estimates that more than three-quarters of the couples he has worked with have had difficulties ranging from frequent arguing to eventual divorce.[1] His 20 years of experience in the field has undoubtedly taught him that it is hard for people to live with construction.

Re-making communication at work requires you to get comfortable with construction. I am obviously not talking about physical construction, but many of the same tolls that remodeling a home can take on people are relevant in our patterns of interaction with others. Frequent and unpleasant surprises, extra time and costs required to address unforeseen problems, differing expectations that are hard to work out, and the stress from being out of a comfortable routine are among the most common challenges of a construction project. Some words of wisdom that can assist people in their survival during construction include: pick your battles and stand your ground on things that matter; choose your moment to bring issues and concerns up with others; listen to all ideas and make it a collaborative process; take advice from the professionals; and laugh and try to enjoy the ride. The same can be said about the challenges and words of wisdom for re-making communication at work.

Avoid the Fix-It Mindset

In my early career I trained conflict resolution practitioners, many of whom were lawyers seeking a better way to practice law. Their intentions were often to get out of litigation and serve their clients in ways that left them feeling a bit more whole than the win-at-all-costs approach could do. Some of these attorneys were the sharpest people I knew, with analytical skills and reasoning abilities that were off the charts. Despite these strengths, the challenge for them was to understand the fundamental concept of interest-based negotiation and the goal of a neutral mediator practicing a facilitative approach (i.e., it is the parties' job to ultimately find the solution, not the neutral mediator's role).

In my trainings, rather than teaching from a mediator-as-judge model, I taught mediators to draw out their clients and develop workable solutions to conflicts that would be reflective of their truest challenges and durable after implementation. It was a hard concept for them to get, and many of them would not accept that they were not there to solve people's problems and give advice. When the light bulb went off for my students I began referring to them as "reformed problem solvers." They finally realized that the quick identification of the problem and the spoon-fed solution was not what their clients needed or wanted. A more flexible process that allowed people to unburden themselves from the effects of the conflict, talk through their frustrations, hopes, and needs, and then work collaboratively to author solutions that would meet the interests of both parties was more effective.

This fix-it mindset is tough to get rid of for all of us at times, particularly with the really dysfunctional patterns that we want to end as soon as possible. If we begin to see the pattern of communication for what it is, we often experience a few phases, beginning with: Eureka, I see a pattern I want to re-make and I know the solution...to...Wow, this goes much deeper than I thought...to...What was I thinking, this is way too complicated...to...The critical moment that leads to giving up, or possibly to the recognition that...Of course this is tough, complex, and overwhelming but it wouldn't be interesting if it wasn't...I may not be able to change it entirely, but a small victory will matter...Small changes can lead to bigger results!

I always say that it is better to try to re-make an unwanted pattern and fail than to let it live on without a fight. Only in this case we are not fighting with the pattern or wrestling it into a solution; we are seeing what can emerge when we learn to talk differently about the things that matter most to us.

Learn How to Talk about What Matters

The implicit reality of re-making communication at work is that you must know what you want to re-make if you are going to achieve it. While we are unfortunately well-versed in the experience of knowing what we do not want (and learning to live with those unwanted patterns of communication and interaction), identifying what is really important to us can be a struggle by itself. It is another challenge all together to learn how to talk about what matters with others. These challenges can persist because of the plague of diverse commitments that pull us in different directions, as well as the conflicting voices of influential people in our lives who may expect or demand certain things from us that may at times clash with our values, needs, and wants.

Re-making unwanted patterns requires the capacity to talk about what matters; therefore, it is necessary to develop skill and confidence in this area. This is not a psychology book, nor do I have any desire to summarize the complex reasons why some of us suppress our desires or fail to willingly advocate for our interests at certain times. However, there are four common issues that, if addressed, can be turned into opportunities for sharper insights and better communication about our individual values and priorities.

The first issue is that in the absence of clearly stating what matters, "you will make people guess and they will likely guess incorrectly." Most conflict in the workplace occurs due to unmet needs. The irony of unmet needs and expectations is that they are often left unspoken. So when we rationalize ourselves away from clearly stating what we want, or what is most important to us in a specific situation or relationship, we may think that we are avoiding the pitfall. The fact is we are simply digging the hole deeper by forcing the other person or people to guess our relative perspective and priorities and to take action accordingly. And this is the reason why unresolved conflict in the workplace is such a significant, repetitive problem. We are all pretty bad guessers when it comes down to it.

The second issue is that "getting what you want requires active movement toward it." It is self-deception to want something, but to make no active move toward it. The first move is usually naming what that thing is—no matter how vague it may seem at the moment. Gaining the confidence to talk out loud about what matters, being fearless about the word choice and how inarticulate it might sound at first, is an active move. As the picture of the desired pattern of communication and interaction comes clearer into focus, the next moves to re-make the unwanted pattern are more easily clarified.

The third issue is that "we are often very good at wanting what others want, but unpracticed at wanting stuff that is consistent with who we are and what we value." The interesting aspect of this is that we are continuously in the act of striving toward something—even when it feels as though we are not. So, if we are going to make something, wouldn't it be better to strive to make it reflect what matters to us? In his 2009 TED talk,[2] Alain de Botton, the internationally acclaimed writer, philosopher, and commentator on work, described the challenge of distinguishing what matters to us and the noise we hear from the world:

> One of the interesting things about success is that we think we know what it means. A lot of the time our ideas about what it would mean to live successfully are not our own. They're sucked in from other people… [It] is not that we should give up on our ideas of success, but that we should make sure that they are our own. We should… make sure that we own them, that we're truly the authors of our own ambitions. Because it's bad enough not getting what you want, but it's even worse to have an idea of what it is you want and find out at the end of the journey that it isn't, in fact, what you wanted all along.

The fourth and final issue is that learning to re-make unwanted patterns requires us to "say yes and no in the right ways, at the right times." In other words, we need equal amounts of courage and willingness to start doing the things that, despite their potential difficulty, are required to make something different. We also need the courage and willingness to say no, draw a line in the sand, and avoid doing certain other things that would either reestablish the old unwanted pattern or simply get in the way of making what we want.

Saying yes to new things is a bit more straightforward than saying no. However, when the patterns that you want to re-make are built on following others' expectations, putting things on the "stop doing" list may be just as hard as beginning new attitudes and behaviors. We know that there are truly no individual actors in organizations and, regardless of your title, tenure, and power in the organization, you need other people. But when the writer and cartoonist Hugh MacLeod said, "The best way to get approval is not to need it," he points to a very important theme with regards to re-making patterns. When there is something we want, we have to be willing to talk about it in the language of priority. If we are willing to share our own vision of what matters and work openly with others, we naturally move beyond the need for "approval" to active "engagement" and support for our goals.

Name What Is Missing

Earlier I talked about what Kingsley Davis called the "double reality." This is where on the one hand we have a complete system of attitudes and beliefs about *what ought to be*, or what should happen in a given circumstance. On the other hand, there is the factual order of *what is*. These two realities are not identical, but neither are they ever really separate.[3] The constant tension between our beliefs about what people ought do and say and how they should behave and act confound us time and again when they simply do not conform.

This double reality is often in play when we assess our overall patterns. A good way to clear the clutter from this dynamic is to assess the tension between the reality of your situation, and the aspirational nature of what you want. The space between the unwanted pattern you are experiencing and the preferred pattern you hope for provides a path to move from left to right.

Work Past the Flash Point

It is rare, but I have been introduced to some organizations where healthy relationships, vibrant habits of communication and interaction, successful performance, and high-quality experiences of people in the organization are consistently reflected in everyday working life. In some cases I have been asked to find out "what they are doing that works" and in other cases leaders have invited me in to help develop ways to sustain and even increase that level of success.

This is unique because most inquiries I get start with a request to address some sort of breakdown in relationship, communication, performance, or quality of experience at work. Many organizations are not fun places to be, and perhaps a more typical condition of real work life matches what communication expert Steven Axley said: "Miscommunication is the normal state of affairs in human communication...miscommunication and unintentional communication are to be expected, for they are the norm."[4]

Getting to the place our teams and organizations aspire to often requires us to move past a current flash point. In many ways this book is about what we do when episodes of communication and interaction go wrong, which is the quintessential flashpoint of a communication breakdown. Although there are numerous activities and models presented that more fully answer this question, in essence when episodes of communication and interaction go wrong we can shift from crisis and reaction to focused attention when we undertake the following:[5]

1. Tell better stories about what happened.
   - Doing this builds understanding of our selves, other people, and the context in which the stories are experienced.

2. See the pattern of communication and interaction that produced those stories.
   - This distinguishes people from their stories and allows you to look "at the communication" with a degree of curious objectivity.
3. Take ownership of the roles people play in making and sustaining the pattern.
   - Patterns are made in coordination and accepting shared ownership for making unwanted patterns, specifically the attitudes, choices, and actions taken in the sequence that sustained the pattern, is the catalyst for leveraging the capacity to make something different.
4. Alter the conditions of context so something different is possible.
   - If an existing pattern is no longer desired, new patterns can be made when the context is changed. Context evolves as new and different things are considered important, as new respect and appreciation for others increases, and as the rules that influence meaning and action are challenged by new assumptions.

This basic sequence is embedded in the more detailed exercises and models used in the chapters that follow in part III and continue in part IV's guided coaching activities. It does not really matter how the communication issue is labeled initially (i.e., I feel stuck, we need teambuilding, morale is down, people can't trust each other, we aren't on the same page, our culture is declining, etc.), the principles reflected within the sequence have a relevance across the spectrum of organizational life and particularly in the traditional areas we often look for communication breakdowns to occur.

The Re-Making Communication Mindset

The concepts and tools in this chapter will guide you to the starting lines and give you insights for navigating the process of re-making communication at work. As far as mindset, perspective, and focus there are a few essentials to keep in mind. These recast some of the concepts that have already been shared and the summary list should serve as a useful cheat sheet to follow. They include the following:

1. Seeing communication as an ongoing, generative force that makes things.
2. Stepping away from our own expectations with curiosity and objectivity.
3. Spotting the connections that form our patterns of communication and interaction.
4. Understanding the storytelling instinct and using our stories to make shared meaning.
5. Investing time to carefully coordinate actions and stay aligned as things evolve.

6. Embracing more than one "best option" so there is room for outcomes that meet multiple needs.
7. Communicating for pattern, always considering a single episode as part of a larger system of interactions.
8. Valuing creativity and the unexpected.

If there is a manifesto in all of this, it is: *go make the patterns you want to experience.* If work is a miserable bore, make something more interesting. If your relationships with colleagues are threatening and void of respectful trust, make something more trustworthy. If you are more or less engaged in your work but feeling a little complacent, make something more challenging. After all, you are already a central figure in the everyday patterns of communication and interaction you live. If you keep your distance, erroneously thinking that you are separate and apart from them, you surrender your leverage for transforming them. If you take ownership of your role and if you focus your attention on the turns that align episodes and the episodes that open patterns, you take back your power for crafting your own working life.

Conclusion

The practice of re-making communication at work is based on principles, not process steps. There are single-step practices that can be used to peek inside communication interactions and there is the M-A-I-D sequence that can be used to re-make entire patterns of communication and interaction. The specific approach to using the practices include reminders to: avoid the "fix-it" mindset, learn to talk about what matters, name what is missing, and work past the flash point. Chapter 13 provides a detailed description and related examples of the single-step practices.

13

Single-Step Practices for Re-Making Communication at Work

The next chapter introduces multi-step processes that can be used to re-make communication at work with individuals and teams. Those are useful in a variety of contexts and organizational circumstances, however the horsepower they offer may not always be necessary. The purpose of this chapter is to introduce a variety of single-step practices that can be used by themselves or in combination with other single-step practices to make communication better. The following summaries provide enough detail for you to put them into use and discover your own ways of customizing them to add value to whatever unique situation you encounter.[1]

Visualizing the System

I have described our working lives as a reflection of the patterns of communication and interaction we engage in. And I have described organization culture as the collective ecosystem of everyone's patterns inside the organization. If we see communication and organizations as systems, then all of the patterns embedded in them are simultaneously connected to and influenced by others within the system. With a systemic point of view we can make communication visible in some pretty simple, but useful ways.

In the practice of CMM there is a tool referred to as a "Daisy" whereby you draw the people, events, and important features in a system (using an image akin to a set of flower petals). When an event or interaction is complex and/ or appears deeply textured, the Daisy offers a way of illustrating how a given situation is made by multiple and overlapping people, attitudes/beliefs, stories, or turns. When we take steps to understand our episodes and patterns, we often oversimplify these variables in order to wrap our heads around the situation. The Daisy helps to slow it down and methodically identify the multiple and intersecting details that are in play.

Depending upon how you frame the center circle, each of the petals can be used to differentiate the strength or salience of particular relationships or aspects of the circumstance. Here are several distinct examples that show a progression of versatile ways to visualize the system. These are from an individual who took a communication perspective at work in his efforts to increase the possibility for a promotion. The 15-minute exercise began by drawing a circle with the framing statement in the center. As he brainstormed additional aspects related to the core idea, he drew a new circle and filled in the peripheral circles as his thoughts progressed. After a few scratch-outs and do-overs, figures 13.1–13.4 show what he came up with.

In these four examples you can see that the first and fourth are almost mind maps that simply organize information. The middle two get more complicated as they reveal the hidden aspects of perception and behavior that unfold in communication. As you scan each example, you can imagine the rich conversations that occurred and the useful questions that each potentially brings up. For example, if you compare the response to "what I believe about my potential" with "the stories people tell about my contributions" where are there similarities and where are there gaps? In appendix 1 there are other examples of using the Daisy in more sophisticated ways to tease apart many of the complex nuances that unfold in our patterns of communication and interaction.

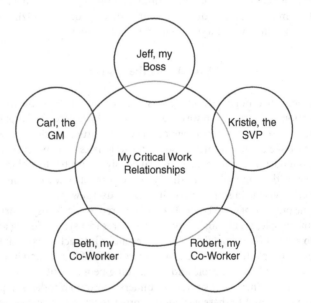

Figure 13.1   Visualizing the system: work relationships.

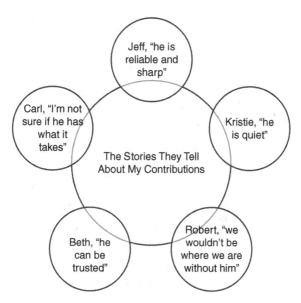

Figure 13.2 · Visualizing the system: stories about my contributions.

Figure 13.3 Visualizing the system: what I believe about my potential.

Figure 13.4   Visualizing the system: intersecting episodes.

Hierarchy of Values, Stories, and Contexts

A deeper way of exploring our patterns is to examine what is most important to us in a given moment using a "hierarchy." This can reveal how our priorities can vary by context and situation. The visual image of a tiered hierarchy allows us to sort through the subtle and powerful values, stories, and contexts that we place above others and subsequently use to interpret and take action on what is happening around us. The hierarchy can be used to sort any number of variables; however it is quite useful in exploring the relative influence from our values, stories, and contexts. First I will describe how to use this single-step practice with values.

Values are the silent but powerful forces that influence the way we speak and act. They may never be discussed openly, but they are ever present. The values we hold dear may be consistent with our experiences, and when that happens we have full integrity. When they are compromised either by our own behaviors or by the circumstances we find ourselves in, we can experience the cognitive dissonance that comes with the gap between what we know is important *and* what we get.[2] This makes it both important to identify the underlying values that drive us, as well as to examine the consistency between our espoused values and actual behavior.

There are numerous ways to clarify one's values, which involve a variety of methods to sort key words or values statements that most reflect what matters to a person in a given frame of reference (i.e., at work, etc.). One of the reasons that many of these attempts to clarify values only leads to temporary, superficial outcomes is because the process does not go to the next step of examining the ways in which our values are negotiated in hierarchies throughout the different episodes/situations we experience.

Imagine that a person holds a set of core values that guide their professional life, including fairness, commitment, open communication, being challenged, and maintaining great relationships. In a perfect world, the actual experience that the person endures would be a deep sense of integrity between their values and lived experience. Absent any specific situation, these five values mesh pretty well. However, in the course of a working life there may likely be multiple scenarios where one's own values are in conflict with each other. It is only the hierarchy, or sorting of the values in order of greatest priority, that reveals which one has the predominant influence on the attitudes, choices, and behaviors of the person in the moment.

The following example of using the Hierarchy Model with values can be used to explore the underlying drivers of our attitudes, choices, and behaviors that influence the way we perceive and act upon the unfolding action in a given episode. The example in figure 13.5 was created when a manager explored a situation in which they were accused by a subordinate of being

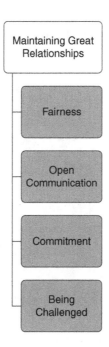

Figure 13.5   Hierarchy of values.

unfair and acting inconsistently with the interpretation of the company's vacation policy. For someone who valued fairness, this was a difficult issue to confront. The two hierarchies illustrated the way in which the manager's decision (i.e., choice to interpret the policy) shifted when a certain value was at the top of the list as seen.

In this example, which led to saying "yes," the manager realized that when requests for vacation came in, it was important to accommodate people as much as possible. Doing this showed a sense of concern and support for employees' efforts to maintain work/life balance and saying "yes" often seemed to bolster the quality of relationships. Even when the workload justified saying "no," it was always hard to do so when people had places to go and events to attend that were important to them.

Figure 13.6 provides the next example, which led to saying "no." None of the values changed, however, the shift in the hierarchy of values explained the different outcome. While this was difficult to see, the manager realized that in different circumstances the value of "fairness" had more or less of a relative emphasis on how they handled requests for time off. When fairness was at the top of the list, they felt that a strict interpretation of the vacation policy was needed and any flexibility would be unacceptable. This was

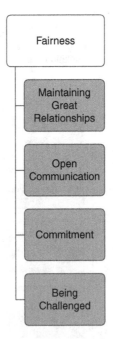

Figure 13.6   Hierarchy of values within decisions.

a considerable contrast to the kind of thought process and decision-making that happened when "maintaining great relationships" was the governing value in the last one.

Similar to the way our values silently shape the attitudes, choices, and behaviors we act out in our patterns of communication and interaction, the stories we believe and tell also powerfully shape our communication. Because we rarely tell only one story about what is said or done, the Hierarchy Model enables us to express multiple stories that each has a varying degree of relevance for us. The story held as the highest context often holds the most power, but until that is revealed and understood, it is difficult to make productive use of that power or see its effects on our patterns of communication and interaction.

In this example, a new hire was struggling to adapt to the pace of work and the different expectations placed on her by her supervisor. Some days were better than others and so when asked about all the possible stories she could tell to explain her feelings and interpretations about recent interactions with her manager, she said: "I want to be challenged, this is new but I'll adjust to it, I think the scrutiny will make me better, and I feel like I'm being singled out and don't deserve this grief." Using the hierarchy to sort them out, figure 13.7 shows the order she put them into when asked the pivotal question: "What story is the loudest and most influential influence on your behavior?"

Seeing this sequence gave her the opportunity to notice that the only negative story that explained the dynamic with her boss was the one dominating her experience. The other stories, each of which seemed positive, failed to energize her due to their place in the hierarchy. The next step was to imagine

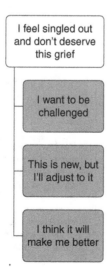

Figure 13.7   Hierarchy of stories.

what would change in her attitude, motivation, and behavior if a different story was the loudest and most believable. "I want to be challenged" was the statement that most captured the professional mindset she wanted and she chose to intentionally act into episodes of communication and interaction that made it a real part of her experience at work.

Finally, the hierarchy single-step practice can also be used to sort personal perspectives we take across multiple contexts. In CMM theory, each action is "simultaneously responding to the previous act and eliciting the subsequent act"[3] and the Hierarchy Model can reveal how each act is influenced by several contexts simultaneously. Common references to the hierarchy of meaning and contexts in CMM often include a progression from: culture, self, relationship, episode, and turn. More specifically, these reveal how the various influences from culture, sense of self, existing relationships, and prior episodes trigger a sense of logical force and response to a given situation.

In the world of work, the hierarchy of meanings that seem most impactful on the turns we take and episodes we engage in include; organization culture, team dynamics, manager-employee relationships, and individual working life scripts. When these are identified and sorted it can reveal the way one participates in patterns based on the relative influence from the hierarchy of meaning each context brings.

For example, this hierarchy illustrated in figure 13.8 was created when four team members proactively met to discuss "how they would decide" a big company decision. They began by listing the various contexts and the related "shoulds" that each one seemed to invite. After they listed them, they

Figure 13.8   Hierarchy of strategies and decisions.

worked together to project the likely decision paths as the stories rotated in the greatest position of influence. After multiple iterations, they agreed to move forward in the sequence.

Throughout the session, the team vacillated between two desired scenarios: slow and steady versus a home run. They eventually chose a strategy of "growing responsibly," however consider how drastically different things would have been if the top context was "cash is tight and we need a big win." The likely outcome from that shift would have had a cascading effect throughout the organization and it would have produced a dramatically different result for the team of leaders. It was not until they surfaced the complexity of their different stories that they were able to talk through the implications and then choose the path that was most useful to them.

Listening for Stories

There is always tension or difference between the stories people live and the stories people tell. One reason for this difference is that stories told tend to have a narrative unity or coherence, while stories lived are contingent on what two or more people do—each with their own varying stories—in specific sequence and in particular circumstances. When these gaps between the story "told" and the story "experienced" surface, what CMM refers to as the LUUUUTT Model can be used to diagram the connections between

Table 13.1 Listening for stories

Purpose: To reveal the tension between the unknown, unheard, and untellable stories—including the gap between what is said and what is actually experienced—in order to spot the causes of fragmented turns, closed episodes, and unwanted patterns of communication.

Type of story	Meaning of the story	Impact
Unknown story	You do value our working relationship	I didn't know the story, so I assumed... • You didn't care • My efforts wouldn't matter
Unheard story	You are making an effort (I just expected your approach to look like mine)	I didn't hear the story, so I felt... • I was the only one trying • Like it wasn't worth the effort
Untellable story	Our organizational culture sometimes suppresses healthy communication by ignoring conflict	I didn't imagine the story, so I would not have thought... • We both had to fight hard to get help in resolving this • People seemed to just "wish it would go away"

conflicting stories. Likewise when there are untold, unheard, unknown and/ or untellable stories, this model builds a graphic image to emplot the various visible and invisible elements of a narrative.

A simplified version of this can be used as a single-step practice to expose and take notice of the hidden side of communication at work. By revealing the unknown, unheard, and untellable stories (including the gap between what is said and what is actually experienced) we can spot the areas prone to the greatest potential for past, current, and future communication breakdowns. The example provided in table 13.1 provides an example that was created by two people who experienced a conflict with each other at work. After several failed attempts to "talk it out" they required a more formal process to try to address their deeply held concerns. One of the individuals originally labeled the cause of the conflict as "mis-communication," but after listening for stories he realized precisely what was missing. A picture of the unknown, unheard, and untellable stories that did not make it into his experience and therefore could not influence the way they interacted.

Seeing Past Speech Acts

Speech acts are actions that you perform while speaking and they can take on many forms, including promising, forgiving, ordering, greeting, warning, challenging, inviting, disinviting, congratulating, and so on. In the world of work there are speech acts at every turn, from the way management interacts with employees, to the way the company is structured. When a CEO announces that there will be an all-hands meeting with an open forum for employees, and that no hard question is off the table, that speech act is a promise, an invitation of participation, and an offer to listen. If the CEO avoids difficult questions during the company town hall, or if s/he does not allow for equal participation from people throughout the company, then that could be seen as a speech act of "failed integrity," which says the leader cannot be trusted to follow through on their promises.

When you read the company handbook and it states that the organization offers an equal employment opportunity (EEO), this is a speech act that says everyone is welcome and nobody can be discriminated against on the basis of age, sex, ethnicity, and so on. In the event that there is a case of clear discrimination against an employee that violates the EEO statement, this is a policy and practice-driven speech act that says the company does not consistently follow its policies.

When leaders decide to institute a hiring freeze in the company, they make a speech act that says the company's finances are important and must be protected by reducing costs. This speech act has other meanings of course, and some people may interpret it to mean that leaders are frugal and unwilling to invest in the necessary personnel to get the required work done. In a worst-case scenario, the speech act could suggest that existing employees are not valued by management and that the practice whereby one person does the work of two or three people is not only tolerable, but desirable.

The single-step practice here is to simply learn how to identify and become accustomed to the recurring speech acts that are used by you and others in the world of work. Because speech acts often communicate more complexity than we first notice, learning to see them and unpack the details they contain can show us the power of what we make in our patterns. The following example was created by a leader who was interested in becoming more familiar with some of the unwanted patterns she experienced. The responses to each prompt were simply the "first thoughts" that popped into her mind. Table 13.2 illustrates what she said in her effort to see past speech acts.

Table 13.2   Seeing past speech acts

Purpose: To identify recurring speech acts that are used by you and others in your world of work and to gain insight into the patterns of communication and interaction they trigger.

Prompt	*Response*
What speech acts do you use most in the world of work?	• I sometimes pull the authority card and preface a decision with "As the director of this department, I…" • Because I value service so much, I often say things like "Let's look from the customer perspective…" This is my way of saying I don't like where this is heading
What effect do these have on people when you deliver them?	• I bet people roll their eyes when I pull rank; I don't know why I just can't say "this is what I want to do!" • I think the customer perspective speech act gets us focused back on what matters; it isn't about us, it is about serving the customer
Is there a speech act you use that communicates something you do not want to say? If so, which turn seems to draw that speech act out?	• I think I need to pay attention to my confidence level and not lead with my title. Rather than modeling, "trust me, I'm a good leader" I am just saying "you have to go with me on this because I'm your boss" • The next time we are at a staff meeting and there is a disagreement about the course of action, this is the time to drop the act
What recurring speech acts do you see/hear company leaders use?	• I hear a lot of veiled threats when it comes to "how difficult the economy is" and "how we might have to tighten our belts"
What effect do these have on people and on the cultural overall?	• I think these things just scare people and cause them to pull back and polish resumes

Deconstructing and Re-Making Patterns

Re-making communication at work involves recognizing the unwanted patterns of communication and interaction that produce experiences and outcomes that are not aligned with our values, priorities, and goals. Once an unwanted pattern is recognized, it can be re-made into a more satisfying pattern that will potentially produce more of the experiences and outcomes that are desired. The first step toward re-making unwanted patterns involves seeing the presenting and constructing levels of the existing pattern to reveal the attitudes, beliefs, and behaviors that influence the episodes that make it. While more extensive processes (presented in the next chapter) may be needed to fully re-make more complex patterns, you can begin to see the presenting and constructing levels of patterns in a single-step practice.

The presenting level of patterns is reflected by the Ws (who, what, when, and where). The constructing level is reflected by a more precise naming of the turns and episodes that shape the pattern. Table 13.3 shows the specific questions that can be used to distinguish between these two layers of an unwanted pattern.

In this grid you can see an existing, unwanted pattern of communication and interaction that is tightly packed together. At the top level, the experiences and outcomes that the pattern produces are listed. Just below it, a simple name is given to it. Giving voice to patterns of communication and

Table 13.3   Deconstructing a pattern (of communication and interaction)

Purpose: To dissect the anatomy of an unwanted pattern of communication by mapping the presenting outcomes it brings, as well as the underlying building blocks (i.e., attitudes, beliefs, and behaviors) that influence the episodes and turns that shape it.

What is the pattern of communication and interaction making?		What possible name(s) could you give to this experience?	
Presenting level	Who is involved in making the pattern and when/where does it seem to take effect?	What challenges or difficulties does it produce, and specifically, how does it impact the quality of your working lives?	Even if it is contradictory, does it produce any benefits for the people who make it?
Constructing level	If there is an episode that captures what the pattern is all about, what would it be and what would you name it?	In this episode, what are the critical turns, or moments of transition, where specific interactions sustain the pattern?	What types of values, attitudes, and behaviors fuel these turns and seem to be holding the pattern together?

interaction that are lived is important because it begins the process of making it discussible. Depending upon the types of names we give them, this also is a first glimpse of the impact and depth of patterns and their effects on us.

Moving from left to right, the presenting level includes three question paths that reveal the basic moving parts (who, where, when, what, etc.) that reflect the presenting conditions that are outwardly experienced. The final level one question prompts you to consider what kinds of potentially competing commitments could exist that work to hold the unwanted pattern in place.[4] Delving briefly into the contradictions that often plague our unwanted patterns provides an early opportunity to test the readiness and ability for people to see the hidden side of communication.

Going down to the constructed level, the questions shift from the presenting conditions and visible experiences and outcomes from the pattern to the inner elements that actually combine to make it. These questions initiate the process of unpacking the pattern by focusing on a specific episode and the precise turns within that episode that seem to sustain the pattern. The final question at the constructed level goes directly to the often unseen forces that shape the choices we make during our "turns" in communication.

Moving from concept to application, the following example demonstrates how a team collaborated to deconstruct an unwanted pattern. In a 60-minute meeting they used this sequence of questions to unpack the key elements of the pattern and discuss their different perspectives on what made and sustained it. In this example, the individuals were given an opportunity to map the pattern according to their own views first. The version in table 13.4 is a consolidated snapshot of the pattern that reflected the various priorities and perspectives of everyone in the room.

Prior to the meeting, this team of eight struggled with a variety of challenges. Chief among them was what they called their "meeting culture," which included more than 12 hours of standing meetings each week, in addition to the other impromptu meetings that took place. They felt frustrated by the fact that the urgency of the changing economy and a more competitive market was exacerbated by too much talk and not enough action. On the other hand, several senior leaders remained committed to "staying on the same page" during an intense period of change and, for them, the meetings were a critical tool for doing that. By exploring the presenting and constructing levels of the pattern they were able to put their finger on a few glaring gaps that most of them had felt, but were unable to express.

In the example you can also see how each level, including the specific question sequences within them, worked together to help the team create a basic map of their existing pattern. The discussions that resulted from the prompts were more valuable than "answering the questions" so you can imagine that the written worksheet acted as a flexible guide to discovering what was going

Table 13.4 Example of deconstructing a pattern (of communication and interaction)

Purpose: To dissect the anatomy of an unwanted pattern of communication by mapping the presenting outcomes it brings, as well as the underlying building blocks (i.e., attitudes, beliefs, and behaviors) that influence the episodes and turns that shape it.

	What is the pattern of communication and interaction making?	*What possible name(s) could you give to this experience?*	
	"We feel stuck, we feel underutilized, and we are afraid we are going to miss a big opportunity."	"Stuck in Neutral"	
Presenting level	*Who is involved making the pattern and when/where does it seem to take effect?*	*What challenges or difficulties does it produce, and specifically, how does it impact the quality of your working lives?*	*Even if it is contradictory, does it produce any benefits for the people who make it?*
	Everyone in our team contributes to this situation. We feel it most at our weekly meetings that sometimes run as long as two and a half hours!	People leave the meetings frustrated, and the piles of work that accumulate during our meetings just grow. There is a constant feeling of "not enough time to keep up."	Yes, our senior leaders have charged us to "stay on the same page" during this intense period of change. The best way we know how to do this is to spend time face-to-face sharing valuable updates. In this case, doing something good makes something bad.

Constructing level	If there is an episode that captures what the pattern is all about, what would it be and what would you name it?	In this episode, what are the critical turns, or moments of transition, where specific interaction sustains the pattern?	What types of values, attitudes, and behaviors fuel these turns and seem to be holding the pattern together?
	"Last Week's Blow Up" We gave it this name because it was an intense meeting—long, full of updates, and heightened by the fact that our numbers had just come out. People were already worked up so it was just the perfect episode to paint a picture of what everyone was feeling. We spend too much time talking about what we'll do and not enough time getting it done.	It seems like the beginning of the meeting is a critical moment where things could either get focused or "just start." If people just launch right into things (often thinking they will do us all a favor and "get through their updates") they end up taking more time. There is a glaring absence of strong facilitation since nobody really "owns" that job. We don't have turns of clarification, time-management, or strategic summarization.	We enjoy each other's company, we know it is important to have regular standing meetings, and we do not want to get our signals crossed when there is an expressed expectation that we should be meeting frequently to stay on the same page.

on and what really mattered to the people involved. As a result of the experience, the participants were energized by the process of looking past the presenting level to the constructing level of their episode. The experience was a catalyst for them to want to make something different, something more in sync with their individual goals and team priorities.

With this momentum, the team used a similar single-step practice to visualize the desired pattern of communication and interaction based on the same elements. In essence, they reverse engineered the process. Table 13.5 includes the full question sequence that they used to transform the first, completed product (the deconstructed pattern) into something better.

The group spent about 25 minutes working together on their version of the Pattern Constructor and table 13.6 illustrates the product they came up with.

You can see in this example that the path forward was clean and simple. There really were no controversial turns that required deeper discussion or patient consideration. The ease with which the process came together was in part due to the content of their pattern and its focus on meetings (as opposed to personality conflicts, etc.), but also due to the work they did leading up to this moment that created a clear sense of priorities and a flexible mindset to achieve them. The group's new pattern, "Moving Full-Speed Ahead," became their common refrain any time things started to get bogged down.

Table 13.5   Constructing a pattern (of communication and interaction)

Purpose: To build a preferred pattern of communication in reverse by mapping the underlying building blocks that will make it, then planning for the presenting outcomes it will bring.

Constructing level	What signature episode will capture the essence of this new pattern and what would you name it?	In this episode, what are the critical turns, or moments of transition, where specific communication will be needed to sustain the pattern?	What types of values, attitudes, and behaviors will positively fuel these turns and hold the pattern together?
Presenting level	Who must be involved to make the pattern and when/where can it take maximum effect?	What benefits and outcomes will it produce, and specifically, how will it improve the quality of your working lives?	How can additional priorities and commitments be aligned with this, so that it is not undermined?

What name(s) could you give to this experience that will remind us to work toward it?

Table 13.6 Example of constructing a pattern (of communication and interaction)

Purpose: To build a preferred pattern of communication in reverse by mapping the underlying building blocks that will make it, then planning for the presenting outcomes it will bring.

Constructing level	*What signature episode will capture the essence of this new pattern and what would you name it?* "Get in, get out, get it done" This is the goal we will hold for our meetings in the future. It will remind us each week that we have to communicate in this way if we want to avoid the unwanted stuff we get when we drift.	*In this episode, what are the critical turns, or moments of transition, where specific communication will be needed to sustain the pattern?* The first turn occurs before the meetings even start. We all need to identify agenda items in advance and consider which ones are true priorities. This will help us to keep each other honest about the choices we make on time management. When the frustration is triggered, the turn we take has to be one that refocuses us on priorities. Perhaps the question: "Okay, it feels like we're starting to drift. What is most important right now?"	*What types of values, attitudes, and behaviors will positively fuel these turns and hold the pattern together?* They are: • Commitment to getting as much done before meetings as possible. • Openness to finding alternative venues to communicate. • Willingness to meet as much as needed when it is the best approach to getting great work done.
Presenting level	*Who must be involved to make the pattern and when/where can it take maximum affect?* This requires all of us to be in it together.	*What benefits and outcomes will it produce, and specifically, how will it improve the quality of your working lives?* If this tilts the scale of our "meeting culture," then it should alleviate quite a bit of stress for all of us. The reduction in frustration from "wasted meeting time" should have a positive chain reaction on our productivity.	*How can additional priorities and commitments be aligned with this, so that it is not undermined?* Because this is about getting in, getting out, and getting it done, we can look for other things that drain our efficiency too. For example, we should reevaluate the way we send our monthly email updates.

What name(s) could you give to this experience that will remind us to work toward it?

"Moving full-speed ahead"

Conclusion

Single-step practices can be used by themselves or in combination with others to take a communication perspective at work and distinguish the building blocks and influential factors that make and sustain fragmented turns, closed episodes, and unwanted patterns. Whether it is a tool to visualize the system, set the hierarchy of values, or listen for stories, they produce a picture of the hidden side of communication. Chapter 14 introduces the M-A-I-D sequence, which integrates the single-step practices into a guide for re-making patterns from start to finish.

14

M-A-I-D: A Guide for Re-Making Patterns of Communication and Interaction

Significant terrain has been covered in this book so far. In part I you were challenged to forget the conventional wisdom about effective communication at work. Along with this challenge you were introduced to a new approach to communication that debunks the old myths and replaces them with a new set of principles regarding what works with communication at work. You reviewed the knowledge guide in part II that explained how these principles can be applied in the real world and you have just been introduced to a set of single-step practices to start re-making your unwanted patterns of communication and interaction.

This chapter introduces M-A-I-D, which is an array of signposts that will guide you in the implementation of the concepts and tools of re-making communication at work. The M-A-I-D sequence includes the following:

- Map influential patterns of communication and interaction
- Assess the quality of the experience and outcomes produced by those patterns
- Identify candidate patterns to re-make
- Determine the partners and sequence of action necessary to re-make the patterns

When to Use It

You have already learned many of the most important aspects of re-making communication at work. The M-A-I-D sequence is simply a way to organize the process of "putting it all together." There are a variety of situations in which you could use this flow, including those given below:

- evaluating the general status of a working relationship, either with a coworker, subordinate, or supervisor;

- reviewing a specific episode of communication with a colleague that produced an unwanted outcome or experience;
- identifying patterns that may need to be altered in order to successfully implement a specific change in the team or organization;
- exploring potential causes of unexpected changes (e.g., decreased engagement among employees, silence where there was active communication, etc.);
- reviewing the quality of a collaborative effort; and
- planning a new project and considering the people, roles, and configuration of responsibilities required for success.

These are just a few examples of when and where you could potentially apply the M-A-I-D sequence. With these scenarios in mind, here is a description of each phase of the four-part sequence, including suggestions for putting them into practice. You will notice that M-A-I-D is not a recipe. Rather than a formula, it is a simple progression that flows from principles in order to remain flexible, which is precisely what your challenges with communication at work require. Each of the four case examples that follow shows off the customizable nature of M-A-I-D, including diverse applications of the process with both individuals and teams.

Map Influential Patterns of Communication and Interaction

The first phase involves looking closely at specific episodes of communication and focusing on distinct patterns of interest. Bringing this focus to a specific set of interactions allows you to punctuate episodes and determine where a given pattern starts and stops. This is important because our working lives can often feel like one continuous, interconnected pattern with little difference between the conversations and interactions that take place throughout the day. The mapping process takes a big job—disentangling influential patterns of communication—and breaks it down into a smaller and more manageable starting place. In order to map influential patterns of communication and interaction you can start with the pattern finder, episode mapper, or turn selector tools described in chapter 9.

Assess the Quality of the Experience and Outcomes Produced by Those Patterns

This phase involves an honest review and assessment of the impact of the pattern across two dimensions. First, look at the impact it has on the quality of your experience. Does it diminish or enhance your working life in some way? Does the overall experience act as a catalyst for you to engage more fully in your work and express your best contributions more consistently, or does it cause you to shrink back, disengage, and limit your performance?

Next, look at the outcomes produced by the pattern. Do they contribute to effective learning, performance, and success at work? Do they make better collaboration? Do they directly or indirectly lead to higher-quality work? Do they foster more aligned relationships that produce better synergy? Do they impact the bottom line?

These questions assess the levels of both relationship and task and each perspective is important to analyze. At the relationship level, you are looking for clues about the impact of the pattern on people. Does the pattern seem to strengthen the bond between people and result in increased trust, positive regard, and the likelihood of productive interactions, or does it disrupt teamwork and reduce the likelihood of trust-based partnering on future projects and activities? At the task level, does the pattern make something useful that is required to achieve the priorities and goals of the people engaged in it (i.e., increased innovation, improved decision-making, better meetings, enhanced products/ services, etc.) or does it complicate matters and work against stated goals?

In order to assess the quality of the experience and outcomes produced by those patterns, you can use the "reality test" framework in table 14.1 or begin with the sample questions listed earlier. In addition to these two resources the tools for "deconstructing" and "constructing patterns" can also assist with assessing the quality and impact of specific communication.

Table 14.1   Reality test framework

Purpose: To assess the quality of the experience and outcomes produced by specific patterns of communication and interaction.

People/experience	*Task/outcome*
Does the pattern strengthen the bond between people and result in increased trust, positive regard, and greater likelihood of productive interactions, or does it disrupt teamwork and reduce the likelihood of trust-based partnering on future projects and activities?	Does the pattern make something useful that is required to achieve the priorities and goals of the people engaged in it (e.g., increased innovation, improved decision-making, better meetings, etc.) or does it complicate matters and work against those stated goals?
1 2 3 4 5 6 7 8 9 10	1 2 3 4 5 6 7 8 9 10
(−) (+)	(−) (+)
Why?_____	Why? _____
_____	_____
_____	_____
_____	_____

Identify Candidate Patterns to Re-Make

This is the careful process of selecting patterns to potentially re-make based on a set of criteria that you choose. This is technically the third step in the sequence; however, it often happens simultaneously with the first two stages of M-A-I-D. The assessment can include comparing the potential upsides and downsides of re-making it. You can weigh your options with questions such as the following:

1. If this pattern was re-made, would it likely improve a relationship, outcome, or other important aspect of the quality of my working life?
2. If so, how important is that to me right now?
3. How entrenched is this pattern and how many people would likely be involved in changing it?
4. What available time, energy, and motivation do I have for re-making this pattern now?
5. What, if any, are the potential risks of engaging people in the process of re-making this pattern?
6. Overall is this a pattern of communication and interaction that matters enough to me to invest in re-making it?
7. Can I afford not to try to re-make it?

Answering questions like these requires a level of decisive judgment about what matters and what will make a difference based on the gap between what you have and what you want. This is a learned skill and the most important aspect of the process early on is to identify candidate patterns that are equal parts "headache and frustration" and "positive potential for something better."

Determine the Partners and Sequence of Action Necessary to Re-Make the Patterns

In this final step, you ask "who," then "what." You begin by determining the partners who are necessary for re-making the pattern. Traditionally, the term "partner" (i.e., strategic partner) was used in reference to an external stakeholder, person, or group that was outside of the organization. The notion of partnering has increasingly turned inward. For example, in human resources or other functional units that are service hubs within an organization, it is not uncommon to refer to those who are served as business "partners."

I think this change in terminology is more than a new addition to business jargon. It implies something fundamental: a shared responsibility for understanding what is important and working effectively together to achieve it. And what, you may ask, is one of the greatest success factors in any effective partnership? It is *communication*, of course.[1]

Once you know the who, then you focus on the what—the specific sequence of actions necessary to re-make the pattern. For every diverse issue you face there is an equally diverse range of potential sequences to employ. The previous chapter on single-step practice for re-making communication at work introduced a variety of those tools that can all be put into action. When determining sequence and approach, I suggest the simplest combination of tools and approaches that can be used to most effectively alter the underlying system of attitudes and behaviors that holds the unwanted pattern in place.

M-A-I-D Case Examples

The following case examples using the M-A-I-D sequence show four different configurations of the tools for re-making communication at work. The selected real-world examples reflect a variety of people, organizations, and issues in order to give you the widest perspective on what is possible when you take a communication perspective at work. In addition to the diversity of content within the examples, there is also diversity of delivery. Some of these cases were facilitated by a coach or consultant and others were self-directed by the participants themselves. This mix illustrates the ways in which M-A-I-D can be used both independently and with the assistance of a consulting third party.

A Boomer in Her Third Act and Patterns of "Inflexible Thinking"

Barbara spent more than 35 years working in the finance division of a large multinational company. After a successful career she was ready to give back to her community in retirement. It was not long before she was asked to serve on the board of directors of a local nonprofit. And it was not much longer after that when the executive director quit unexpectedly. The board president nominated Barbara to take on the interim role of executive director acknowledging that her business experience and practical focus would be invaluable as they put together a recruitment plan for a full-time executive director.

After accepting the role, Barbara quickly found out that there was much more to the organization than she saw in her role as a board member. Once the three-month interim period had careened into its ninth month, Barbara realized that she needed to take a much more deliberate approach to leading the nonprofit. It seemed like the staff and volunteers were at odds with each other over various matters and she felt it was time to explore the origins of these potentially destructive issues. After participating in a short webinar that introduced the concepts and tools of re-making communication at work, this is how Barbara used the M-A-I-D sequence in a self-guided process.

To start things off and get a feel for the bigger picture, Barbara used the six-question "pattern finder" to identify a specific pattern of communication and interaction to potentially re-make. The summary of her finished product, given here, revealed a set of challenging experiences that produced a variety of unwanted outcomes. The very real impact from these patterns affected her own quality of working life, as well as the organization's capacity to meet the demands of its mission.

Pattern Finder

1. What recurring experiences or outcomes do I have at work?

   To keep things moving along I will often make some kind of executive decision and then roll it out at a staff meeting. After that, things just stop. Rather than efficient problem-solving, there is no implementation and the action just stalls.

   When we have our combined staff and volunteer meetings each month, the room is pretty chilly. It seems like there is a real lack of trust and I'm not entirely sure where it is coming from.

   The two longtime program coordinators and I seem to be butting heads regularly. I thought they would appreciate my experience and the way I lead, but their resistance and lack of contribution is really frustrating.

2. How do I know that these experiences and outcomes are real?

I say, think, feel, and act...	Others say, think, feel, and act...
A. I announce a decision or decisive action with an email, memo, or verbally during the staff meeting	A. They say "we need more time," "that won't work"...I get blank stares, and rather than change, it's just status quo
B. I share news, information, and updates with volunteers and staff and feel like people just glare with their arms folded	B. I hear volunteers talk a lot about "what we used to do" and the old guard really seems to rev people up
C. I can be blunt because we have so much to do and so little time, I run our leadership meetings like a CEO	C. They bristle whenever they see me rolling up my sleeves to plow through a pile of issues

3. When and where do the interactions that produce these experiences and outcomes take place?

   Our weekly staff meetings, the monthly combined staff/volunteer get together, and my biweekly leadership meeting with my two program coordinators.

4. If I connect the dots, what story does all of this tell and how would I name it?

I am willing to be forceful, task-focused, and ready to move past pleasantries to get to the bottom line, but other people seem to want greater connection and involvement in the way work gets done. I'll call it: "Corporate Thinking Is Not Appreciated Around Here!"

5. Where does it sit on the continuum?

Unwanted..Preferred

$$-3 \qquad -2 \qquad -1 \qquad 0 \qquad +1 \qquad +2 \qquad +3$$

For me: It fluctuates a bit. On a bad day it is a −2. The reason is that the harder I push, the worse things feel and the less stuff gets done. I would take a 0 at this point, let alone a +3.

For them: I would guess it is about the same. It might even be -3 on a bad day.

6. Does it need to be re-made in some way?

Yes, this pattern is increasingly destructive. I feel stressed and it is not leading to the kinds of outcomes we need. I could lose staff if things don't get better soon.

After completing the six-question Pattern Finder Barbara realized she wanted to focus specifically on the relationship with her two program coordinators. The staff meeting and the issues with volunteers were important, however, the Pattern Finder allowed her to see that the main issue for her was the clash of her leadership team.

In order to better understand the reasons behind her actions and behaviors, Barbara used a single-step process, the "hierarchy of values," in order to expose the "physics" of the pattern and try to discover where this "CEO mindset" was coming from. This is what she came up with.

Hierarchy of Values

1. In my role as the interim executive director, what are the most important priorities and values that guide the work I do?
   - Challenging others to be their best
   - Keeping the doors open and lights on
   - Bringing an efficient business mentality
   - Making a difference
   - Proving that I can lead and succeed
2. Considering each of these priorities and values, which are the strongest influences on the way I communicate and interact in this specific pattern?

After organizing her values and priorities in order from "most" to "least" influential (shown in figure 14.1), Barbara had a moment of insight. She saw that when her attitudes and actions were driven—first and foremost—by her value of "bringing an efficient business mentality" to the organization, the pattern of "Corporate Thinking Is Not Appreciated Around Here!" was

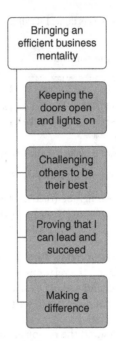

Figure 14.1   Barbara's hierarchy of values.

re-made daily. That CEO mindset subsequently colored the pace, tone, and structure of her approach to work.

For example, when Barbara moved quickly through the meeting agenda to "get more done," her program coordinators felt "bossed and disrespected." When Barbara unilaterally changed things for the sake of achieving greater efficiency, her team pushed back to preserve what they thought was good and necessary in the old way of doing things. Her values and priorities to "make a difference" and "challenge others to be at their best" were not seen or felt by anyone.

Barbara considered each of the biweekly leadership meetings to be the recurring episodes in the pattern. As she thought back on the last few episodes, she realized that her program coordinators were not being challenged to contribute and help lead the organization; they were just being challenged to "do what Barbara asked."

Continuing in her process, Barbara decided to find out if there was more going on below the surface. She understood that her business background was the origin of her CEO mindset, but she wondered if there were any unknown, unheard, and untellable stories in the mix. To explore these, she completed another single-step process in table 14.2 to see what else was contributing to the unwanted pattern.

Table 14.2   Barbara's unknown, unheard, and untellable stories

Listening for stories

Purpose: To reveal the tension between the unknown, unheard, and untellable stories—including the gap between what is said and what is actually experienced—in order to spot the causes of fragmented turns, closed episodes, and unwanted patterns of communication.

Type of story	If there is a story, what does it mean?	What is the impact of the story?
Unknown story	One of the reasons I retired was because I wanted something different than Corporate America. Why am I trying to take this nonprofit back to a place I don't even want to go?	I didn't know the story, so I assumed… • Doing what came naturally put me on the right path • My career experience was enough to "get people on board"
Unheard story	The program coordinators have a lot to give and they actually want to make positive changes	I didn't hear the story, so I felt… • They were just resistant to me due to their own fear and uncertainty
Untellable story	Much of my business experience does not apply here, though saying so could reduce my credibility	I didn't imagine the story, so I would not have thought… • I may be acting out of insecurity • People may already know this and I'm just catching up to it…

Listening for Stories

By revealing these unknown, unheard, and untellable stories Barbara made a few more discoveries about what she was making. The rhetorical question she posed to herself—Why am I trying to take this nonprofit back to a place I don't even want to go?—was a liberating moment for her. She reported that what was clear in that instant was that she was now free to lead in a more flexible way. She could give team members room to try their own novel approaches and overall she could relax the pace of work and invest more in the connections of people that would lead to deeper commitment to the mission.

With growing momentum to re-make the pattern, Barbara checked in with the M-A-I-D sequence. Without effort to track the steps and keep up with the process, she realized that she already moved through most of the sequence. Now, she was ready to finish the process by completing the "pattern constructor" exercise. This was her way of involving the right people and planning the concrete next steps she would take in the upcoming leadership meeting. This would be the "next episode" in the pattern and she wanted it to mark a shift to something different. Table 14.3 shows the preferred pattern she designed.

Table 14.3 Barbara's new pattern

Constructing a preferred pattern of communication and interaction

Purpose: To build a preferred pattern of communication in reverse by mapping the underlying building blocks that will make it, then planning for the presenting outcomes it will bring.

Constructing level	*What signature episode will capture the essence of this new pattern and what would you name it?* "At the next leadership meeting, we will do things differently. I'll call it 'The Program Coordinators Lead.' There will be no agenda, just two questions: (1) What do we need to change in order to work better together as a leadership team; and (2) What can I do to help you succeed in your jobs?"	*In this episode, what are the critical turns, or moments of transition, where specific communication will be needed to sustain the pattern?* "When things feel like they are drifting a bit and my knee-jerk reaction to 'roll up my sleeves and fix things' is triggered, the turn I will take is to put my concern in the form of a question (i.e., 'How will you handle this potential challenge?'). Then, I will simply listen."	*What types of values, attitudes, and behaviors will positively fuel these turns and hold the pattern together?* "I want to flip my values so that the new hierarchy is: 1. I am here to make a difference 2. I can challenge others to be their best 3. We will keep the doors open and lights on 4. If my decisions and actions are influenced by these three values first, I won't need the 'CEO Mindset' to prove my value."
Presenting level	*Who must be involved to make the pattern and when/where can it take maximum effect?* "I need both program coordinators to want this change to happen. If so, we can start by re-making our bimonthly leadership meetings. I will also give them more leadership opportunities during the volunteer meetings in order to shift that dynamic too."	*What benefits and outcomes will it produce, and specifically, how will it improve the quality of your working lives?* "I can still speak in a no-nonsense manner, but I will be more diplomatic. This will avoid offending people and increase trust. They will have more autonomy and feel like they can get back to doing what they love. With less friction, we will all be more productive with our priorities."	*How can additional priorities and commitments be aligned with these new episodes so that they are not undermined?* "We have volunteer recruitment goals, as well as two new programs coming on line next year. Rather than me leading each of these priorities, we can share the load and each champion one. This structural change will help us to consider multiple perspectives and share the challenges we face."

What name could you give to this preferred pattern to remind you to work toward it?

"We are in this together."

Following the successful effort to re-make her unwanted pattern, I asked Barbara what was the most useful aspect of using the concepts and tools of re-making communication at work. Barbara wrote a simple summary about her experience using the M-A-I-D sequence and shared the following highlights:

> For me the most useful thing was "looking in the mirror" and coming to terms with what I brought to the table. Before this, it was convenient to blame people for not being on board or just "not getting it." Seeing my hierarchy of values and listening for the deeper stories revealed a lot. The questions and work-sheets were helpful because they made me "look at the communication" as I was making it. I could see how each turn caused these reactions that nobody wanted. I like the M-A-I-D sequence because I did not have to follow a complicated 12-point plan. There was no worry or stress on my part about "getting the process right." I just checked in with each part of the sequence periodically and realized I was doing it all as I went along. I'm glad I did this exercise, although my team may be even happier than me. We have come a long way from "Corporate Thinking Is Not Appreciated Around Here!" all the way to "We are in this together."

A Next Generation Leader and the Pattern of "Getting In Your Own Way"

For the first time in our history we have four different generations in the workforce simultaneously. The cohorts range in ages from their early twenties through their eighties. A whole cottage industry has sprung up to explain the various features of this blended workforce, including all of the challenges and opportunities that hinder or encourage their working well together. The upshot of this is that the trend will not last.

Despite the downward economy that has delayed retirement for many people, the Silent and Baby Boomer generations have begun their mass retirement. It is widely expected that there will be a shortage of experienced managers once this succession process accelerates. This means opportunities for rapid promotion and career advancement for people like Robin, who was identified as a "high-potential" candidate in her fast-growing technology company.

Robin's manager was pretty astute and he told her frankly that "she could run this company one day" and the only thing that could get in her way was *her*. He was invested in her success and so he arranged for a coach to work with her in order to develop her leadership abilities for long-term success. Her potential was off of the charts. Robin got a lot done, she had fresh thinking and innovative ideas, and she was willing to work harder than anybody else. Unfortunately, her strengths also had a shadow side. As others in her generation were sometimes known for, she had a tendency to be impatient with others' pace of change and expected that everything should be done yesterday. During meetings she would often monopolize conversations, over-power others, and solve problems in a way that felt confrontational to people.

This was not a question of intention, as much as it was a lack of awareness and attention to the way her actions affected others.

The impact of this was that her results-oriented mindset compromised the quality of some key working relationships. And no matter how great her upside was, Robin's climb on the ladder of success was threatened by these patterns of communication and interaction that caused people to question her potential and their willingness to "bet on her" to be a key leader.

Robin's case demonstrates the effectiveness of starting small with re-making communication at work. The activities and discussions presented in her story were completed during a single 90-minute meeting where Robin and her coach used the M-A-I-D sequence. The coach was not an "expert" in communication nor did Robin read advanced materials or participate in preparatory training.

Learning to See What You Make

One of the first challenges for Robin was to learn how to see her patterns of communication and interaction, especially the impact she had on making them. After listening to her describe "a day in the life at work" her coach became curious about the specific way Robin expressed her contributions. Using a single-step process to "visualize the system," Robin produced a picture of her definition of success at work. The center circle in figure 14.2

Figure 14.2 Visualizing Robin's story of success.

framed the exercise and each peripheral circle described an idea, value, or story that explained her picture of success.

After looking at the picture she made, Robin had a laugh at her own expense. She said that it looked like a "bad handout from a motivational speaker." With this bit of humor as a lead-in to something real, the coach asked her to reflect on the question: "If these are some of the definitions that shape your idea of success, what ripple effect do you see them have on others you work with?" With this question as the starting place, here is how the next few turns in their coaching session unfolded:

> *Robin*: "Well…I see somebody who is confident, probably too cocky some-times. One effect on people is that they know that they always have to push and cannot relax; the pace I lead my team with will leave them behind if they are not on board…I'm sure that for some people I am a challenge to work with; my boss has told me as such. Honestly, I see some-one with high expectations for herself and others—a potential CEO!"
>
> *Coach*: "I can definitely see the values and commitments of someone quite successful here too. As I look at your picture I notice that something that many leaders describe as *a key to their success* is missing from yours. I'm wondering if you see it too."
>
> *Robin*: "Are you talking about having great people? Yes, I thought about that. It is interesting that I didn't list it. I guess I thought it was implied."

Seeing that Robin was starting to look beyond her own tightly packed ideas of what mattered, the coach asked her to make a second picture of the system. Going in a clockwise direction, in figure 14.3 Robin added a new circle and wrote something specific that connected the first definition of suc-cess with the "people-side" of what would drive successful outcomes.

> *Robin*: "Looking at this now, I notice how little I actually think about the people aspects of our work. As a manager I probably just sounded really bad by saying that; but, it's true. I get so focused on what we're doing—and I want to meet the high-standards of our executive leader-ship team—I just push and push."
>
> *Coach*: "You are not the first new manager who has lost that balance. In fact, I think rather than sounding really bad by saying that, you just did something important that will help you throughout your career: you were truthful about what you see regarding your contribution to the situation. I don't believe I have ever worked with a truly successful leader who didn't have that trait of self-candor and honesty."
>
> *Robin*: "Okay, so I can admit that I'm not perfect: what do I do? I'm not going to go all 'touchy feely' with my group; that's just not who I am."
>
> *Coach*: "I would not want you to be someone you're not. That said, if the patterns of communication you're making are limiting your potential career success and alienating people in the process, then do you think it could be worth a few strategic adjustments on your end?"

Figure 14.3   Robin's expanding story of success.

Episode Mapper

Robin was in the room because her answer to that last rhetorical question was "yes." To keep the momentum going, the coach invited Robin to map a recent episode that produced a really difficult outcome. He explained that mapping an episode is a way to pick apart the specific communication interaction to see exactly what it makes and how it makes it. The coach believed that this exercise would reveal whether Robin was taking enough of a communication perspective to see what her boss knew about the potential of her negative contributions to undermine her success. Using the "episode mapper" worksheet, Robin told the story of the last staff meeting where things got pretty tense.

1. Who are the players?

   At the end of the meeting, it was just me, Tim, Jeanne, and Trent who were left in the conference room. The others had already left.

2. When/where did it begin and when/where did it end?

It definitely started when I called Jeanne out after I learned she had not finished the presentation that was supposed to go live the next day. I don't know if it has even ended; she was really angry at the way I handled it.

3. Frequency and impact checklist:
   - Does it repeat? How often?

     This is the only specific incident like this regarding the launch. But I would have to say that yes, my tendency to overreact and expect everything to be done yesterday happens a lot.

   - Does it have a minor, moderate, or major impact on my day when it happens?

     This one seemed to have a major impact. I know that my boss found out about it, which is kind of why I'm in this coaching program. In my mind, they do not have that big of an impact, but I guess that is part of the problem—I don't realize that my fire hose approach can hurt people.

4. When the episode plays out, the results are more:

   Closed..Open

   | −3 | −2 | −1 | 0 | +1 | +2 | +3 |

   Well, I guess that depends on the definition of success. If the goal is a "home run with the new launch, get ahead of the tectonic shifts, game changing use of technology, and go big or go home" then they are open. Now that we are working on this, I think that in reality these kinds of episodes are quite closed when you think about the goals of "everybody working on the same page, anticipate, communicate about change with everyone, use technology to help people perform better, and motivate the team to commit to these big goals. I give it a -2."

5. What name would I give the episode?

   I would call this one "Robin Went Too Far."

6. What adjustments could be made to *open the episode* in a positive way?

   Slow down enough to listen and let others do their thing...The ironic thing is that if I would have listened a little bit longer, I would have had all my concerns addressed. I just saw flashing red lights that said "Jeanne Dropped the Ball."

After mapping this episode Robin now had an objective blueprint of the staff meeting that went off the rails. Without the need to challenge her with hard questions, Robin naturally began to take ownership and responsibility for her actions. And, more importantly, the prompts led her to recognize that she had a "pattern on her hands." This segue was what the coach needed for the final exercise in their first session.

> *Coach*: "Okay Robin, you just put your finger on the hidden part of communication. *When our everyday episodes of communication and interaction repeat they make ongoing patterns.* When the patterns are consistent with our values and goals, they are *preferred*. When they clash with what matters to us, they are *unwanted*. If we want to know why we get the experiences and results we make at work, all we have to do is look at the patterns of communication and interaction we engage in. In a future session we can look at how this particular pattern is playing out in the big picture for you. However, since you are still involved in an on-going episode, I think we should focus our attention on your next 'turn' to see if we can open it up a little bit."
>
> *Robin*: "Agreed. I need to clean this mess up so that the launch is not impacted by what just happened. I have already spoken with Jeanne to apologize so I think she and I are good for now. It is the 'next time' I'm worried about."

In order to bring attention to the next move Robin could make, the coach used the "turn selector" worksheet to help her map the specific approach she would take. Rather than completing the full six questions, the coach wanted to accommodate Robin's desire to move quickly, so he modified the exercise and only used the last two.

1. What shift in your next turn could lead to more alignment?

   I think the shift has to be in my overall tone. Rather than going at a million miles per hour, I need to slow it down and focus on one thing at a time. Not only will this match the pace that my team prefers, it might help us catch some last minute mistakes.

2. When will you take the next turn to change the trajectory of the episode?

   As far as the team, we have another meeting tomorrow to go over the final preparation before the launch. Typically I start those walkthrough meetings with a very crisp "okay, where are we at?" I think I need to acknowledge the hard work that has gotten us to this point. I'll announce that the goal of the meeting is to make sure we are on the same page and that we will take as much time as needed to get prepared for the launch. Although it will be hard for me, I need to hang back a little bit and let others contribute.

After discussing these two questions, Robin said that she felt like she had a concrete game plan for moving forward, which was important to her. Throughout the session the coach was very deliberate in the way he introduced only a few concepts and tools to re-make communication at work. Wherever possible he avoided jargon and kept things as simple as possible. The flexibility of the M-A-I-D sequence allowed the exercises to be applied in a useful way during their first session, and it ensured that the next coaching session would be an opportunity to look more deeply at the patterns of communication and interaction Robin was making with her colleagues at work.

A Sales Team Got Stuck in a Pattern of "Change Traps"

There is nothing easy about working in sales. The grind, the competition, the rejection, and the need to innovate and find new ways to connect with customers can be exhausting. This was the case for Kyle and his sales team. Despite the fact that Kyle, Sophia, and Jamie all chose the profession because they liked the constant commotion and steep challenges it presented, over time they collectively seemed to grow more and more comfortable with the status quo. A period of stability in the market, coupled with a string of successful accounts, made the team prone to several common change traps that resulted in unwanted patterns of communication and interaction. With the assistance of a professional facilitator, here is how Kyle and his two colleagues used the M-A-I-D sequence to re-make their unwanted patterns of communication and interaction.

Listening for Stories

After an introductory discussion that got the group talking, the facilitator spoke briefly about the power of stories, including the ways they shape our interactions with people at work. He introduced the concept of "working life scripts" by saying, "These are the professional narratives you believe and tell about your anticipated experience at work. Specifically, they tell a story about the kinds of episodes you expect to participate in at work. These scripts are 'written' from past experience, as well as from the beliefs and expectations you have about the future."

After sharing a couple of sample working life scripts, the facilitator invited Kyle, Sophia, and Jamie to tell their own stories about how they look at their working lives. The goal of this short exercise was to keep things loose while finding entry points toward deeper and more substantive conversations about their concerns. As an example of the outcome from this activity, table 14.4 shows Sophia's finished product.

Along with Sophia, Kyle and Jamie described their working life scripts too. The total time required to individually create them and share the results with the group was about 25 minutes; however, it was time very well spent. During the discussion the facilitator heard several recurring themes that gave him the opportunity to introduce another exercise to listen for stories. Rather than doing three individual versions of this one, the facilitator chose to do one together as a team. The working life script activity produced an honest exchange that was enough to talk out loud about the unknown, unheard, and untellable stories in the team. Table 14.5 shows the consolidated version of what they made.

By revealing these unknown, unheard, and untellable stories Kyle, Sophia, and Jamie made a few more discoveries about what they were making together. It turned out that each of them had been feeling quite similar to

Table 14.4   Sophia's working life script

What is your working life script?

Purpose: To tell a story about your working life, including the beliefs that influence your patterns of communication and interaction and shape your everyday experience at work.

Describe the plot of your working life?	*Who are the influential characters in your story and what past events may influence what you believe about your working life?*
A college graduate lands a job in sales and dives in head first. Before she knows what kind of career she wants, she is five years into it. In this story, the high points are very high and the lows could not be lower.	Besides me, Kyle and Jamie are important players...our regional manager Jim is too. Jim was my first boss, I guess the one thing he really helped me do was "pick myself up off the mat." I see myself as tough and determined.
	As far as influential events, going through a major economic crisis was my most defining career phase. I was still new at the time, so I did not know what the "good old days" were all about. I am pretty cautious because I know it could happen again any time.
What typical episodes do you engage in?	*Imagine that these episodes are part of larger patterns of communication and interaction...which recurring pattern shapes the quality of your experience and outcomes the most?*
• We have a lot of "whirlwind meetings" where we compare notes, check-in, and try to coordinate our leads.	
• It is common to "commiserate about the challenges" we face. These are informal venting sessions.	Speaking for myself..."the old ways are not working anymore." The toll from episodes like the "whirlwind meetings" and the "what have you done for me lately" conversations with clients do not seem to be move us forward. Sometimes I wonder if I am burning out because I just don't seem to have the energy to figure out what could be better.
• With clients we have a lot of "what have you done for me lately" conversations. These are phone calls and face-to-face meetings to reestablish value to keep the business.	
• With prospects, the most common episode is "we love the idea, but the timing is just not right." For every account I land there are a dozen high-potential pitches that end like this.	

the others, but the sales culture in their group was one that prompted them to "always be up" and to project "steady confidence" in the face of adversity. The consequence of this was that there were quite a few stories that needed to be heard. This is a brief excerpt from the conversation that took place after the exercise:

Table 14.5   The team's unknown, unheard, and untellable stories

Listening for stories

Purpose: To reveal the tension between the unknown, unheard, and untellable stories—including the gap between what is said and what is actually experienced—in order to spot the causes of fragmented turns, closed episodes, and unwanted patterns of communication.

Type of story	If there is a story, what does it mean?	What is the impact of the story?
Unknown story	We are actually losing ground to our competitors—it is slow, but noticeable	I didn't know the story, so I assumed... • Continuing with our regular efforts was enough
Unheard story	We have been relying on our past success and the hunger has faded a little	I didn't hear the story, so I felt... • We were just in a slight dip and things would balance out soon
Untellable story	The incredible energy and hard work we invested to make the last few years so successful may have left the tank empty	I didn't imagine the story, so I would not have thought... • The grind may be too much • In small ways we've been resistant to change and okay with the status quo

Kyle: "This is really interesting to see. We have all been feeling and acting a certain way, but we were not talking about it with each other. I hope you both know that we can talk about things like this. Getting remotivated and relying on the support of the team is an important aspect of sales success."

Jamie: "I'm glad we're doing this too. It really seems like our celebration of success in 2010 evolved into resting on our laurels. We weathered the financial crisis of 2008–2009 and we did have a lot to be proud about. But, now that we have to hustle more, we're really slow to get off the starting block."

Sophia: "Well, it's not like we haven't been working. In fact, I've been as busy as ever. I know you both have too. It seems like the unheard story about *losing market share* is the wakeup call. We will need to work differently now. And honestly, I don't know if I'm up for the 70-hour weeks we pulled back then."

Jamie: "I hear you. It seems like we have more of a balance now, which is nice. The fact is that maybe we are just not as hungry."

Kyle: "I think I've been as guilty as the next guy of sweeping some of these signs under the rug. It definitely seems like we are at a turning point. Maybe we need to look at how we structure our work in relation to our changing position in the market."

Facilitator: "Listening to this open exchange reminds me about the high level of trust you have with each other. I think this willingness to share what is real will help you through the transition. Before we shift gears to the strategy and tactical work flow issues, I think it would be valuable to look specifically at how these *unheard, unknown,* and *untellable* stories have actually found their way into the everyday patterns of communication and interaction you engage in."

Kyle: "Okay, that sounds good. It may help us to see more about what is going on here before we try to leap into change mode."

Deconstructing and Constructing Patterns

With Kyle and the rest of the group's endorsement to continue exposing their hidden communication, the facilitator introduced an activity to help the team "deconstruct" a pattern of communication that was the direct result of their complex stories playing out together. The facilitator could have used the "pattern finder" to help the team more specifically identify the character and details of the pattern. However, he deemed that unnecessary due to the fact that a relatively clear picture of the pattern had already emerged in the first two exercises.

Instead, the facilitator wrote out a rough description of the pattern profile that was starting to emerge for the group. The information he used to draft the pattern profile was taken from the prior discussion about working life scripts and unheard, unknown, and untellable stories in their everyday experience at work. Without too much emphasis on wordsmithing, he invited comments to adjust the wording and intent as needed. This is what the final product said:

> *Pattern Profile Description:* We do things to balance change and stability, but we have leaned too far toward stability. Now that the competition is heating up, we worry that too much intensity will cause burnout. There are already signs of fatigue and resistance to necessary changes.
>
> *Typical Episodes:* We stay busy but we do not tackle big issues, we talk a lot about the past (i.e., how good we are), and we make sure our meetings follow the same routine updates without venturing into more challenging topics.
>
> *Potential Alternative Episodes:* Honest conversations about the right balance of change, accurate assessments about the roles and accountabilities required to meet our current priorities, letting busy work go and investing in top goals, and creating pockets of continuity to rest from change and avoid burnout.

With this pattern profile on the white board, each individual considered its implications and then completed their own worksheet to deconstruct the pattern. As individuals shared their responses, the facilitator consolidated their thoughts into one. The purpose of that sequence was to shift from individual ownership of the attitudes and behaviors involved in the pattern to a team investment in re-making them. Table 14.6 shows the finished version they created.

Table 14.6 Deconstructing the team's unwanted pattern

Deconstructing a pattern of communication and interaction

Purpose: To dissect the anatomy of an unwanted pattern of communication by mapping the presenting outcomes it brings, as well as the underlying building blocks (i.e., attitudes, beliefs, and behaviors) that influence the episodes that shape it.

	What is the pattern of communication and interaction making? • Superficial collaboration where we avoid certain issues • Good work/life balance and reasonable stress levels • A potential disaster if we do not make changes to get more competitive	What possible name(s) could you give to this experience? "It was a good ride, but we have to call it like we see it."	
Presenting level	*Who is involved in making the pattern and when/where does it seem to take effect?* We are all involved in making this happen. Although we have met the numbers in such a way that has satisfied corporate, we know we need to be doing more.	*What challenges or difficulties does it produce, and specifically, how does it impact the quality of your working lives?* We are losing market share and have not done enough to boost the new business pipeline. If we do not make adjustments, this could have long-term effects.	*Even if it is contradictory, does it produce any benefits for the people who make it?* Yes, it seems like by clinging to our past success, we avoid the need to confront changes in the market. This preserves the balanced pace we have come to rely on.
Constructing level	*If there is an episode that captures what the pattern is all about, what would it be and what would you name it?* The episode that captures this best is probably our weekly sales meeting. Knowing what we know now, it is almost comical that we just go through the motions—everybody knows it but nobody says anything.	*In this episode, what are the critical turns, or moments of transition, where specific communication sustains the pattern?* Whenever we talk about high-potential pitches that failed to close the deal, we avoid talking about the honest reasons why: We are failing to innovate. Instead, one of us will say something about the good accounts we still have or the fact that those prospective customers don't get it.	*What types of values, attitudes, and behaviors fuel these turns and seem to be needed to hold the pattern together?* We seem to have all of these "get out of jail free cards" and nobody is willing to speak up about the ways we are falling short. We have all worked together for a few years and so it is done out of genuine regard for each other.

If you look at their finished product you can see that Kyle, Sophia, and Jamie got to an even deeper level of conversation about the pattern of communication and interaction that dominated their recent work experience. Looking at the last question (i.e., values, attitudes, and behaviors that fuel these turns), the facilitator shared the concept of a "master contract." A master contract is the previously defined relationship among the communicating participants, or what each believes they can expect of the other in a specific episode or within ongoing patterns. These are often implied, unwritten agreements that coworkers develop with each other. The facilitator asked if anybody noticed a master contract that suggests "We Will Not Challenge Each Other." Here is the dialogue that followed:

> *Sophia*: "Absolutely, I see it clearly. While I know we do these things because we respect the dues that we have all paid, hearing us talk like this would have embarrassed us a few years ago."
>
> *Jamie*: "Sophia is right: this must mean we are part of the old guard. If we saw a sales team take the convenient path as much as we do we would criticize them pretty hard."
>
> *Kyle*: "I guess the thing to do is 'renegotiate the contract.' I think we can have a higher degree of truth telling without compromising the respect we have for each other. Do you both agree?"

As the facilitator listened to the discussion unfold, it was clear that the team was now taking a communication perspective. They understood that in order to make something different, they would have to change the fundamental drivers of their ongoing communication habits. Seamlessly, the facilitator invited them to complete the final exercise of the session saying: "After you have deconstructed a pattern to see what it is and what it makes, you can use the 'pattern constructor' to flip the sequence and create a plan to make something better."

Following a similar process, each individual created their own version and then the facilitator led a discussion to consolidate them into one team picture. This finished version in table 14.7 became the "first step" in the strategic and tactical changes that Kyle knew were needed for his team.

You can tell from the tone of the final response that Kyle and his team were excited about the work that was done. They had no illusions that the questions about their long-term engagement were resolved, but they had done enough to start moving forward in their process.

If you review the steps the facilitator used to work with the group you will notice that M-A-I-D acted as a flexible array of signposts that guided the implementation of the concepts and tools of re-making communication at work. Throughout the two-and-a-half-hour session, the group *M*apped an influential pattern of communication and interaction, gained a greater sense of urgency for change by *A*ssessing the quality of the experience and outcomes produced by the pattern, *I*dentified a candidate pattern to re-make,

Table 14.7 The team's preferred pattern

Constructing a pattern of communication and interaction

Purpose: To build a preferred pattern of communication in reverse by mapping the underlying building blocks that will make it, then planning for the presenting outcomes it will bring.

Constructing level	*What signature episode will capture the essence of this new pattern and what would you name it?* Substantive meetings with "Truth Telling"—at our sales meetings we need to make time to dig a little deeper into why we are not closing more business.	*In this episode, what are the critical turns, or moments of transition, where specific communication will be needed to sustain the pattern?* If we revert to our old ways of covering up our shortcomings by talking about the glory days, we need to help each other make the turn that says, "That was the past, what do we need to do right now to be successful?"	*What types of values, attitudes, and behaviors will positively fuel these turns and hold the pattern together?* • Commitment to be open, honest, and engaged in our work • Respect for our past contributions without using them to cover up our gaps
Presenting level	*Who must be involved to make the pattern and when/where can it take maximum affect?* We all have to be in this together, consistently.	*What benefits and outcomes will it produce, and specifically, how will it improve the quality of your working lives?* Going through the motions has caused stress by itself. Our open approach should alleviate that and help us see our challenges squarely. While we will need to work differently, it is possible that we can avoid a return to the crazy survival mode.	*How can additional priorities and commitments be aligned with this, so that it is not undermined?* We already have our benchmarks for this year so we know what we need to do with the numbers. To make sure we stay on track, each of us could create personal action plans that reflect the changes necessary to stay consistent with this new approach.

What name(s) could you give to this experience that will remind us to work toward it?

"Down, but not out. We may be slower, but we are smarter!"

and *D*etermined the partners and sequence of action necessary to begin re-making the pattern. They accomplished all of this without ever really knowing that they were "using a process."

A Start-Up Company, Starting Up Patterns of "Bad Habits"

The environment of a start-up company is unlike any other work environment. Things move fast, the stakes are high, and the particular mindset and skill-set of those who can thrive in the entrepreneurial environment are unique. Like a blank canvass, a start-up company provides an amazing opportunity to create a winning business model and an organization culture "from scratch." The chance to establish healthy and productive patterns of communication are matched only by the potential to create unwanted patterns and bad outcomes. In both cases, the trajectories that they make are potentially long-lasting and full of high-impact effects (unless of course they cause the business to fail early).

When Jason, Michelle, and Gary sat at their kitchen table and decided to be business partners, they did not know what to expect, but they were ready for the journey. They believed that their new software "App" had the potential to set the world on fire and meet a glaring gap in the personal productivity market. What they didn't realize was that the patterns of communication and interaction they made would have just as much impact as the code they wrote for their new software.

When a few early bumps in the road threatened to delay the first deliverable, it started to concern a few of the investors. With a clear suggestion from the primary backer of the business, Jason, Michelle, and Gary brought a consultant in to "work on their communication." With time at a premium, they agreed to one three-hour session with the promise that they would follow-up on their own after the consulting engagement ended.

The experienced consultant they hired was familiar with re-making communication at work. As she spoke with the three partners during the advance one-to-one discovery session interviews, she quickly decided to use that as the focus of her work. The two primary reasons she chose this set of tools over other organization development interventions were: (1) Jason, Michelle, and Gary were seasoned professionals and they were interested in more than superficial responses to challenges with communication; and (2) the habits they were forming created a few unwanted patterns of communication and interaction that could potentially be re-made quickly with concentrated effort. The fact that the company was new meant that the pattern echoes of these difficult situations were still relatively fresh. Patterns that have not had time to form deep, well-worn grooves are always easier to shift.

On the day of the session, the consultant wanted to keep things simple. It was an intentionally stripped-down design to get right to the point. This was a client that did not want to waste time on gimmicks. She had the M-A-I-D sequence on a poster and introduced the agenda like this:

> We are going to do these four things in our time together. My hope is that after our work is finished, yours has just begun. The three of you can use this flexible sequence to address a range of issues that may surface as your challenges shift. When you get past all of the acronyms and exercises we will complete, this is all about getting your business off the ground. It is about working in a way that enables your best contributions to have their full effect in the roles you play. And, it is about redefining the term *partnership* so that the three of you are aligned, gaining momentum toward the launch of the business, and sending a confident, focused message to your backers. So let's dive right into it!

Following the individual conversations she had with each person, the consultant had written a few pattern profiles that reflected common challenges the group faced. After her preamble, she presented these along with the question: "If these are clues about what may create the unwanted experiences and outcomes you get, which one are you most curious about?" She framed the question with the word "curious" in order to set a tone of open-mindedness, rather than judgment. To demonstrate this, here are three of the pattern profiles she presented and the dialogue among Jason, Michelle, and Gary that followed.

Patterns of Multitasking
Description: There seems to be a pattern of pervasive multitasking, which is a by-product of the busy schedules everyone keeps. Rather than successfully juggling diverse tasks in a way that allows people to accomplish more with less time, the quality and accuracy of work suffers.

Typical Episodes: Interactions are paused/concluded before there is closure, the quality and accuracy of work declines, and incomplete discussions and missing information prevent effective, on-going collaboration.

Potential Alternative Episodes: Focused conversations and work sessions that tackle one priority at a time, interactions are given sufficient time for closure, and realistic expectations about sharing workloads are established.

Patterns of Unfinished Business
Description: The interactions of the three partners are prone to quick check-ins and short meetings. People seem to want premature closure due to pressure from deadlines, fatigue, or avoidance of uncomfortable issues that end up leaving important business unfinished. The result of this is that staff meetings end without real resolution, discussions are started with no closure, and problems are partially resolved, but not fully addressed.

Typical Episodes: Meetings feel endless because things never sunset, frustration from lack of closure, and constant problem chasing decreases motivation.

Potential Alternative Episodes: Investments of time and energy in specific collaboration in order to match our priorities with the right cycles of interaction to address issues.

Patterns of Internal Competition

Description: Unhealthy internal competition can lead to a duplication of efforts. There seems to be a pattern of cutting corners on collaboration in order to personally accomplish individual tasks. This has led to a decrease in information sharing and joint problem-solving. (This appears to be the trigger that the business investors are concerned about most.)

Typical Episodes: Information sharing declines, a win/lose mentality pervades decision-making, and companywide goals are diminished in light of individual accomplishments.

Potential Alternative Episodes: Information sharing increases, a win/win mentality pervades decision-making, and innovation and great ideas come from anywhere because they advance the larger cause.

> *Gary*: "For me, I am curious about all of them. I have been wearing the title 'Expert Multitasker' like a badge of honor, but I think I have been too scattered to get things done at the standard I expect. There is definitely something here for me to think about."
>
> *Jason*: "I think the elephant in the room is the one about competition. I'll speak for myself: I've seen some things lately that I could assist with but I have just stayed in my lane and done my own thing. I hadn't really thought about it as internal competition so I'll sit with that label for a few minutes."
>
> *Michelle*: "Unfinished business is the one I care about. My role in this partnership has always been less as a technology-driven contributor and more of a business management role. I have been incredibly frustrated as our discussions have dwindled down to the bare minimum investment of time and attention. I know we are busy, but I'm really curious to know what we can do about this within the time constraints we have."
>
> *Consultant*: "Okay, these are all fantastic insights. These are your words, reflected back to you in a slightly different format. If you take notice of the word 'pattern,' it implies that there are everyday communication interactions that repeat and become part of your ongoing daily experience. Since each of you highlighted a different one, let me ask you: on a scale of #1–#10, how frequent does the pattern show up and how damaging is it to your productivity when it does (#10 is the most frequent and impactful)?"
>
> *Michelle*: "I would give the 'Unfinished Business' pattern an #8. To me it is nearly a daily occurrence and I think it is really driving down the quality of our work."
>
> *Jason*: "I'd give the 'Internal Competition' pattern a #5. It is fairly consistent for me, but I also think there are some good parts about pushing each other to raise the bar."

Gary: "The 'Multitasking' pattern gets a #9 from me. It is a near constant issue and there is no doubt that it is getting in the way of focusing and following through on the right priorities."

Consultant: "Great, these scales are nice because they give us a way to gauge the relative importance and urgency of the pattern. Judging by your responses, these are all hitting home in some way. Let's talk about the irony of this. You are all very bright people, and as you look at these patterns you can see they are producing some unwanted experiences and outcomes. Yet, they persist. There is often a kind of 'physics' to our patterns of communication and interaction and if we look closely at them, we may see what forces hold them in place."

Logical Force Radar

The consultant got their attention by creating a personally relevant connection to the team issues at hand, so she introduced the next exercise by saying:

> Logical force is an aspect of the "physics of communication" and the simple exercise of "logical force radar" is a way to give each person a sense of the subtle, often unseen reactions that play a role in keeping the unwanted patterns in place. The goal of the exercise is to reveal a clear picture of the specific "shoulds" and "oughts" that prompt us to act in ways that are inconsistent with our values and desires. Noticing these gives us the awareness to question them and introduce alternative choices that are more in line with our needs.

Each person completed a 'logical force radar' worksheet. At the end, they shared their results with each other. This discussion proved to be a very respectful exchange of some pretty sensitive disclosures. To illustrate the nature of what the exercise produced, table 14.8 shows Gary's finished product and the dialogue that ensued.

When Gary shared his perspective there was a moment where the other two partners sat up in their chairs. When he said—"I guess it is just easier to keep my head down and continue multitasking rather than slowing down to assess how we are really doing."—Michelle was the first to speak up:

Michelle: "Wow! That could not have been said any clearer. I will join Gary in saying that I am guilty of avoiding these kinds of honest assessments myself. The startup plan put us all in motion and we have just been following that trajectory ever since. Things have evolved, but our way of working together hasn't."

Jason: "Yeah, thank you Gary for being so frank. That hits home for me too. It is embarrassing that we needed a consultant to jolt us to this insight—no offense. We cannot just keep our heads down and hope that we're on course."

Consultant: "No offense taken. You all came up with these insights without much help from me. Since it does seem like you are ready to make something different with your pattern of communication and interaction, let me show you a way to start. We will do the first take right now, and then as you move forward in the coming days and weeks you can build on it. Because Gary's work revealed a lot of common ground with the pattern of multitasking, we will use that one as our example."

Constructing a Pattern of Communication and Interaction

The consultant introduced the pattern constructor worksheet as a tool to help the group create a plan to start making something better. Each individual created their own template and then the consultant led a process to consolidate them into one. This finished version in table 14.9 became the starting place for the three partners to get back on track.

Table 14.8   Gary's logical force radar

Logical force radar

Purpose: To identify the specific "shoulds" and "oughts" that prompt you to act in ways that are inconsistent with your values and desires.

In a few words, describe the pattern you want to explore:
Rather than successfully juggling diverse tasks in a way that allows me to accomplish more with less time, the quality and accuracy of my work is suffering...and the pressure keeps building.

What do you see, hear, think, and feel during a typically episode in this pattern:	*The logical forces or sense of "should" that compels me to respond in a certain way...*
• The loudest things I hear are "time is running out," "our investors expect results," and "our window to get to market is closing."	• I feel like I "should" be further along on the code than I am. I project this feeling of being behind the eight ball to my team and we end up working at a fever pitch.
• At our meetings, I see us sidetrack a lot. When a phone buzzes, we often end up leaving the meeting to go put out some fire. But we fail to see that we just potentially created a new one by failing to follow through on the task at hand.	• I see how ineffective we are, but I convince myself that this is "just how it has to be." I don't challenge our practice because nobody has time to sort things out.
• The left hand doesn't know what the right hand is doing. Where our roles overlap there is often incomplete information that prevents us from moving forward on things.	• I want the other partners to know that I trust them, so I have the sense that I "should not question them." With all of the time pressure, I guess it is just easier to keep my head down and continue multitasking rather than slowing down to assess how we are really doing.

Table 14.9 Constructing a new pattern

Constructing a pattern of communication and interaction

Purpose: To build a preferred pattern of communication in reverse by mapping the underlying building blocks that will make it, then planning for the presenting outcomes it will bring.

	What signature episode will capture the essence of this new pattern and what would you name it?	*In this episode, what are the critical turns, or moments of transition, where specific communication will be needed to sustain the pattern?*	*What types of values, attitudes, and behaviors will positively fuel these turns and hold the pattern together?*
Constructing level	"Meetings That Make a Difference" We don't necessarily need more time in meetings, we just need to be present, focused on priorities, and willing to hang in there long enough to get closure on critical issues.	When the phones buzz, we have to be okay with letting things wait. Everything can't be a crisis if we are going to build a company. Also, when things are really overwhelming we will need to remind each other that doing three things at one time is the equivalent of doing three things poorly!	• No more "keeping our heads down"—we need to speak honestly about what we see. • Our commitment to excellence has to be applied to the way we work, not just the product we are trying to produce. • If we don't lead differently, the culture we are creating here is going to burn people out.
	Who must be involved to make the pattern and when/where can it take maximum effect?	*What benefits and outcomes will it produce, and specifically, how will it improve the quality of your working lives?*	*How can additional priorities and commitments be aligned with this, so that it is not undermined?*
Presenting level	We are critical, and so is our board. If we change our approach to working together, that will surely translate to the tone we set in the board meetings.	We may still be just as busy, but we will not be frantic. The feeling that time and the quality of our work are slipping should be replaced with the feeling that we are building toward the successful launch.	Since the three of us are leading our own small teams, we need to practice the same approach with them. This will prevent us from getting fragmented. We do not need to make some big announcement, we'll just lead the next round of staff meetings differently.

What name(s) could you give to this experience that will remind us to work toward it?

"Doing the right things with the time and resources we have!"

As the meeting closed Michelle said something that got everybody laughing. It was a perfect way to transition from the facilitated session to their self-directed efforts to keep re-making communication at work:

> *Michelle*: "Okay, it looks like we are going to have this new goal and related pattern of communication to keep us on track. The only question I have is, 'what is the right thing when we run out of capital next month?'"
>
> *Jason*: "Hah, and that is exactly why we need to do the right things, right now—so that doesn't happen."

In these four case studies you were introduced to specific, real-world examples that put the concepts and tools of re-making communication at work into practice. The M-A-I-D sequence reminds you—whether you are working in a self-directed manner or with a coach or consultant—to hold loosely to the process, but tightly to the principles. The guided coaching activities in part IV also provide practice examples to further assist with the application of the book's key themes.

Conclusion

The M-A-I-D sequence is an array of signposts that will guide you in the implementation of the concepts and tools of re-making communication at work. The M-A-I-D sequence includes: *M*ap influential patterns of communication and interaction; *A*ssess the quality of the experience and outcomes produced by those patterns; *I*dentify candidate patterns to re-make; and *D*etermine the partners and sequence of action necessary to re-make the patterns. Case studies from the real world of work demonstrate the ways in which the sequence acts as a loose guide, rather than a strict set of process steps to follow.

The M-A-I-D sequence can be used in a variety of situations, including: Evaluating the general status of a working relationship, either with a coworker, subordinate, or supervisor; reviewing a specific episode of communication with a colleague that produced an unwanted outcome or experience; identifying patterns that may need to be altered in order to successfully implement a specific change in the team or organization; and exploring potential causes of unexpected changes (e.g., decreased engagement among employees, silence where there was active communication, etc.), among others.

15

Applying Part III to the Real World of Work

Re-making communication at work is open-ended. No strict process is required and there are no right ways to do it. This inherent flexibility is intentional as it matches the need to customize your response to each unique communication interaction. There are Single-Step Processes that can be used alone or in combination within the M-A-I-D sequence for a more comprehensive approach.

Regardless of where you begin and how you start, change is always hard. This can be especially true when the change you want to make is wound tightly around habits of interaction you engage in regularly. To successfully implement these concepts and tools in the pursuit of the changes you seek, remember what you have at your disposal to respond to your everyday communication challenges. Table 15.1 provides a summary of the tools and what they will make when you apply them in the real world of work:

Table 15.1 Summary of the tools for re-making communication at work

	Tool	What it makes
1. Start here to see what your communication makes	Pattern finder	Scan your world of work in six questions to develop a clear picture of the unwanted and preferred patterns in your experience that matter most
	Episode mapper	Follow another six-question sequence to see the specific episodes that shape the influential patterns you engage in
	Turn selector •	Take notice of the specific turns that can shift the quality of the episode in a way that will potentially re-make the overall pattern
2. Use these to look more deeply at what you are making and how it is made	Logical force radar	Expose a clear picture of the specific "shoulds" and "oughts" that prompt you to act in ways that may be inconsistent with your values and desires
	Visualizing the system	Diagram the people, events, stories, and other important features in a pattern of communication that shed light on the way it is made and sustained
	Listening for stories	Reveal the tension between the unknown, unheard, and untellable stories (including the gap between what is said and what is actually experienced) to spot the causes of communication breakdowns
	Hierarchy of influence	Map the values, stories, and influential contexts in order of significance to examine the often silent, but powerful forces that shape patterns of communication

Seeing past speech acts	Identify recurring speech acts used in the world of work that trigger assumptions and sustain fragmented turns, closed episodes, and unwanted patterns of communication
Looking at the chemistry of communication: checking for contextual elements	Discover the contextual drivers that influence patterns of communication, including the powerful stories found in master contracts, working life scripts, and preexisting patterns
Setting the pattern, episode, and turn continuum	Identify the quality and character of patterns of communication and contrast their impact along a visual continuum of effect
Looking at the physics of communication: checking for invisible rules	Explore the often invisible rules that are used to interpret communication events and determine how to respond based on that interpretation
3. Use these to re-make new patterns	
Deconstructing patterns	Dissect the anatomy of an unwanted pattern of communication by mapping the presenting outcomes it brings, as well as the underlying building blocks (i.e., attitudes, beliefs, and behaviors) that influence the episodes that shape it
Constructing patterns	Build a preferred pattern of communication in reverse by mapping the underlying building blocks that will make it, then planning for the presenting outcomes it will bring

Part IV

Creating Big Change by Starting Small

16

Where to Begin: Individual, Team, and Organizational Starting Lines

One of the ironies exposed by this book is that the thing we do most in everyday organizational life—communicate and interact with other people—is the thing we spend the least amount of time considering. My hope is that the concepts and tools I have introduced, including the urgent reasons for making use of them in your own working life, will change that paradox.

Rather than waiting for communication and performance breakdowns to reach a fever pitch before you give them reasonable time and attention, you can invest early and often in ways to make patterns where the next crisis cannot emerge. And, rather than the all-too-often reactive and crisis-driven response to communication emergencies that involve "putting out the fire" and trying to get back to "business as usual" as soon as possible, you can commit to re-making communication at work as the new "business as usual." The focus of this chapter is to provide a few final insights to help you make these transitions and find your individual, team, and organizational starting lines.

Start a Fire

Can't start a fire worrying about your little world falling apart.

—*Bruce Springsteen*

Describing the starting line for change makes it hard to avoid the metaphor of "catching fire." A blazing fire evokes light, swift movement, and intensity. But, it can also invoke fear, loss of control, and hesitation, which are necessary obstacles to overcome with any desired change. What I appreciate about the Springsteen quote is that it simply states the tension we often feel between the desired change and the familiarity trap we get stuck in with our known, comfortable surroundings (even if they are unwanted).

In this instance "little world" is not meant as a pejorative reference; we all have our own little worlds where our tightly packed systems of belief and expectation provide us with a modicum of security in their predictability. The starting line for re-making communication at work marks a transition toward unknown elements and away from the well-worn, familiar expectations about what effective communication at work is. If we let our little worlds collapse, they can be re-made into something more expansive.

Opportunity Is Everywhere, Just Start Somewhere

When you wade into the stuff of everyday working life you quickly see many performance improvement opportunities. Whether they are individual goals and hopes for the quality of your working life, or whether they are broader team and organizational performance ambitions, these opportunities are everywhere. The first starting line is to just start somewhere.

Start with Stories

We make sense of our world by translating our lived experience into the stories we tell. In the workplace, stories are the way people make sense of their working lives and share their experience with others. Within organizational life, stories are viewed as the justification for the decisions and actions people take and they are a source for clues about the individuals' underlying values and beliefs.[1] In this regard, we are the stories we tell about ourselves. Organizational culture is just a reflection of these stories about our experiences and the beliefs we draw from them and the actions we take as a result. Re-making communication at work, like other forms of narrative analysis, can reveal the stories lived and told by members of an organization, which become the path toward seeing the hidden side of communication at work. To begin to re-make anything, start with stories.

Start with Your Working Life

One of the best places to begin re-making communication at work is with your specific aspirations for your working life. If maintaining a healthy, high-quality working life is important to you, remember that any of the indictors you use to judge what you have (i.e., great job title, competitive pay, strong supervisor-employee relationship, work/life balance, reasonable challenges in your role, opportunities to grow, etc.) are only a reflection of the underlying patterns of communication and interaction that are required to make them.

To create the conditions for these preferred patterns, which in turn can shape the experiences you want in your working life, you do not need to look further than the strong, recurring patterns you engage in. These patterns hold predictions of their own consequences and that is why naming a pattern precisely and following the trajectory of its impact out into your everyday experience provides so much leverage to understand the outcomes it will create.

Changing in the Changes

The author Jules Verne planted a profound message through his lead character's (Captain Nemo) crest. The mysterious symbol included the phrase "mobilis in mobili," which translated from the Latin means "changing in the changes." To change the culture of your team and organization, you must first change yourself. Team and organizational change always begins with the individual. You have to care about the experience and outcomes you make and recognize them as forces that impact the rest of your team and the larger organizations. If you have this intrinsic motivation, then you can actually direct change. While you cannot control it, you can influence the flow.

Not All Blocks Are Equal

The differences between a "block" and a "building block" could not be more divergent. That one word—building—is the scaffolding for transformation. What is required to go from a block, which is a solid mass that obstructs someone or something by placing obstacles in the way, to a building block is the commitment to make something different. The first time you hit a block in your efforts to re-make communication at work, and you surely will, do not focus on the obstacle right in front of you. Instead, focus on the word "building" and that will lead you back to the reasons you want to make something better, as well as the motivation, resources, and perseverance to keep going.

Long-Term versus Short-Term Accomplishments

My career is dedicated to helping people succeed at work. I don't consider many of the conventional definitions of success at work—a great title, high-value compensation, formal power in the organization, and so on—to be the most helpful measures of success. I define success at work as the "long-term achievement of your best possible working life." While landing a great job and achieving excellent performance and rewards in the short term can be examples of valuable success factors, I think that the ultimate measure of success is the ability to learn how to work well through the course of a long, winding career. When you think about a successful working life in this way, you understand that the horizon you keep in focus requires persistence, patience, and the careful selection of priorities that relate more to how you work, than what you achieve at work.

At the time this book goes to print, the *Harvard Business Review* just announced Jeff Bezos, from the online retailer Amazon.com, as the world's number one living CEO.[2] His leadership philosophy, which dictates that the "customers' experience comes first" above all short-term profit gains, provides an interesting parallel to striking this balance between learning to work well in the long term and pursuing short-term accomplishments in our own working lives. According to Bezos, many of the successes that have helped make that company great are a direct or indirect result of putting the customer first. For example, products like the Kindle e-reader and other related technological advances within their web platform would never have happened if short-term gains were placed above a long-term investment in the customer experience.

In a similar way, if you define the quality of your working life by a great title, high-value compensation, formal power in the organization, or some other combination of short-term benchmarks, this will affect the way you choose to invest in making patterns (i.e., you likely will not consider the most challenging ones important enough to stick with). If, on the other hand, you define the quality of your working life by the quality of the experiences you make, then the investment cycles you tolerate will grow longer, but so will the potential for long-term, positive, residual effects that go well past the short-term gains of superficial achievements.

Bezos says that when things get complicated for his leadership team, their path toward simplifying business dilemmas always returns to the question: "What is best for the customer?" They trust that if they pursue that question and follow it wherever it leads, things will work out in the long term. When faced with your own challenging situation at work that requires you to slow down, dig in, and invest in making something better, try leading with this question: "What is best for my working life?"

Build on What You Know Works

Re-making communication at work builds on many existing organizational improvement practices, it just adds a missing step. Here is one of many possible examples. It is common for teams to work together to increase their working knowledge of shared values and related expectations for communication. While the processes may vary, the typical steps include values clarification exercises for individuals, consolidating those values for a list of "team commitments," and then outlining a set of shared expectations for professional communication and interaction that are consistent with those values. This can be quite useful, however something significant is missing.

The missing piece here is the entire set of rules that influence how we make meaning and take action, which can be examined to identify the gaps between what we say we value and how we actually behave. The integrity gaps that exist between our espoused values and lived experience either erode our performance and credibility with others, or show us the way toward "one more damn growth opportunity" as the old bumper sticker says. All of this goes right back to the chemistry, physics, and design of communication you learned about in part II. If you were already going to look at your team's values and expectations for communication—no matter how traditional the intended approach would be—this is a chance to start. Re-making communication at work does not require a mandate from the CEO or a formal announcement. The best starting line is often the one you are already.

Leave People Whole

Exploring patterns of communication can be challenging when they lead into sensitive areas. It can often be hard to separate the people from the issues, but it is important to leave people feeling whole. Interrogating a pattern too aggressively can hurt feelings and break people down. This is why re-making communication at work places so much emphasis on making communication something to look at, which is apart from the people viewing it. The objective distance can help to avoid unintended consequences of bruised feelings and egos when patterns are deconstructed and re-made.

Good Results Come from Small Irritations

Pearls are formed inside oysters when a small grain of sand or rock gets inside the shell and lodges against the mantle, the oyster's soft inner fleshy body. The animal has a biological defense mechanism against this foreign particle and it secretes a protective substance called nacre that covers the irritant layer by layer. Remembering how pearls are formed is a useful lesson with re-making communication at work. Good results can come from small irritations. In this case, rather than covering it up, we can use small irritations to notice troublesome turns within difficult episodes that can be explored and potentially shifted. A curious mind and an orientation to questions (as opposed to quick judgments and rash solutions) can help this pursuit of "communication pearls."

Some Melt Downs Are Good

In the popular vernacular, a meltdown is something to be avoided. It usually means that a person's capacity to handle a stressful situation or time of change has reached its peak and the reactionary cycle of "survival mode" kicks in. There are, however, good meltdowns. Kurt Lewin, considered the father of organization development, described his straightforward model of change in three phases: unfreeze, change, refreeze.[3]

Unfreezing is when you get ready for change by acknowledging that it is needed, testing the pros and cons of change, and loosening your hold on the status quo so that something different can emerge. Change is the transition that takes place, not necessarily the events, but the process of making the actual changes. Finally, freezing (or refreezing) involves the habits that form once the accepted change becomes the new norm. I often refer to Lewin's model of change when there is a pitch of stress in the room and a solid joke about "good meltdowns" can break the ice.

Make the First Move

I recall coaching a rising star in an organization. He was working on a leadership philosophy for himself and our process included a few exercises to identify his core values and to determine how consistently he experienced those values in the workplace. By the end of the exercise the value of trustworthy relationships was near the top of his list; however, he indicated that although it was an important value he seldom, if ever, experienced it. I asked him how frequently trust "showed up" in his everyday interactions and he said "not at all." When I asked how consistently he enacted trustworthy gestures toward people, he said, "Well, not at all because I can't trust them." This is the problem of first moves.

Similar to trust dynamics where only trustworthy behaviors can actually build trust, first moves and new turns in old patterns are what ultimately re-make them. Making the first move is hard at times. In the case of a breach of trust where some hurt was caused, there are often multiple reasons to avoid trusting back. This dynamic is indicative of re-making communication at work. The reflexive pattern between people means that for every action there will be a related reaction. So if you want that second move (i.e., somebody acting trustworthy toward you), you may need to move first. And, if you won't take the first turn, who will?

Let Go of Bad Habits

There are often a few faulty assessments and bad habits that keep us stuck at the starting line and unable to start re-making communication at work. Here are a few of the most typical attitudes and behaviors that—if recognized and released—can set you free. These are five things not to do:

- *Believe that certain people should be avoided at all costs, and certain topics are just off limits for discussion.* When this belief is held, some of the most important patterns are taken off the table. The precise elements of organizational life that could be re-made into something better are treated like they do not even exist.

- *Expect that people do not have your best interests in mind, but try not to show it.* When people begin with the mindset that trust must be earned they often will not make the first move. If you expect the worst in people you often get it, which further prevents people from finding the starting line and jumping out of the gate.

- *Talk about your frustrations with people who are the least involved in the situation.* Excluding the people who matter prevents the pattern from being looked at or re-made. While it may feel "safer" to tell others rather than confronting the people involved in the matter, nothing gets re-made until the right people are talking about what matters most to them.

- *Take a default contrarian stance.* Believing that it is helpful to challenge "for the sake of challenging" is a pattern of interaction itself, and when it persists, it can be a roadblock for re-making unwanted episodes because it serves as a constant distraction to the primary pattern in play.

- *Ease your way out of uncomfortable and difficult situations when they surface.* The discomfort that occurs when something real is happening is the precise moment we need to stick with it. These are the moments of creation, where the turns and episodes shift and something different can show up in the patterns of our communication and interaction.

Some Moments Cannot Wait

It has always confounded me that in our organizational lives we often wait to say the things that really matter until it is too late to do something about it. I heard about a send-off party that was held for a team member who was leaving her organization after 16 great years of service. The full story was unknown, but it was believed that the person would rather stay and felt as though recent changes left her with no choice but to leave. One of the changes she felt most acutely was the lack of appreciation for the distinct contributions from herself and others. Ironically, at her going away party there was a tremendous outpouring of appreciation, thanks, and sincere moments of gratitude for everything she had contributed.

Why couldn't those same people live the other days like it was that last day? Would that person have felt more acknowledged for the value-added contributions she had made and would the stress of compounding changes have been alleviated a bit by the slow and steady moments of thanks, appreciation, and recognition? It is important to learn how to precipitate these moments of honest expression, without waiting until the inertia of "deciding" has already set undesired change in motion.

Find Allies

Developing communication mentors is an effective way to extend the concept and capabilities of re-making communication at work. In a typical mentoring relationship, the mentor helps to enhance our network of contacts, spends time meeting with us to talk about issues of the day, helps us to pinpoint our strengths/opportunities and our weaknesses/challenges, uses their influence to help create connections for us, and most importantly, provides us with timely advice and feedback. Imagine if these supportive relationships were intentionally established with a focus on helping you learn how to re-make unwanted patterns into experiences and outcomes that drive individual, team, and organizational success? For these reasons, finding "communication allies" and developing supportive relationships is an important priority to pursue.

Separate Confidence from Competence

The American writer, Glenn O'Brien, famously said, "You start out as a phony and become real." This may sound like a foreign concept, but it is important to conjure a level of confidence to experiment and try things even at a time when your level of skill and competence is still rising. I have actually found that the small mistakes are the greatest teachers, and the confidence to act differently "the next time around" is as valuable as the confidence I have gained from doing something well. If you can distinguish confidence from accomplishment and pure competence, you give yourself enough of a running start to actually attain those things in time. Failing to muster sufficient confidence to start, and waiting (a long time) for the competence to develop within you, is a recipe for stalling.

Things Are Never Finished

We continuously make our patterns of communication and interaction. Things are never completely made. This can be an exhausting realization, or inspiration if you see the possibilities.

Re-Make Patterns, Not People

This book can be distilled into these four words—re-make patterns, not people. The minute you begin to look away from the tangible patterns of communication to personalities, you edge toward the subject (away from the object) and lose the objective curiosity that allows you to say the malleable—"Isn't that interesting?"—rather than the immovable—"I wish you were different." Trying to change other people is an endless pursuit of the unattainable.

Builders, Watchers, and Breakers

There is an evaluation tool used in marketing called the Net Promoter Score. Created by Fred Reichheld, the Net Promoter Score is based on the idea that a company's customers can be categorized into three groups: promoters, passives, and detractors. By asking a fundamental question—How likely is it that you would recommend your company to a friend or colleague?—you can establish a clear measure of company performance and brand value through the customers' perspective. Using the assessment, customers respond on a 0–10 point rating scale, which is categorized in the three groups:

- Promoters (score 9–10) are loyal enthusiasts who will keep buying and refer others, fueling growth.
- Passives (score 7–8) are satisfied but unenthusiastic customers who are vulnerable to competitive offerings.
- Detractors (score 0–6) are unhappy customers who can damage your brand and impede growth through negative word-of-mouth.

What I like about this simple, but powerful process is that it allows you to see the relative distinction between segments, it demonstrates how conceivable it is for people to slide up or down along the scale based upon changes in their experience, and it shows how focused the niche of the promoter category really is.

Using this concept as a starting place, I use a different version of this during communication audits intended to identify the active builders in a given organization. There are three levels in this revised model:

- Builders (score 9–10) understand their role in making the patterns of communication and interaction that shape their experience at work and are active and empowered to make them.
- Watchers (score 6–8) are not convinced that they have a role to play, but could be swayed to constructively participate by builders.
- Breakers (score 0–5) knowingly or unknowingly build or sustain unwanted patterns through their combined action and inaction.

The Final Word: Empathy

In a way, the final word is the most important. With the sweeping premise of this book—we get what we make and we make it in our communication and interaction with others—there is a fundamental truth: we are all builders. The starting line for great design and the capacity to build to the reflection of what we desire is *empathy*. The ability to be patient, approachable, generous, well-meaning, and concerned for the process and result of our effort to make something gives us room to fail and also to continue on until we succeed. Our empathy toward others' efforts, however imperfect they may be, is what gives them both the space and incentive to try again in order to make something better. Without empathy there is judgment and this can lead to fragmented turns, closed episodes, and unwanted patterns much more quickly than an empathetic mindset that, by its very nature, is a blueprint for aligned, open, and preferred ways of interacting.

Conclusion

There are clear and accessible starting lines to begin the practice of re-making communication at work. The range of suggestions includes: starting with stories, drawing on aspirations for your working life, using change as a catalyst, and finding allies, among others. One of the reasons it is vital to identify specific starting places for change is because of the strong hold that the old myths of effective communication maintain. Learning to bring others along in the process is a critical step and it can be accomplished simply by engaging "builders" and "watchers" who are willing to participate in the effort to make something better with communication at work. Chapter 17 extends these starting lines and introduces a range of guided coaching activities to accelerate your progress.

17

How to Accelerate Your Progress: Guided Coaching for the Essentials

The goal of this chapter is to provide you with a variety of easy-to-use tools and thought exercises to help you apply the concepts and practices of re-making communication at work. Each guided coaching exercise has been designed to be self-administered, however, discussing your ideas and responses in an interactive way with someone else can also be quite beneficial. As you read, I encourage you to select the activities that seem most useful to you and then return later to others as you run into related and relevant challenges with implementation.

White Boards

Throughout the chapter there are white boards that you can use to take notes and respond to various questions and prompts that are designed to facilitate the application of concepts. Feel free to use them as a sounding board for your own ideas and responses to the challenge of re-making communication at work.

—————————————————————————————————

White Board—Example

(Jot notes, answer prompts, or doodle right here!)

—————————————————————————————————

Quick Pattern Scan

Sometimes you just need to take stock of where things are right now, in this moment. An effective way to do that is to conduct a quick pattern scan of your current work flow and the predominant interactions you are involved in on an ongoing basis. Seeing your challenges and concerns and establishing a sense of personal relevance to them can help you decide which ones to pay attention to. For a short and simple way to check for interesting patterns, complete the following white board:

———————————————————————————————————

White Board—Quick Pattern Scan

Of all the recurring conversations and interactions I engage in at work, which ones bother, frustrate, hurt, or inconvenience me the most?

What names would I give to the two most challenging patterns?

Why should I consider re-making one or both of them?

Who else is involved with me in making these patterns?

How much do these patterns block the experiences and outcomes I value?

———————————————————————————————————

When the Thing We Don't Like About a Pattern Is...Ourselves

Our own individual attitudes and behaviors create performance patterns for us. These undoubtedly influence those we work with directly, but their primary effect is on the quality of our own working lives. When our individual patterns reflect our values and priorities they can set a positive tone and lead us toward the outcomes we desire. However, when our experienced patterns are not in sync with our aspirations, values, and priorities they can lead to chronic integrity gaps, performance anxiety, stress, and severe impacts on the quality of our working lives.

Seeing these networks of conflicting intrapersonal attitudes and behaviors is tough because we are closest to our own patterns; therefore gaining objectivity is difficult. This requires separation to examine them in the light of day and challenge the beliefs that keep them in place. This white board offers prompts to help you create enough separation between you and the pattern you make:

———————————————————————————————————

White Board—Seeing Ourselves within Our Patterns

Even if it is unwanted in some way, is there anything you like about this pattern of communication and interaction? (Come on, there must be something!)

What don't you like about this pattern of communication and interaction?

What are you contributing that keeps it going? (Be honest!)

If you could replace the unwanted parts of this pattern with something better, what would it be?

Considering where things are at right now, when is the next possible turn you can take to alter the next likely episode in the pattern?

Take an Inventory of Your Favorite Speech Acts

In previous chapters I talked about the basic chemistry of our patterns of communication and interaction, including the building blocks that shape them. "Speech acts" were identified as one of the fundamental elements we need to understand in order to grasp the way we make (and potentially re-make) our patterns. Speech acts are the actions you perform while speaking. They are what you do to someone by what you say to them.[1]

If you just pull out a speech act from everyday life, it would be informative but incomplete by itself. What gives greater coherence to a speech act is its relationship to other turns and speech acts within an episode of communication. For example, one type of speech act is a "threat" and, among many possible examples, one common expression of that speech act in the world of work is the statement "If we don't meet our numbers, there will be hell to pay!"

Speech acts are all around, and despite their powerful impact on patterns of communication and interaction, they go unnoticed because of their complexity and ubiquity. One coaching exercise I use to help people accelerate their progress with re-making communication at work is to take an inventory of their favorite speech acts. "Favorite" is meant here as the ones that are most challenging, problematic, interesting, liberating, confusing, and frustrating.

White Board—Your Favorite Speech Acts

1. What common speech acts do *others* express?

Select one favorite from your list and consider the following:

- When you hear this speech act, what "next turn" are you most likely to take?

- How do both the speech act and likely next turn influence the episode and greater pattern of communication and interaction?

2. What common speech acts do *you* communicate?

Select one favorite from the list and consider the following:

- When another person hears this speech act, what "next turn" are they most likely to take?

- How do the speech act and likely next turn influence the episode and greater pattern of communication and interaction?

3. What common speech act(s) do you hear the *leaders* in the organization express?

- In what ways do these speech acts potentially enhance or detract from the quality of your work and overall performance outcomes?

- How do these speech acts reflect or contradict the values of the team/organization?

- What new speech acts, if expressed in genuine patterns of interaction, could create opportunities for something better?

Increase Your Visual Capacity

If you can see communication, you can remake it. Creating an elaborate "storyboard" that captures the moving parts and subtle detail of a complex pattern of communication and interaction is not always necessary to see communication and subsequently re-make it. However, drawing your communication with a few lines and circles does help. With practice you will learn to rely on images and pictures to sort through your trickiest episodes. To start, you are just going to draw a few productive doodles that accomplish the same positive change. As Sonni Brown and others have confirmed, there is a Doodle Revolution afoot.[2]

Now that left-handed and right-brained people, with their soft skills, introvertedness, and other previously scorned traits, are seen in their full glory, we have permission to embrace new ways of thinking about being productive. The premise is that anyone can put pen to paper and draw ideas. The visual literacy of seeing ideas and concepts in visual form, in addition to what we can communicate with language, creates a more dynamic way of understanding our experiences with complexity and change, as well as everyday life. If you need a quick refresher, you can refer to chapter 13 in this volume. It has lots of details about how to visualize the system, hierarchy of contexts, and more.

————————————————————————————————————

White Board—Increase Your Visual Capacity

In the space below, draw a picture of your working life, including the most important, ongoing pattern of communication and interaction you engage in. Use words, phrases, symbols, images, pictures, or anything else you can think of to make a picture of it:

————————————————————————————————————

Look Inside Your Stories

Our ability to observe our own process of interpreting and making meaning from experience is an important element of re-making communication at work. The way that we tell our stories reflects the specific filtering that shapes our perceptions and sustains our belief systems. The stories we tell are the very stuff from which we take action. Stories themselves then become a critical tool for noticing and then challenging our assumptions about how we perform in our patterns of communication and interaction.

Some of the power for re-making communication at work emerges from particular ways in which we talk about what matters to us, which makes our stories critical for opening up new opportunities, or constraining the way we interpret and make meaning from our experiences. One way to dig deeper and tell better stories is to ask "why."[3]

————————————————————————————————————

White Board—Look Inside Your Stories

Briefly summarize the "story" about a current pattern of communication you are engaged in.

For example, "A frustrating pattern that I'm experiencing at work could be called 'everything is wrong, but nobody is to blame.' The story of this pattern is that everyone says they want stability and a break from change, but nobody is willing to follow through and be accountable to things. They quickly point to everything that is wrong, but nobody takes responsibility for changing it."

Using you own short story as an example, dig deeper by simply asking the question "Why?" five successive times. This will reveal layers of the story that should help you understand it better.

For example, select a specific element of the story and ask the five whys to see what layers of insight can be revealed: "People say they want stability need a break from change," why...and so on?

Learn to Watch Your Tricky Episodes

In part II I introduced the basic chemistry of our patterns of communication and interaction, including the elements that shape them. Episodes were identified as important building blocks that combine to form our larger patterns of communication and interaction. One simple way of thinking about episodes is to imagine two or more people interacting in conversation, each taking one or more turns in the process of making meaning and coordinating action. If these turns can be held together by a noticeable beginning and end, then you may have an episode. Episodes are transitional in nature, meaning how one specific episode goes likely reflects how the previous one ended, and often dictates how the next might begin.

Similar to speech acts that go by common names, there are frequent episodes that we could name and recognize across the everyday experience of our organizational lives. Some of them are fleeting, like "the unexpected chat with a colleague in the hallway" and some of them are more structured, like "a weekly one-on-one check-in with the boss" or "the quarterly conference call to review financial performance." In each of these episodes speech acts are coordinated and people often interact in predictable ways. Announcing to your overly chatty colleague that you "have to get back to work" is a speech act that signals the end of that episode, and the start of the next one. Congratulating people on a good annual report with the speech act "if we keep this up, we are going to weather the storm of the economic downturn" is a powerful signal that the meeting is over, and that everyone can rest easier in their job security for the rest of the quarter.

For most of us, the majority of our day-to-day episodes likely unfold with little controversy. However, some specific episodes can be quite tricky, and those warrant greater attention. Learning to watch your tricky episodes is an important practice in learning to re-make communication at work. I am deliberately using the phrase "watch your episodes" to draw a parallel between everyday communication at work and channel surfing on the couch. When you sit down to watch television you may come across a 30-minute or 60-minute show (i.e., sitcom, drama, etc.) that features a single episode that is in the context of a larger pattern (in this case the series). The question is, "Are you making some good reality television in your world of work?" If so, use the following white board to map your tricky episode(s):

White Board—Watch Your Tricky Episodes, Part 1

What are some of recurring episodes that you participate in?

Which of these are "tricky" and worth watching?

How do these tricky episodes related to the larger patterns they belong to?

What makes the episode special and in potential need of attention?

Learning to watch an episode requires a bit of objective distance from ourselves and the other people involved. To get this perspective, try shaking yourself from the assumptions you hold about the people and their intentions.

White Board—Watch Your Tricky Episodes, Part 2

For Other People:
Right now, what do you assume the other people in the episode care about?

What do you believe they want to experience or see as a result of the action they take?

Does the episode contribute to a pattern of communication and interaction that makes that experience for them?

For Yourself:
Right now, what do you care about while you are engaged in the episode?

What do you want to experience or see as a result of your contributions?

Does the episode contribute to a pattern of communication and interaction that makes this experience for you?

Polish Your Turn-Taking

You know you have an episode when a combination of conversational turns, held together by a noticeable beginning and end, occurs. Turn-by-turn, we make meaning and coordinate our actions within these episodes that ultimately clump together to form our patterns of communication and interaction. If we want to re-make communication at work, then we have to learn to get down to the level of turn.

If episodes are the building blocks that combine to form our larger patterns of communication and interaction, then turns are the choices we make about where to place each block. Speaking of stone blocks and the art of laying them in just the right place, the deeply thinking environmental artist, Dan Snow, said, "The skill one wishes to have is the ability to cast a gaze across a stockpile and immediately reduce the number of possible picks to one. Knowing why one stone and not another is needed is the result of understanding principles."[4]

If we could develop the capacity to see a range of turns like a stockpile of stones, each an option at our disposal to create something slightly different from the next, then perhaps we could use that knowledge to make intentional choices in the turns we take to shape the episodes and patterns of communication we want.

One coaching essential for re-making communication at work is to polish your turn-taking, specifically within your tricky episodes. In the last coaching exercise you identified a few examples of tricky episodes to watch. Here you will focus in on the specific turns that you contribute to those episodes. Maybe it is a particular speech act that prompts a reaction from the other person/people and shapes the whole episode. Or, perhaps the typical turn you take has little to do with words and more to do with silence and nonverbal cues that clearly say, "I do not approve of this." Using one of your tricky episodes as a guide, consider a critical moment where one of the turns you take seems pivotal and then chart it in this white board:

———————————————————————————————————

White Board—Polish Your Turn-Taking

As you think about the words, nonverbal cues, or speech acts that are part of your turn, what are you really saying?

What is the logical force behind this statement (i.e., what is the sense of "should" that compels you to take that specific turn)?

Is the assumption within this "should" helpful to you?

If you kept making a similar turn, how will the pattern likely continue?

If you want to change the specific episode in hopes of re-making the overall pattern, what other options do you have for a new turn to take?

———————————————————————————————————

Envisioning Your Working Life

In the modern world, our lives are working lives that span many decades, industries, organizations, and roles. One of the keys to staying relevant at work and remaining competitive in the job market is to consistently increase our learning and performance while dealing with the challenges of change. The ability to do this will help you add increasing value to your organization while going beyond your regular job description. Re-making communication at work is part of this essential tool set because it allows you to identify patterns of communication and interaction that reduce learning and performance and produce unwanted outcomes that potentially diminish your success. More importantly, the concepts and tools can be used to intentionally craft the quality and day-to-day experience of your working life.

So, if your work life does not currently match your aspirations, and if you want a different experience for your career, then you will have to make it. Before you can make those experiences you need a vision for your working life.

———————————————————————————————

White Board—Envisioning Your Working Life, Part 1

Think about your working life of the future...

What kinds of experiences do you hope to have on a daily basis?

What kinds of relationships do you want?

What kinds of opportunities do you wish to encounter?

How do you envision yourself tackling new challenges that come your way?

What specific milestones do you want to reach throughout your career?

What names would you give to the most common, recurring episodes of your desired working life?

If your ideal working life was a story, what title would you give it and how would you describe the plot in just a few words?

———————————————————————————————

Now that you have a basic picture of what your ideal working life is, you can go to the next level of "making" it through the patterns of communication and interaction you engage in.

White Board—Envisioning Your Working Life, Part 2

What specific patterns of communication and interaction could create the conditions for your future working life to emerge?

In order to transition from what you have now, to what you would like to experience in the future, what critical moments are needed to get things on a different trajectory?

How can you precipitate these critical moments?

Specifically, what kinds of episodes do you need to engineer in order to generate momentum toward the patterns you want to experience?

Who do you need to involve in these episodes and what turn will you take to invite them into the process?

Reading the Rules of the Game

In organizational life there are rules that influence: (1) how we make meaning of our experience; and (2) take action based on our interpretation of what we see, hear, feel, and think. These rules are powerful and they often go unnoticed. Any unexamined rule controls us at some level. To gain greater leverage over our decision-making in the present moment, we must understand the rules that influence us and selectively limit which ones guide our choices.

Constitutive rules guide the way we make meaning of situations. For example, because we believe that our company is the best, our competitor's recent surge must be explained by luck. Regulative rules guide the way we take action on them. For example, because our competitor got lucky, we don't really need to change our approach to innovation.

If we do not bring attention and focus to our constitutive and regulative rules, we simply carry the existing mix of rules with us for better or worse. Carrying old rules in new communication settings just reproduces the same patterns with different names. If you want something different, you have to understand how the context of the situation you are in triggers the constitutive and regulative rules that impact you. Here is an exercise that can help you expose your "rules of the game" by borrowing from the sports metaphor. Organizational cultures sustain these written and unwritten rules and you likely know what they are, whether or not you have ever discussed them. Use this white board, take inventory of the following:

———————————————————————————————————

White Board—The Rules of the Game

What are some of the "rules" that influence how people interpret the messages from our leaders?

What are some of the "rules" that influence how people act in response to their messages?

What are some of the "rules" that influence how people interpret messages from me?

What are some of the "rules" that influence how people act in response to my messages?

What are some of the "rules" that influence how I interpret messages from my boss?

What are some of the "rules" that influence how I act in response to my boss' messages?

———————————————————————————————————

Making Moments Critical

I have discussed the importance of critical moments, or bifurcation points, that mark a distinctive turn where something different becomes more inevitable or less unlikely all depending upon the nature of the interaction in that specific moment. "Moment" does not necessarily refer to clock time, although in many cases they happen quickly. This makes them all the more important to notice in the emergent space after they are possible and just before they pass.

In a manner of speaking, any turn within an episode fits the definition of a critical moment because of its pivotal nature. However, if you recall a relationship that crashed, a decision that backfired, or a plan that failed due to a single event, then you know that not all moments are created equally.

Imagine you are at an exit interview, which is the last formal conversation that takes place concerning an employee's work experience in the organization. Across from you sits a 22-year veteran of the company who proceeds to do some serious truth-telling about the state of things, including a series of important issues that would be critical for leaders in the organization to know about. She explains that these issues have been going on for months and years in some cases. For a variety of reasons, however, they were never shared. It wasn't until that precipitous moment of the exit interview that the employee felt ready to share. Why did it take that long? What might have happened if the moment of honest exchange occurred sooner? Examples like this remind us about how important it is to learn how to precipitate these moments of honest expression, without waiting.

The way to identify critical moments of choice within episodes begins with surfacing the powerful stories, messages, and underlying values that shape our attitudes and beliefs and push us toward action. These are what guide our decision-making and influence our relationships and if we develop active attention toward them we can use them to overpower the logical forces and constitutive and regulative rules that might cause us to leap when we should hold still, or stay put when we should boldly step toward something different. The practice of precipitating critical moments can intentionally cultivate a critical moment early, before it is too late.

Get Back to Basics

If the prospect of forgetting everything you learned about effective communication at work and learning to see complex patterns of communication and interaction seems like too much, start by selecting an area of your working life that is not going exactly how you want it to go at the moment. The first question is simply: What is happening? Now, follow that path where it leads using some of the building blocks of patterns.

- Punctuation—Where would you say this situation started? Is it still ongoing or is there an end point that paused it or brought it to closure (for now)?
- Turns—Okay, now that we have a sense of where it starts and stops, let's look at what happened inside of those boundaries. What kinds of things did they say and how would you guess they were feeling when they said them? When it was your turn, how were you feeling? What did you say next? What were you trying to get them to think/do based on that?
- Critical moments—Was there a particular turn that either you or the other person took that you think was more important than the others because of what happened next? Sometimes there is a particular thing someone says and it shifts the next response, escalates the emotion, or raises the stakes because of what it communicated—did you notice any critical moments?

If you are addressing individual patterns, here are some helpful reminders that can make things easier along the way:

1. The present moment counts double. If you stay present in the here and now you gain powerful leverage at the point of pattern creation. Whether you are lagging just behind the present moment by being influenced by the past, or whether you are one step beyond thinking about the future state of things, you lose the precision of the present moment and its potential to fully create what's happening now. Reflecting on the past counts, as does imagining the desired future. But for each increment of value these bring, the present counts double for that is the place where experience emerges in the interactions of people.

2. What we focus on becomes our experience. This notion was articulated clearly in the famous quote by William James, considered by most to be the father of psychology: "My experience is what I agree to attend to." Modern research has caught up with this profound idea and confirmed that the power of mental activity and the focus of our thoughts is a key driver in our perceived experience. As it relates to re-making communication at work, I cannot stress enough the importance of selecting what to focus on and having the courage to value that enough to ignore everything else (at least momentarily).

3. Learning to take ownership without attachment. This is the ability to recognize your role in making patterns and being willing to "step up to the plate" of participation. If you can do this without feeling the need to stay attached to the structure and outcomes, you open possibilities for the unexpected.

4. Little turns can shift big patterns. If you can increase the level of intention and active choice-making in the turns you take, it can undermine the logical force of a given episode.

5. Give full voice to what matters (and what is too often unsaid). When the source of most workplace conflict is examined, unmet expectations are very often at the core. The ironic thing about unmet expectations is that they are often never mentioned in the first place. Holding our colleagues accountable for doing or not doing things that we never asked them for is mind-bending, yet part of our standard operating procedure. Maybe it is because we make assumptions about what people hear us say and see us do, and maybe we trust their interpretation and meaning-making process to know more about our needs and wishes than is realistic. Either way, giving full voice to what matters is a strength and skill that is required for re-making unwanted patterns of communication and interaction.

A Meaningful Picture of the Pattern You Want

Creating the patterns of communication and interaction we want will not happen by luck or accident. Getting there requires a meaningful picture of what is possible. This core vision acts as a beacon that helps to translate focused action into desired results. Often a meaningful picture is aspirational as it reflects the elements/details that characterize the desired future. At other times it can be based on a signature alteration, characterized by the differences that would be experienced if something specific changed. Not only does it help to possess a clear focus on this meaningful picture, it facilitates opportunities to share this picture and inspire others around its potential.

More than just a vision, a meaningful picture is the first tangible glimpse of what you hope to bring focus to in a given endeavor. Holding close to a meaningful picture should not be confused with the proverbial "bolt of lightning from the sky." In some instances, the process starts out looking murky and requires living with a set of questions over time in order to slowly nurture a meaningful picture into an energetic, focused vision for change.

Pattern Echo Test

Sometimes the subtler and more ambiguous communication issues we face can be identified by a quick "pattern echo test." If you are able to start your day and end it with a clear focus on what is right in front of you, then that possible issue—the one you have been stewing on since the last uncomfortable or ambiguous episode—is likely not all that relevant. If, however, you are unable to fully focus on what is right in front of you because the pattern echo of an unwanted episode will not subside, then it matters enough to give it some attention and explore it further. Giving it attention by walking it through the episode mapping exercise will help you determine if a wider effort is needed, including the potential involvement of other people.

Pattern Profiles

A pattern profile is a simple way of focusing on the core issue(s) involved in unwanted patterns of communication and interaction. It includes a snapshot of the challenge, related episodes, and potential alternative episodes required to re-make the unwanted pattern into something better. The first time I created a pattern profile and shared it with a leader, I immediately recognized the value it had in simplifying the complex, multilayered communication issues that individuals and teams face in the real world of work.

I worked with a vice president who struggled for months to fix what she called their division's "dysfunctional family." I spent time with a few of her key people and led the team through a re-making communication at work session that explored the dominant patterns of communication and interaction they experienced. On the fly I created a simple summary of the key issues that surfaced throughout the day-long session. After the vice president read it, she said "I've been banging my head against the wall for nearly six months on these issues; what you just outlined in two pages is what I have been struggling to put my finger on this whole time!"

Once you see an example you can make your own pattern profiles to pull apart the layers of complex issues and organize them in a simple framework. To get started, here is a sample pattern profile. Appendix 2 has a complete set of individual and team pattern profiles that reflect familiar challenges in the real world of work. You will notice that the language used to describe the "typical episodes" and "alternative episodes" reflects activities and general ways of working with others. This task-focused language is useful because it directs you to the practical attitudes and behaviors within productive episodes.

Patterns of Self-Handicapping

Description: This pattern shows up when intentional self-sabotaging acts such as setting unattainably high goals, taking on too much, procrastinating, or purposefully reducing effort become forms of self-handicapping that precipitate failure. Not surprisingly, these behaviors severely undermine a person's chances of performing effectively and they can impact patterns of communication and interaction that include collaborative elements. Self-handicapping suggests that an individual's expectation about their likelihood of accomplishing a given task affects their success in completing it.[5]

Typical Episodes: Low levels of individual morale, reduced self-efficacy and confidence, missed deadlines, repeated conversations about follow through and shared accountability, and reduced trust among colleagues.

Potential Alternative Episodes: Realistic goal setting, strength-based work planning, proactive support checks from management, and increased trust among team members.

Other Roadblocks to Watch Out For

"Pattern fatigue" can set in when we live with unwanted patterns over a period of time. These patterns can zap our energy and lead us through sluggish cycles of frustration that drain us. In addition to pattern fatigue, the following list provides a series of reminders about common hiccups and roadblocks that can potentially block efforts to re-make patterns of communication at work:

- focusing on patterns of communication and interaction between people when organizational problems are the cause of the unwanted outcome;
- spending too much time focusing on past communication patterns at the expense of being present;
- insufficient personnel to initiate and support efforts to re-make communication at work;

- believing in the readiness for change when the conditions, timing, and willingness are not adequate; and
- giving away our story about what matters for the sake of agreeing with others. Sometimes we can feel compelled to surrender what is important to us, or stop the pursuit of understanding others' point of view when we feel that the tension it creates could be harmful to a relationship. Alternatively, if we push too hard and advocate too aggressively for our own perspectives and priorities, we alienate people. Getting this balance right prevents patterns from getting stuck in this in-between space.

With these challenges to watch for, the following tips of encouragement will help. These are adapted from the "typical challenges faced by entrepreneurs when professionalizing their organizations" by Barry Dym, Stephen Jenks, and Michael Sonduck.[6]

- Keeping a clear check on reality without losing hope;
- Striking a balance between decisiveness and rigorous inquiry;
- Acting even in the face of your own doubts and uncertainties;
- Resisting the temptation of returning to familiar ways of solving problems when things don't go as expected;
- Being okay with progress and unconcerned with perfection; and
- Realizing that, even when you've gotten it right, it will need to be done again—organizations are never in a finished state.

Conclusion

There are a variety of easy-to-use tools and thought exercises that can help you apply the concepts and practices of re-making communication at work. The practical activities can be used to address a wide range of everyday communication challenges and help you develop the confidence to apply the book's lessons in your world of work. As it is with any learning experience, the pace and approach is best determined by the learner so these exercises can be customized according to your unique needs. Chapter 18 continues with the theme of creating big change by starting small as it establishes a clear link between effective leadership and organization culture change with the concepts and practice of Re-making Communication at Work.

18

Re-Making Leadership and Organizational Culture with Communication

Whether we consciously choose to or not, we build the ongoing patterns of communication and interaction that shape our relationships, decisions, performance, and the quality of our working lives. Collectively, these patterns reflect the character of our teams and give the culture of our organization its identity. Although every member of the organization contributes, leaders have extreme influence over the specific patterns that influence culture via their active engagement in overlapping contexts (i.e., meetings, reporting relationships, decision-making venues, etc.) where communication gets made and reinforced.

The goal of this chapter is to make the connection between the tools for re-making communication at work and effective leadership and culture change. The chapter begins with leadership and, following a transitional summary, it concludes with organization culture.

Organizational Leaders: Architects of Their Patterns of Communication and Interaction

A new approach to communication at work opens an opportunity to explore the relationship between the communication perspective and the purpose and effectiveness of leaders. We already know that the research and practice of leadership has evolved significantly over the last few generations. The accepted norms from the old hierarchical, top-down models of effective leadership called for one strong, charismatic figure whose job it was to know the right problems, the right answers, and to have the right solutions to organize people and resources in order to effectively meet the demands of work.

This model eventually gave way to more facilitative approaches that emphasize the leaders' capacity to involve others' strengths, build on diversity, know processes that can be applied across contexts, and decentralize decision-making in a faster, leaner world of work.[1] Re-making communication at work builds on this facilitative model. When you take the communication perspective at work that I advocate, you can define organizational leaders as *the lead architects of the patterns of communication and interaction that take place in organizations*. While it is the collective effort of every person in the organization to contribute to the patterns that ultimately shape the culture and performance of the company, leaders play a significant role in influencing the day-to-day experiences of staff, which in turn create and sustain many of the major elements of organizational culture.

In this definition, leaders play a critical role in fostering that talent and making the most productive use of it. Leaders enable discussion, champion follow through, and reward people for what matters. The authority and resources to do this put them in a unique seat of influence for re-making communication at work. And these all shape the culture of organizations in significant ways, depending upon the relative strength and influence of the leader(s) in relation to the followers. By virtue of their cross-cutting function, leaders are players in shaping many of the central patterns that exist in an organization.

Architects at Work

I have argued that everyone has power in the constructive process of shaping the organization in which they work. Leaders, however, have exceptional potential power due to their position of influence and the inherent acknowledgment of their (presumed) ability to be effective stewards of organizational turning points such as strategic decision-making, financial management, major personnel decisions, and setting the policies and accountabilities that influence culture and set standards for employee contribution and performance, to mention a few.

Operationalizing the notion of leaders as architects of patterns starts with monitoring the quality of the patterns of communication and interaction that occur within their teams. Most leaders I know work very hard to do the right things and to pay attention to what matters. Now that we have debunked the myths of effective communication at work that have prevented leaders from looking at communication as the powerful leverage it can be in shaping organizational outcomes, we can associate effective leadership with three skills:

1. Scanning current patterns of communication and interaction
   a. Continuously observing what happens within the organization
   b. Focusing on a clear picture of what matters
   c. Clarifying the desired future that realistically matches that picture
2. Selecting preferred patterns to strengthen and unwanted patterns to re-make

    a. Identifying the turns and episodes that can lead to, or which undermine the desired future

    b. Using the practice of re-making communication at work to address them

3. Reversing the roles of responsibility

    a. Engaging with others in the entire process

    b. Turning followers into leaders by empowering them to actively contribute to the necessary pattern changes

The rest of this section on leadership offers more constructive insights and ideas to facilitate your knowledge and awareness about how re-making communication at work can complement existing leadership knowledge, skill, and practice. Overall these can be used to develop a versatile toolkit for understanding people, relationships, and organizations and for acting effectively in difficult situations.

The Fundamental Question: What Matters Right Now?

Leadership is a situational pursuit that requires a reflective mind and a flexible set of hands. In order to keep pace with change and respond to increasingly diverse challenges, leaders must approach every situation with confidence in principles that work and a willingness to apply those proven principles and related practices in new combinations. The fundamental question for every leader, at every moment, is what matters most right now? In a process of continuous assessment leaders want to understand what is most important and—if conditions are not fully aligned with values, priorities, and objectives—what are the possibilities for something better. The implication of learning how to focus on what matters is that you can then manage to what matters.

In previous chapters I described the contradiction between what we say about how important communication is at work and how we act quite differently from those definitive statements. I indicated that the cause of this paradox is the fact that the transmission model of communication is not effective, therefore despite the fact that communication is really important, we are still unable to fundamentally alter the issues that consistently surface when it breaks down. Leaders can do three things to resolve this contradiction: (1) Hire like communication matters; (2) engage with their people like communication matters; and (3) see beyond every workplace experience and outcome to the underlying pattern of communication and interaction that made it.

Our Focus Is Our Future

We already know that what leaders focus on and monitor reflects what matters. What is recorded in the excel spread sheet makes it to the board report, which gets air time at the meeting, and captures the attention and focus of the moment. What is overlooked and unmeasured is not often considered. For all intents and purposes, what leaders do not see simply does not exist for them. Re-making communication at work and the process of seeing communication gives leaders a chance to bring greater focused attention to more of the important elements in their organization and to avoid getting surprised by the hidden issues they cause when left unattended.

The practices introduced in prior chapters offered a scaled approach with various vantage points that give a specific perspective at the desired level. Seeing patterns is like the 15,000-foot view. Seeing episodes is like the 1,000-foot view. And noticing turns is being at ground live in real-time. These mixed-level vantage points can help leaders examine

1. the frames they employ to process and understand their experiences;
2. the language they use and the stories they tell to name those experiences; and
3. the actions they take, which affect what gets made into those experiences and outcomes

As leaders go through this iteration, they gain confidence in the practice of seeing the ecosystem of their team's patterns. This in turn leads to better ways of

- recognizing/calling attention to distinctions among stories that indicate where people are not on the same page and priorities/goals could get derailed;
- spotting recurring episodes and patterns of interaction that can produce disruptive experiences and outcomes that reduce performance and productivity; and
- becoming skilled at noticing and naming subtle turns that can get things back on track and aligned with desired team and organizational outcomes.

Doing these things consistently and effectively brings necessary attention to the most important things. Rather than having that casual comment or overlooked rift derail desired outcomes down the line, leaders can proactively integrate a much wider range of information into their picture of what is happening and where their focus can add the most value.

Everyday Shifts

Once you start re-making communication at work, you see how your language changes in the common interactions you have with others. For example, at a staff meeting you might say:

- "As we take care of the business part of our agenda, what kind of team experience do we want to make today?"

- "As we tackle the goals we are setting today, we will need to look closely at the patterns of communication and interaction that will help us achieve those outcomes."

At an annual performance review with a staff member, you might say:

- "Before we dive into the specific feedback, let's talk about the most helpful way for us to communicate right now."
- "Specifically, what do we need to make today in order to effectively review your performance, highlight your strengths and achievements, and focus on your growth and improvement opportunities?"

And, at a strategic planning session, you might say:

- "Now that we see the priorities and goals that we feel will make us successful, what existing patterns of communication and interaction either support or block these goals?"
- "Which specific patterns must be made or re-made if we are to create the conditions to achieve the goals within the timeframes we have set?"

Leadership Episodes

What you do when nobody is watching defines the true character of a leadership moment. That simple scenario implies that your genuine values, priorities, and character will authentically emerge when the lack of scrutiny or influence from others allows your true colors to influence your action. In a similar way, I believe there are leadership episodes that occur frequently, and because they are hidden within the larger patterns of communication, people do not often see them. I define "leadership episodes" as the *interactions between people that set the tone for what is possible*. If the communication interaction is unwanted, closed, and fragmented then that limits the possibility for preferred, open, and aligned outcomes.

When a leader takes five minutes to walk through the office, look a person in the eye and tell them that they are proud to be working with them, others may not notice this brief episode. However, if the person who receives acknowledgment had been struggling to stay engaged and wondered if their contributions had been seen, this small episode could produce a big effect. The converse is also true. When a leader sends a zinger or left-handed compliment toward someone who is unsure of their future in the organization, this micro episode (that others may not have observed) can change the course of their career in the organization.

Despite the fact the more challenging episodes within our unwanted patterns tend to get most of our attention, there are often positive episodes that can just as powerfully shape our desired patterns. Here is a list of some of the most important leadership episodes that can result in useful patterns to recognize and cultivate:

- Openly admitting mistakes and being transparent about known and unknown challenges...can lead to patterns of trust and appreciation.
- Taking time to reflect on disappointments and failures...can lead to patterns of learning and freedom to make "useful mistakes."
- Signaling that disagreement is welcomed by inviting creative dissent... can lead to patterns of conflict resolution and increased innovation.
- Implementing feedback and seeking input from organizational stakeholders about their real experience at work...can lead to patterns of truth telling and policies/procedures that reflect the real needs and desires of people.
- Initiating difficult, but necessary, conversations with people when issues are fresh...can create patterns of respect and accelerated problem-solving.

A Legend with No Map

There is no universal handbook on effective leadership. Despite the many efforts to create one, there is no single definition and related approach to leadership that provides a foolproof script to follow with guaranteed positive results every time. People are different, circumstances constantly evolve, and effective solutions that may work with one person in one context may fail in another. Operating in this type of uncharted, no-script terrain is one of the fundamental challenges leaders face.

However, despite these many variations leaders can proactively engage in specific patterns that allow them to increase their likelihood of success. In a way, this chapter provides a legend with no map. This means there are cardinal directions to navigate, as well as principles to interpret the landmarks along the way. If leaders do invest the time and energy to re-make communication at work, then they can expect some or all of the following positive outcomes:

- *Accomplishing More with Less:* No organization is immune to the inverse relationship of shrinking resources and growing expectations. In the face of continuing competition and resource limitations, individuals and teams are increasingly asked to accomplish more with less. Positioning active, high-performing leaders to re-make communication at work can help organizations to maximize the resources reflected in their human capital, making it easier to solve the equation of doing more with less.
- *The Multiplication of Benefits with the Integration of New Skills:* As leaders exercise their re-making competencies and related skills, those skills and abilities naturally tend to proliferate across the organization. Leaders that re-make communication at work are consistently successful in improving the most impactful patterns, and their success is often emulated by direct reports and even by superiors. As this informal transfer of knowledge/

skill influences others throughout the organization, the benefits of greater capacity and improved team performance multiply as well.

- *Increased Positive Conflict and Greater Team Cohesion:* The costs of negative, unresolved conflict represent one of the most reducible business costs on a balance sheet. However, productive conflict that results in increased creativity and greater team cohesion after positive resolution offers a catalyst for change. Leaders that re-make communication at work by definition often create dissent because of the way in which they push past limited expectations. Because these areas of divergence are substantive, not personality-driven, these are often inspiring challenges and they can be framed as a source of positive conflict and a pathway toward greater team cohesion.

- *Retaining Top Talent, Forgetting the Beauty Contest:* Making a difference in organizations can sometimes be ugly. The polished, glamorous image of change-makers who inspire people and quickly turn troubling situations around is a myth. This is hard work and not for those interested only in image. Investing in leaders who re-make communication at work signals an organization's commitment to success, despite the ways in which this success has a way of showing up in unconventional circumstances. Popularity contests and pretty packages never make change, but when leaders exercise their re-making competencies with grit and determination, it can be contagious for others.

Transitional Summary

There is a clear relationship between leadership and the capacity to re-make communication at work. When they take a communication perspective at work, organizational leaders are the lead architects inspiring the intentional creation of the patterns of communication and interaction that take place in organizations. While it takes the collective effort of every person in the organization to contribute to the patterns that ultimately shape the culture and performance of the company, leaders play a significant role in influencing the day-to-day experience of staff, which in turn create and sustain many of the major elements of organizational culture.

Workplace Culture: The Ecosystem of Our Patterns of Communication and Interaction

An entire series of books could be written specifically about organization culture and the impact communication has on its evolution. As I stated earlier, the limited purpose of this chapter is to establish a basic link between re-making communication at work and its effect on leaders and their efforts to shape organization culture. Seeing this link begins by imagining that organizational culture is a reflection of the patterns of communication and interaction among its people.

This ecosystem of patterns directly influences the quality of working life for people inside the organization and it influences their level of engagement, learning, performance, and overall contribution. Sustaining high levels of these four factors can lead to bottom-line success for the organization and the virtuous cycle that follows: healthy relationships among engaged people, doing their best work, in a profitable company, which produces healthier, more engaged people doing even better work as they contribute increasingly to the long-term success of the organization.

When people join an organization they go through a process of assimilation where they absorb the rules and norms of their new culture. This begins from the very first set of interactions during the recruitment and selection process and it accelerates during the first few weeks of employment. In this process people learn what members of a culture think, do, and say and it helps people make sense of their experience in the organization.[2] While they are in the process of absorbing and assimilating, they also begin to coinfluence these same learned, shared, and transmitted elements of the culture.

Whether you are a student studying communication and organizational life, or if you have spent meaningful time in the world of work, you know that many organizations can be quite challenging places. When the ongoing patterns among people in organizations create negative outcomes (i.e., competition, reluctance to learn and innovate, barriers that make it difficult for people to perform well and deliver their best contribution, etc.) a vicious cycle ensues. These patterns erode the quality of working life for people inside the organization, which means the related cycles of reduced performance over time may threaten the well-being of the company's bottom line.

Surprisingly, much of the popular literature that explains success in organizations is often attributed to a combination of factors such as a killer strategy, amazing C-level leadership, offering rich and diverse benefits to employees, getting the right mix of people/roles on board, betting big on a singular competitive advantage, responding quicker than others to the realities of the market, and being disciplined with these factors over time. While these factors are definitely a significant influence on organizational success, I believe they overlook the obvious and most profound contributor.

Focusing on the patterns of communication and interaction among its people is one of the clearest ways to influence the overall success of organizations. The old business quip that "culture eats strategy for breakfast" confirms the problem with placing too much emphasis away from culture. More precisely, learning to recognize and re-make unwanted patterns of communication and interaction into more productive systems will lead to more desired outcomes. Taking a communication perspective at work and using the philosophy and practice of re-making communication at work to intentionally shape organizational culture is explained in the following concepts.

Officially Redefining Organization Culture...Again

I know, I know...here comes another definition of organization culture and you are thinking that the last 423 will suffice. It is true: organization culture has many definitions. As it relates to re-making communication at work, however, a legitimate update is needed.

Culture can be defined as the learned, shared, and transmitted behaviors among members of an organization. The way people within organizations interpret their experience and assign meaning to the actions they take also reflect culture. I personally like this straightforward definition of culture: it is just the way things get done around here.[3] Re-making communication at work requires a definition that accounts more accurately for the generative power of the patterns that make "the way things get done" in organizations. Therefore, I define it as *the ecosystem of our patterns of communication and interaction*.

Traditional views of organizational culture frame it in objective terms and describe artifacts such as stories, rituals, and symbols as the evidence and representation of what the culture is. My definition combines elements of the interpretive definition (i.e., culture consists of the networks of shared meanings among members) and the critical-interpretive concept (i.e., networks of shared meanings, plus the power struggles generated by negotiating among competing meanings) and blends them together.

Organizations Are Made, Not Found

The intrinsic nature of our organizational lives was summed up perfectly by sociologist Amatai Etzioni: "Our society is an organizational society. We are born in organizations, educated in organizations, and most of us spend much of our lives working for organizations. We spend much of our leisure time playing and praying in organizations. Most of us will die in an organization, and when the time comes for burial, the largest organization of all-the state-must grant official permission."[4] The way in which we live out our lives embedded in organizations can lead to a faulty assumption that organizations exist, as they are, and we simply find them and join them. On the contrary: organizations are made, not found.

Changing an organization's culture begins with taking a communication perspective. It becomes real when you identify and alter the combined patterns of communication and interaction among the people in an organization to create the experiences and outcomes that the organization's intended purpose require and inspire.

In our modern society we live with, depend on, and engage in a complex and interactive system of organizations. Across community, social, cultural, religious, recreational, and vocational vantage points, "we are the organizations in which we live."[5] The sheer number of organizations that exist today is staggering. By default, the vast amount of organizations that any one individual is not a part of is also significant. Even when a person is a member, the organization can still appear *reified*, which means that organizational members may no longer be able to recognize that organizations are made and may be changed. This contributes to the common belief that organizations simply exist apart from themselves and the people within them. While this is a logical notion, particularly when you consider a generations-old institution or a successful brand that has done business decade after decade, there is an alternative way of thinking about organizations.

An organization is made through the ongoing and combined actions of its people. When you consider that the basis for any action is communication, another way of expressing this is that "communication...is the very essence of a social system or organization."[6] This is a really important shift in perspective on what organizations are. The traditional view of an "organization that is a static container that simply holds the interactions of people" vs. an "organization that is the combined patterns of communication and interaction of people" provides the starting point to connect re-making communication at work with culture change.

People Stay or Go Because of This Stuff

People do not leave organizations to seek out other opportunities because of communication or culture. They leave because of what communication and culture makes or does not make in their experience at work. The primary lens through which most people seem to evaluate their ability to remain in a job is the quality of their direct relationship with their supervisor. If the patterns are solid enough, then people typically stay. When they get past the point of tolerable, people who have a choice will often leave that organization.

Beyond the fundamental supervisor-employee relationship, another prominent area that people evaluate is the quality of the organization's culture. In exit interviews around the country right now, people are providing reasons for their voluntary terminations. If they are candid, they may say things like the following:

- "I don't agree with how things are done here, the culture of this organization doesn't match my values."
- "I love our mission and the people that I work with...but the way decisions are made and the amount of procedural 'stuff' we have to go through is just too much."

- "I don't feel like I can trust people here and so I need to move on to a healthier place to work."
- "The culture here is just too toxic; I can't stay here any longer."

While some of these statements may seem extreme, I have heard them many times. When it really comes down to it, this vast thing that we call *culture* is really just the stories we tell about our experience on the job. Whether or not a leader may have their own alternative story about "what the culture is/isn't" doesn't change the fact that individuals write their own stories to some degree. In the case of individuals who choose to leave an organization, it is the power of their stories (and the degree to which their experiences are inconsistent with their values and aspirations) that compel them to take that final step.

Communicating Organizations

In the 1990s there was a successful effort to define the "learning organization,"[7] which is comprised of people who care deeply about continuous improvement and shape a culture of collaboration that learns from past mistakes while questioning the deeper assumptions that created them in the first place.[8] The argument is that people in these organizations are better equipped to manage the onslaught of change and competition, and that learning organizations are themselves environments that foster positively regarded attributes like greater innovation, increased employee engagement, and overall performance improvements.

Considering the substantial importance of organizational communication and the potential that re-making communication has to shape organizational culture, I believe we need another kind of organization typology: the *communicating organization*. I would define this as "a critical mass of influential organizational members who take a communication perspective and actively build preferred patterns of interaction that align with company goals and values."

If We Want Better Organizations, We Will Have to Make Them

After a particularly brutal day-long session with a team who had been living with an unresolved conflict for nearly 18 months, I remember asking myself the question: "How could a team of such talented people, who basically like each other, make such unwanted experiences and outcomes for so long?" In a way this question was the genesis of this book. I began to wonder how these everyday patterns of communication and interaction that produce such unwanted experiences and outcomes get made and then held in place for long periods of time. The toll that these damaging situations can take on people is immense, not to mention the erosion of team and organizational performance that impacts the bottom line throughout the friction, yet they persist so often for so many people.

I wrote Re-making Communication at Work as a tool to create alignment among people, priorities, and performance within everyday organizational life with the goal of avoiding these paradoxical situations. Being miserable at work and literally suffering under the burden of unwanted experiences is not necessary. The cost of transformation runs right through a leader's choice to invest the effort required to re-make communication at work. Doing this over time can transform culture and uproot the many causes and conditions of unproductive, unwanted patterns of communication and interaction that impact people in the world of work.

Conclusion

Although every member of the organization contributes, leaders have extreme influence over the specific patterns that influence workplace culture via their active engagement in dominant contexts (i.e., meetings, reporting relationships, decision-making venues, etc.) where communication gets made and reinforced. This creates a fundamental link between re-making communication at work and its effect on both leaders and the role they play in shaping organization culture.

Seeing this link begins by defining leaders as the chief architects of patterns and organizational culture as the ecosystem of the patterns of communication and interaction among its people. The correlation between re-making communication at work and the effectiveness of leaders' capacity to influence culture has implications on: individual and team performance, alignment between people and goals, retention of top talent, and responses to change, among others.

19

Sharing the Book's Lessons with the "Hard-to-Reach"

Effectively conveying new ideas to people who are naturally skeptical or "hard to reach" can be difficult. Without trying to diagnose the many forms of resistance that you may encounter as you attempt to bring the concepts of this book into your organization, this chapter includes a few tips and examples that have proven useful for me and my clients in the real world.

Find Intersections between the Familiar and the Unfamiliar

In a recent consulting project I met a resistant upper-level manager who wore his blue-collar credentials on his sleeves. With his arms folded through the first part of the session, he sent a clear signal that he was not buying what I was selling. He made his feelings known by asking a question that he did not require an answer for: "Can you try to say everything you've just said in a different way, I am not following you at all!" With my work cut out for me, I began by getting back to an earlier comment he had made about his hobby of running. I thought this could give me a way toward a disarming intersection between re-making communication at work and something important to him.

I had recently read Christopher McDougal's great book *Born to Run*,[1] which documented the culture and practice of the long-distance barefoot running traditions of the Tarahumara Indians of the Copper Canyon region of Northwestern Mexico. The book was a *New York Times* bestseller and it sparked a bit of a barefoot running revolution here in the United States. The unique cast of elusive and full-personality characters, as well as the subplots of extreme endurance races in difficult conditions and remote places made for a good read.

To bring the rest of the group into the loop and set up my best chance of getting him on board, I put my own spin on the gist of the story. I explained that one of the biggest takeaways for me was to "forget everything you've been told about effective running." The conventional wisdom, from complicated training regimens to the requirement of expensive shoes and specialized gear, was challenged by a new set of principles that brought everything down to the basic fundamentals. The author's efforts to understand the secrets of the Tarahumara Indians, also known as the Rarámuri (meaning "runners on foot"), led to a transformation of his own running experience and a legitimate challenge to the establishment of the running industry's long-held, largely unchallenged beliefs.

Bringing it back to my workshop, I said that something similar is going on with communication. I explained that what I was trying to show them was that our understanding of traditional approaches to communication at work should also be challenged and a new set of principles introduced. Just like McDougal presented research and opinions that claimed modern cushioned running shoes are a major cause of running injuries, I wanted them to see that superficial approaches to communication do little to help and can in fact do more damage by sustaining the underlying patterns of communication and interaction that produce the unwanted experiences and performance gaps in the first place. And, just like the thin sandals worn by Tarahumara runners sparked a "back to basics" revolution of running, I challenged them to strip things down to the basics and look at your communication habits at the level of action, reaction, action, and so on. The accumulation of these small exchanges is what shapes the habitual way people work together. Looking carefully at how we work offers a path toward the hands-on changes required to work better.

I can't say that he was jumping for joy, but the arms were no longer folded and he was engaged in the conversation. This intersection, which was nothing more than an anecdote in the moment, helped to simplify the concepts of re-making communication at work and it gave several people an alternative invitation to consider the challenge.

Follow What's Important and It Will Lead Back to a Useful Point

"Find something more important than you are" was the advice of philosopher Dan Dennett when he commented on the secret of happiness. When we try to influence people with the ideas we like we may end up pushing the point too far. It can be really helpful, instead, to listen for elements of importance expressed by other people and just follow them. While you may abandon the pursuit of the point you want to make momentarily, following what's important will often lead to something useful.

At a seminar for nonprofit leaders I was asked to share my perspective about communication between board members and executive directors. This is an important area and so I wanted to offer something that would really help the people in the room focus more on their organization's mission and less on the frustrations of communication breakdowns. I began by introducing some of the concepts in this book, including the necessary shift from the transmission model to the communication perspective.

Five minutes into it I noticed the body language in the room sagging and I might as well have been saying "blabadyblah, blah, blah, blabadyblah" because I was not connecting. In my mind I knew that what I was sharing was important to me, but I realized I had not quite found out what was important to them. I stopped mid-sentence and said, let me ask you a question: "If the average tenure of a nonprofit executive director is 18 months, what do you think some of the patterns of communication and interaction are that accelerate burn out and leave these otherwise dedicated, passionate community leaders running for the door?"

In the moments that followed there was a spirited discussion and lots of stories were shared. I tracked the conversation, inviting everyone to participate as much as possible. I slowly started peppering in my own language about the vocabulary for re-making communication at work and soon I was back on point. This time, however, the points I scored followed along with what was relevant to their real concerns.

Find the Pain

If you anticipate equal parts need for re-making communication at work and potential resistance to the concepts, try to quickly get down to the most fundamental level of "why should I care"—this is the personal pain point. This is not a reference to physical discomfort, but to the everyday challenges, headaches, frustrations, and even trauma that impacts our emotional and psychological health at work.

As with any other presenting condition in your working life, these damaging and painful experiences can be traced back to patterns. There are a number of simple questions you can introduce to get to this basic level and give you the best chance of delving deeper into the patterns that cause the pain. Some questions include the following:

- What nagging, persistent issue keeps you awake at night?
- What important priority or goal does it seem to block?
- To shift this frustrating dynamic, what might need to change?
- Is there any reason you can think of why you should keep the status quo?

After discussing these questions, I introduce a transitional question that usually either opens the door for more, or signals that the time is just not right. The question goes something like this: "If the specific barriers that keep you up at night stymie your goals and prevent you from doing your best work could be more clearly identified and potentially resolved, would you be willing to invest a few minutes of your time to try that out?"

Most people respond to this question positively. Although they may temporarily associate you with a used car salesman, they will hopefully understand that you are really not selling, but rather looking for a way to do the difficult, but potentially transformational work of re-making communication.

Drop the Jargon

Sometimes the words we use to share a new concept with someone else get in the way. If we couch the terms in ways that draw them in with curiosity, that momentary attention can be enough to share the essence of the thought. The opposite is also true; the wrong word choice can trigger closed ears and closed minds quickly. To get past the biases and assumptions that act as our gatekeepers to new ideas, I suggest dropping the jargon.

Jargon is the inside trade language of a particular profession and, to those who are uninitiated, it can come across as unintelligible and pretentious. The practical effect is that unnecessary jargon can often confuse, alienate, and bore others; people seldom listen effectively in those three states. The list of jargon examples to avoid would be too long to include here, so rather than pointing those out, here is a stripped-down version of key themes that might help you reach the "hard-to-reach."

- Those headaches at work that we experience working with others...we can get rid of them.
- One of the reasons they stick around is because we've been calling them by the wrong names.
- Behind every communication breakdown, experience with a difficult colleague, wasted meeting, and failed change effort there are patterns of communication and interaction that actually make that stuff.
- Our experiences and the outcomes we get are actually made by the habitual ways we interact with other people.
- If we change the way we communicate and interact, then we can re-make those headache-causing experiences into something better.

At the end of both part I and part II of this book there were short summaries of themes with an emphasis on applying the concepts in the real world of work. Those two chapters are also a good source of jargon-free language to help share this book's lessons with the hard-to-reach.

Conclusion

Effectively conveying new ideas to people who are naturally skeptical or "hard-to-reach" can be difficult. Proven suggestions for sharing the lessons of this book include: finding intersections of the familiar, focusing on what is important to others, adding value by addressing real challenges and frustrations, and dropping the jargon. Along with the suggestions for applying the book's lessons in the real world of work, these tips can help you take Re-making Communication at Work into even the most difficult corners of your organization.

20

Applying Part IV to the Real World of Work

Perhaps the most inescapable demand of work is the need to communicate with other people. For individual contributors, the quality of the communication they engage in directly reflects their relationships with coworkers, the level of motivation and engagement they feel, the impact and performance they contribute, and the general quality of their working lives. For leaders, the quality of the communication they engage in directly reflects their relationships with their direct reports, the capacity to motivate and engage people, the alignment of team performance with company goals, the capacity to manage complexity and change, and the overall influence of their leadership on vital benchmarks like workforce retention, productivity, and ultimately culture.

Re-making Communication at Work boils down to one simple idea: The experiences and outcomes you get at work are made in the specific patterns of communication and interaction you engage in. If you find the starting lines and use the guided coaching activities presented in part IV, you will start making something better.

If you want something different in your everyday experience at work or in the long-term arc of your career, you have to make that change by altering your fundamental building blocks of communication. If you want to be an effective leader that achieves results, inspires others, and adds lasting value to your organization, you will achieve that impact by creating the patterns of communication that create the conditions for you to deliver these results.

Once you fully integrate this concept, exercise the principles, and practice the tools, you re-make communication at work every time you

1. *take a communication perspective* and understand that meetings are not just meetings and conversations are not just conversations. The everyday episodes of interaction that play out in our working lives are

governed by rules and they move us closer to or further away from the outcomes and experiences we seek.

2. *recognize your patterns of communication and interaction* where decisions get made, relationships are built, organizational culture is solidified, and the trajectory for ultimate business outcomes are set into motion.

3. *examine what you make and select unwanted patterns to re-make.* Spot the critical moments where something different/better could be made, understand how to create the flexible conditions for change, follow a sequence of steps to re-make unwanted patterns of communication and interaction, and learn to avoid everyday pitfalls that can undermine these new patterns and the benefits they bring.

4. *gain a significant competitive advantage by re-making communication at work.* Perhaps one of the most significant sources of competitive advantage is the capacity to literally re-make unwanted patterns into coordinated efforts that align people with priorities, bring out the best in people's talent and motivation, and boost learning and performance by closing the inevitable gaps that emerge when things go bad.

Appendix I: Blank Worksheets for Re-Making Communication at Work

Pattern Finder

1. What recurring experiences or outcomes do I have at work?

2. How do I know that these experiences and outcomes are real?

I say, think, feel, and act...	Others say, think, feel, and act...

3. When and where do the interactions that produce these experiences and outcomes take place?

4. If I connect the dots, what story does all of this tell and what would I name it?
   (What you do here is identify the related items from the first three responses. Once you see them, tell them like a story in reverse order.)

5. Where does it sit on the continuum?
   Unwanted...Preferred
   -3 -2 -1 0 $+1$ $+2$ $+3$

6. Does it need to be re-made in some way?

Episode Mapper

1. Who are the players?

2. When/where does it begin and when/where does it end?

3. Checklists:
   - Does it repeat? How often?
   - Does it have a minor, moderate, or major impact on my day when it happens?

4. When the episode plays out, the results are more:

   Closed..Open

   | -3 | -2 | -1 | 0 | $+1$ | $+2$ | $+3$ |

5. What name would you give the episode?

6. Does it need adjusting in some way?

Turn Selector

1. What are the three pivotal turns?

Starts with me...	Starts with them...
• I say, think, feel, do...	• They say, think, feel, do...
• They say, think, feel, do...	• I say, think, feel, do...
• Then I say, think, feel, do...	• Then they say, think, feel, do...

2. Is there a specific speech act that frames one of the turns, which sets a tone and direction for where things go from there?

3. What rules seem to prompt our responses within each turn?

Me	Them
How I interpret what they say...	How they interpret what I say...
How I act based on that interpretation...	How they act based on that interpretation...
The logical forces or sense of "should" that compels me to respond in a certain way...	The logical forces or sense of "should" that compels them to respond in a certain way...

4. These turns are:

   Fragmented..Aligned

   | -3 | -2 | -1 | 0 | $+1$ | $+2$ | $+3$ |

5. What pivot in your next turn, or in their next turn, could lead to more alignment?

6. When will you take the next turn?

Deconstructing a Pattern of Communication and Interaction

Purpose: To dissect the anatomy of an unwanted pattern of communication by mapping the "presenting outcomes" it brings, as well as the "underlying building blocks" (i.e., attitudes, beliefs, and behaviors) that influence the episodes and turns that shape it.

What is the pattern of communication and interaction making?		*What possible name(s) could you give to this experience?*	
Presenting Level	Who is involved in making the pattern and when/where does it seem to take affect?	What challenges or difficulties does it produce, and specifically, how does it impact the quality of your working lives?	Even if it is contradictory, does it produce any benefits for the people who make it?
Constructing Level	If there is an episode that captures what the pattern is all about, what would it be and what would you name it?	In this episode, what are the critical turns, or moments of transition, where specific interactions sustain the pattern?	What types of values, attitudes, and behaviors fuel these turns and seem to be holding the pattern together?

Constructing a Pattern of Communication and Interaction

Purpose: To build a preferred pattern of communication in reverse by mapping the "underlying building blocks" that will make it, then planning for the "presenting outcomes" it will bring.

Constructing Level	What signature episode will capture the essence of this new pattern and what would you name it?	In this episode, what are the critical turns, or moments of transition, where specific communication will be needed to sustain the pattern?	What types of values, attitudes, and behaviors will positively fuel these turns and hold the pattern together?
Presenting Level	Who must be involved to make the pattern and when/where can it take maximum effect?	What benefits and outcomes will it produce, and specifically, how will it improve the quality of your working lives?	How can additional priorities and commitments be aligned with this, so that it is not undermined?

What name(s) could you give to this experience that will remind us to work toward it?

Reality Test

Purpose: : To assess the quality of the experience and outcomes produced by specific patterns of communication and interaction.

People/experience	Task/outcome
Does the pattern strengthen the bond between people and result in increased trust, positive regard, and greater likelihood of productive interactions, or does it disrupt teamwork and reduce the likelihood of trust-based partnering on future projects and activities?	Does the pattern make something useful that is required to achieve the priorities and goals of the people engaged in it (e.g., increased innovation, improved decision-making, better meetings, etc.) or does it complicate matters and work against those stated goals?

1 2 3 4 5 6 7 8 9 10   1 2 3 4 5 6 7 8 9 10

(−)   (+)   (−)   (+)

Why?_____   Why? _____

_____   _____

_____   _____

_____   _____

_____   _____

_____   _____

Listening for Stories

Purpose: To reveal the tension between the unknown, unheard, and untellable stories—including the gap between what is said and what is actually experienced—in order to spot the causes of fragmented turns, closed episodes, and unwanted patterns of communication.

Type of Story	If There Is a Story, What Does It Mean?	What Is the Impact of the Story?
Unknown Story		
Unheard Story		
Untellable Story		

Visualizing the System

Diagram the people, events, stories, and other important features in a pattern of communication that shed light on the way it is made and sustained.

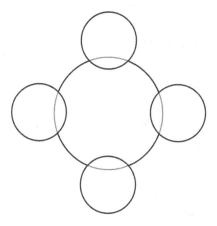

Hierarchy of Influence

Map the values, stories, and influential contexts in order of significance to examine the often silent, but powerful forces that shape patterns of communication.

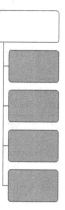

Seeing Past Speech Acts

Purpose: To identify recurring speech acts that are used by you and others in your world of work and to gain insight into the patterns of communication and interaction they trigger.

Prompt	*Response*
What speech acts do you use most in the world of work?	
What effect do these have on people when you deliver them?	
Is there a speech act you use that communicates something you do not want to say? If so, which turn seems to draw that speech act out?	
What recurring speech acts do you see/hear company leaders use?	
What effects do these have on people and on the culture overall?	

Logical Force Radar

Purpose: To identify the specific "shoulds" and "oughts" that prompt you to act in ways that are inconsistent with your values and desires.

In a few words, describe the pattern you want to explore:

What do you see, hear, think, and feel during a typical episode in this pattern:	The logical forces or sense of "should" that compels me to respond in a certain way:

What Is Your Working Life Script?

Purpose: To tell a story about your working life, including the beliefs that influence your patterns of communication and interaction and shape your everyday experience at work.

Describe the plot of your working life?	Who are the influential characters in your story and what past events may influence what you believe about your working life?
What typical episodes do you engage in?	Imagine that these episodes are part of larger patterns of communication and interaction…which recurring pattern shapes the quality of your experience and outcomes the most?

Appendix 2: Pattern Profiles

Patterns of Self-Handicapping

Description: This pattern shows up when intentional self-sabotaging acts such as setting unattainably high goals, taking on too much, procrastinating, or purposefully reducing effort become forms of self-handicapping that precipitate failure. Not surprisingly, these behaviors severely undermine a person's chances of performing effectively and they can impact patterns of communication and interaction that include collaborative elements. Self-handicapping suggests that an individual's expectation about their likelihood of accomplishing a given task affects their success in completing it.[1]

Typical Episodes: Low levels of individual morale, reduced self-efficacy and confidence, missed deadlines, repeated conversations about follow through and shared accountability, and reduced trust among colleagues.

Potential Alternative Episodes: Realistic goal setting, strength-based work planning, proactive support checks from management, and increased trust among team members.

Patterns of Self-Fulfilling Prophecies

Description: Unwanted patterns can be held in place by self-fulfilling prophecies, which are predictions that directly or indirectly cause themselves to become true. If an individual lacks confidence in a novel or challenging situation, they may convince themselves that the situation will result in a specific outcome (i.e., destined for failure), regardless of whether that is likely. As a result of this belief, they will take very real action that reflects the belief and in many cases leads to the anticipated negative outcome.[2]

Typical Episodes: Large-scale change implementation fails, challenging conversations with difficult employees are ineffective, efforts to rebuild trust with colleagues prove disappointing, and stretch goals for personal/professional development are avoided or not achieved.

Potential Alternative Episodes: Focusing on resources and commitment for success, embracing the learning potential of small failures and disappointments, and surrounding people with additional sources of resilience and confidence.

Patterns of Halos and Horns

Description: This pattern shows up when individuals hold and act upon assumptions and biases about other people. In situations where challenges have existed and trust has yet to be established, individuals often feel that those who appear similar to them (i.e., looks, attitudes, beliefs, etc.) are more trustworthy. Individuals who appear different are not granted that same baseline level of trust. Sometimes referred to as the "halo" (angel) and "horn" (devil) effect,[3] if these biases and assumptions are left unchecked, the similarity syndrome can lead to errors, inconsistencies, and inequities that reduce trust.

Typical Episodes: People play favorites, promotions are awarded to those who are liked rather than those who are deserving, people who are different are unfairly rated on performance reviews, and the integrity and fairness of a manager/organization is questioned.

Potential Alternative Episodes: Checking assumptions for biases, using objective criteria for evaluation and promotion decisions, and educating people about the value of diversity in organizational endeavors.

Patterns of Disequilibrium

Description: Individuals naturally seek a balance between the opposing forces that promote and restrain change. When environments produce too much or not enough change people remain in a state of disequilibrium. With too much change, individuals can become fatigued, disengaged, and resistant. With insufficient room to change and evolve, new priorities go unmet, frustration sets in, and morale can suffer.[4]

Typical Episodes: Chasing shiny objects and the flavor of the month, implementing the next change before completing the current change, prematurely abandoning priorities that require long-term commitment, and people cannot get off the treadmill of continuous change.

Potential Alternative Episodes: Honest conversations about the right balance of change, accountability for follow through on commitments to change, letting lesser priorities go for the sake of meeting top goals, and creating pockets of continuity for people to rest from change processes.

Patterns of Multitasking

Description: Patterns of pervasive multitasking seem innocent on the surface, but can be quite damaging. Multitasking has been widely recognized as an important skill to have in today's fast-paced and competitive business environment. The idea that one can juggle tasks in such a way that allows them to accomplish more with less time is a myth. Multitasking not only results in the loss of time, but it reduces overall effectiveness and the accuracy of performance in the specific categories of tasks involved. The task switching reduces valuable self-talk and mental processing time needed for effective decision-making and the overall switch-cost from one activity to the next could represent as much as 20–40 percent reduction in overall productivity.[5]

Typical Episodes: Interactions are paused/concluded before there is closure, the quality and accuracy of work declines, incomplete discussions and missing information prevent effective collaboration, and exhaustion sets in.

Potential Alternative Episodes: Focused conversations and work sessions that tackle one priority at a time, interactions are given sufficient time for closure, accuracy checks on work prevent service failures, and realistic expectations to accomplish reasonable workloads reduce stress.

Patterns of Perfectionism

Description: While perfectionism can be an admirable trait under certain circumstances, being excessive or overly compulsive about obtaining accurate and predictable results can prevent/impede performance. Re-making communication at work by its very nature requires a certain degree of risk through trial and error—the willingness to make something different. Perfectionist behaviors that seek to predictably control experience makes people less likely to have uncharted conversations, admit failure, and risk learning new things. It can also damage interpersonal relationships, decrease productivity, and harm physical and emotional health in its most extreme forms.[6]

Typical Episodes: Things do not get done (unless it is perfect, it is not finished...), too much focus on polish/look and not enough emphasis on substance/impact, the impression that "people are not good enough," and avoidance of uncertainty and change.

Potential Alternative Episodes: Maintaining realistic expectations for finished products, designing work flows that prioritize substance over polish, distinguishing between excellence and perfection, separating people's work from their personalities, and accepting uncertainty in change in staged increments to increase comfort over time.

Patterns of Failing to Change Mental Models

Description: Changing the behaviors that lead to ineffective patterns of communication and interaction is only part of the solution. It is also critical to change the underlying patterns of thinking that sustain those behaviors if lasting improvement will be achieved.[7]

Typical Episodes: Issue identification stops when the presenting issues are named, people feel/know more is involved but do not discuss it because it is too difficult/sensitive, and out of politeness or fear people do not share authentic concerns.

Potential Alternative Episodes: Continue issue identification exercises past the presenting issues to the patterns of thinking that sustain them, increase courage to discuss difficult attitudes, and give permission to share unheard/untold stories that reveal underlying thinking.

Patterns of Defensive Routines

Description: To avoid potentially embarrassing or awkward situations people deflect responsibility, avoid certain topics, and seek ways to maintain the status quo with defensive behaviors. The result is that individuals fail to inquire about their own role in contributing to or causing problems and they may also fail to accept responsibility for their own choices and behaviors.[8]

Typical Episodes: Blaming others for failure, explaining lack of follow-through on external circumstances, avoiding difficult tasks by finding excuses that hide fear and uncertainty, and credibility gaps among colleagues.

Potential Alternative Episodes: Taking personal responsibility for priorities, take ownership and control over the conditions that you can influence, seeking collaboration and increased support to take on necessary change, and increasing credibility among colleagues through honest discussions of performance.

Patterns of Insufficient Margin of Power

Description: When a person experiences more demands on their time and attention than they have available resources to meet them, they experience an insufficient margin of power. This low margin results in insufficient levels of time, energy, and resources available to complete challenging goals that require extra effort to achieve.[9]

Typical Episodes: Stretch goals fail, fatigue from playing constant catch up, increased occurrences of illness and stress-triggered episodes, the quality and accuracy of work declines, and disengagement and apathy increase over time.

Potential Alternative Episodes: Goal setting based on accurate assessment of available resources to meet demands, when margin declines resources are increased commensurately, attendance and productivity increase, and motivation and positive engagement increase as challenging goals are met.

Patterns of Information Anxiety

Description: Information anxiety occurs when people are bombarded with multiple messages and are unable to sort and identify what is important for them to know and understand. This leads to information overload, which increases the gap between what a person understands and what they think they should understand. The apprehension of always "feeling behind" or "knowing that something is missing" can be a constant drain on attention and energy.[10]

Typical Episodes: Actions fail due to insufficient information and planning, service failures increase due to confusion and misaligned priorities, perceptions of unprofessionalism increase, and customers/partners may lose confidence.

Potential Alternative Episodes: Systems of clear information sharing with priority messages, time investment in communication venues that promote clear exchanges, and informal commitments to "compare notes" and stay aligned.

Patterns of Defensive Pessimism

Description: Defensive pessimism occurs when an individual lowers his/her expectations for success and/or imagines a scenario that helps them mentally prepare for the worst. While defensive pessimism can help anxious people, it can prevent meaningful action and the development of greater levels of self-efficacy required for performance improvement.[11]

Typical Episodes: Negative talk about anticipated failure, decline in morale, and failure to fully invest in priorities.

Potential Alternative Episodes: Setting expectations based on actual potential for success, positive reinforcement and encouragement, and increased confidence and resilience.

Patterns of Skilled Incompetence

Description: Skilled incompetence involves the avoidance of difficult priorities. Instead, there is a focus on easier and more convenient tasks of lesser priority. The pattern also shows up when an individual may know that another person is aware of something that is a problem of mutual concern, yet both people choose to act as if neither of the parties knows anything.[12]

Typical Episodes: Problems that persist and fester, busy activity with no valuable accomplishments, and superficial communication that suppresses issues.

Potential Alternative Episodes: Focused conversations on true priorities, less busywork and more value-added contributions, and authentic communication about genuine concerns.

Team Patterns

Patterns of Tunnel Vision

Description: When individuals fail to recognize the impact of their actions on the team, this tunnel vision causes a decline in their capacity to take ownership and meaningfully participate in problem-solving efforts.[13]

Typical Episodes: Bottlenecks—people are left waiting for others to complete their work, scapegoating—people do not take responsibility for their role and contribution, and efforts to change fail because the full system is not considered.

Potential Alternative Episodes: People see their role in relation to the team, people understand the effect of their performance on other people and the system, collaborative efforts have greater opportunities of success due to more accurate big picture thinking.

Patterns of Unhealthy Competition

Description: Unhealthy internal competition results in split allegiances and mutually exclusive goal attainment. Decreases in information sharing, collaboration, and joint problem-solving can undermine loyalty, decrease innovation, and lead to damaged morale and high turnover.

Typical Episodes: Information sharing declines, a win/lose mentality pervades decision-making, companywide goals are diminished in light of department goals, and organizational culture rewards individual behavior.

Potential Alternative Episodes: Information sharing increases, a win/win mentality pervades decision-making, innovation and great ideas come from anywhere, and organizational culture rewards individual and team performance.

Patterns of Fear to Tell the Truth

Description: When team members do not believe they are free to raise concerns in good faith without fear of reprisal or victimization, patterns of closed communication and distrust increase.

Typical Episodes: Elephants in the room roam freely, important errors are left undiscussed, superficial communication, leaders lack credibility to hear and respond to genuine concerns, employees withdraw due to fear and distrust.

Potential Alternative Episodes: Real issues are communicated honestly, difficult issues are considered, leaders are not above criticism, and people engage more in open dialogue that builds trust.

Patterns of Groupthink

Description: When team norms and expectations reinforce conformity, they can lead individuals to censor themselves, create mindguards where innovative thinking is inhibited; develop illusions of unanimity and consensus that rationalize bad decisions and lead to unquestioned beliefs.[14]

Typical Episodes: Doing things because "we've always done them that way," going with the flow even if it is against common sense, and failing to question assumptions.

Potential Alternative Episodes: Challenging the status quo in constructive ways, thinking in alternative formats to spark innovation, and relying on outside perspectives to contrast internal team views.

Patterns of Unfinished Business

Description: Seeking premature closure due to pressure from deadlines, fatigue, or uncomfortable issues can leave important business unfinished. The result of this permanence tendency is that staff meetings end without resolution, discussions are started with no closure, and problems are partially resolved, but not fully addressed.[15]

Typical Episodes: Frustration from lack of closure, meetings feel endless because things never sunset, and people get burnt out on the merry-go-round of constant problem chasing.

Potential Alternative Episodes: Investments of time and energy match needs, meetings are longer but achieve closure, and people are energized from successfully addressing issues.

Patterns of Failure to Report Bad News

Description: The "mum effect" that occurs when people are silent or distance themselves from bad news out of fear of being blamed by association can significantly undermine necessary learning and performance feedback required for corrective action.[16]

Typical Episodes: Critical issues are shoved under the rug, disingenuous interactions hide truthful exchanges, trust, and credibility among leaders erodes.

Potential Alternative Episodes: Truth telling is an expected norm, the messenger is rewarded—not "shot," and open communication builds trust as critical issues are spotted and addressed early.

Patterns of Too Much Complacency and Not Enough Urgency

Description: Bringing about change requires teams to maintain a sense of urgency around their priorities. Complacency limits the energy and actions of people to get things done, however, a meaningful and positive sense of urgency can catalyze action and consolidate the power, credibility, and influence necessary to meet the challenge at hand.[17]

Typical Episodes: People wait on important priorities, opportunities are missed, and challenges arrive and people are unprepared to meet them.

Potential Alternative Episodes: People feel enough urgency to move but not too much pressured that they get stressed, opportunities and challenges are addressed proactively, and leaders use appropriate motivation (not fear) to get people engaged.

Notes

Introduction: Forget Everything You Learned
About Communication at Work

1. The transmission model, or standard model of communication, is described in greater detail throughout the introduction. It was established in 1949 by Claude Shannon and Warren Weaver for Bell Laboratories and the concept of the model suggests that communication is the process of sending and receiving messages or transferring information from one person (sender) to another (receiver). The four-hundred-year link from Locke and Hume is made by the relative emphasis on the pure transmission of ideas, rather than accommodation for the ways in which they are expressed and exchanged.

2. Originally introduced in 1976, the theory of the coordinated management of meaning (CMM) was a system of ideas most often used to understand interpersonal communication. The versatility of the concepts and the usefulness of their applications led many CMM scholars and practitioners to extend its use to different areas outside of traditional speech communication. In recent years numerous scholars and practitioners have taken aspects of CMM into the traditional practice areas of leadership and organization development, which is where my primary interest lies. One of the challenges with the transfer of CMM's core concepts and ideas has been the complexity of terminology and the lack of meaningful examples that bridge the theory with the real world of work.

3. Stan Deetz, "Difference between the Organizational Theory and the Communication Theory," accessed on January 10, 2013, from: http://www.youtube.com/watch?v=O3hzz0J_Bzo.

4. Robert Craig, "Communication Theory as a Field," *Communication Theory* 9. 2 (1999): 199–161.

5. *History of Organizational Communication*, referenced on January 9, 2013, from: http://en.wikipedia.org/wiki/Organizational_communication.

6. Stephen Axley, "Managerial and Organizational Communication in Terms of the Conduit Metaphor," *Academy of Management Review* 9 (1984): 428–437.

7. Robert Craig, "Communication," *Encyclopedia of Rhetoric* (Oxford University Press, Version of 3/9/00), accessed on January 9, 2013, from: http://spot.colorado.edu/~craigr/Communication.htm; emphasis in the original

8. Matt Koschmann, professor in the Department of Communication at the University of Colorado Boulder. YouTube Video: *What is Organizational Communication?* accessed January 9, 2013, at http://www.youtube.com/watch?v=e5oXygLGMuY.

9. Karen Ashcraft, *"Major Eras of Organization (Communication)Theory in the 20th Century,"* Applied Organizational Communication Overview, accessed January 8, 2013, at http://issuu.com/professor/docs/eras.

10. A good book that describes the human relations and human resources approach, along with all of the other major bodies of theory is Eric Eisenberg and H. Lloyd Goodall Jr.'s *Organization Communication* (New York: St. Martin's Press, 1997).

11. Karl Weick, *The Social Psychology of Organizing* 2nd ed. (Reading, MA: Addison-Wesley: 1979).

12. Matt Koschmann, Professor in the Department of Communication at the University of Colorado Boulder. YouTube Video: *What is Organizational Communication?* Accessed 1/9/2013 at http://www.youtube.com/watch?v=e5oXygLGMuY.

13. Karl Weick, *The Social Psychology of Organizing*, 2nd ed. (Reading, MA: Addison-Wesley, 1979), 358.

14. Robert Craig, "Communication," Encyclopedia of Rhetoric (Oxford University Press, Version of 3/9/00), accessed on January 9, 2013, from: http://spot.colorado.edu/~craigr/Communication.htm.

15. Paul Watzlawick, Janet Beavin, and Don Jackson, *The Pragmatics of Human Communication: A Study of Interactional Patterns, Pathologies, and Paradoxes* (New York: Norton, 1967).

16. Eisenberg and Goodall, *Organizational Communication.*

17. Jim Lukaszewski, *Rethinking Employee Communication: A Strategic Analysis* (Jim Lukaszewski's Strategy Newsletter No. 5, 2006).

1   Old Myths and New Principles for Re-Making Communication at Work

1. Joseph DeVito, *The Interpersonal Communication Book*, 9th ed. (New York: Longman, 2001).

2. Ibid.

2   Taking a Communication Perspective at Work

1. I have heard Barnett Pearce and other CMM scholars and practitioners use the analogy of scaffolding to get a better vantage point for seeing communication. I think the analogy is quite appropriate, which is why I included subtle images of scaffolding on the cover of the book.

2. Kingsley Davis, *Human Society* (New York: Macmillan, 1942).

3. Peter Bregman, *A Good Way to Change a Corporate Culture*. Published on June 25, 2009. Referenced on January 18, 2013, from: http://blogs.hbr.org /bregman/2009/06/the-best-way-to-change-a-corpo.html.

4. Tina Fey, *Bossypants* (New York: Little, Brown and Co., 2011).

5. Robert Kegan, *In Over Our Heads: The Mental Demands of Modern Life* (Cambridge, MA: Harvard University Press, 1994).

6. Barnett Pearce and Kim Pearce, "Extending the Theory of the Coordinated Management of Meaning (CMM) Through a Community Dialogue Process," *Communication Theory* 10.4 (November 2000): 420.

7. Peter Vaill, *Learning as a Way of Being* (San Francisco, CA: Jossey-Bass, 1996), 43.

3   Where Communication Counts Most in the Changing World of Work

1. *What is a Great Place to Work*, referenced on January 12, 2013, from: http:// www.greatplacetowork.com/our-approach/what-is-a-great-workplace.

2. Walter Kiechel, "A Manager's Career In the New Economy," *Fortune*, April 4, 1994, 68–72.

3. Dell Hymes, "On Communicative Competence." In J. B. Pride and Janet Holmes, *Sociolinguistics: Selected Readings*. Harmondsworth: Penguin. 1972, pp. 269–293.

5   Applying Part I to the Real World of Work

1. Anecdotes like these were originally presented in the CMM Solutions Field Guide. Barnett Pearce, Jesse Sostrin, and Kim Pearce, *CMM Solutions Field Guide for Consultants* (San Mateo, CA: Lulu Press, 2011).

6   Communication Chemistry: What Makes Patterns

1. Chris Argyris, *On Organizational Learning*, 2nd ed. (Malden, MA: Blackwell Business, 1999).

2. Jack Mezirow, *Learning as Transformation: Critical Perspectives on a Theory in Progress* (San Francisco, CA: Jossey-Bass, 2000).

3. Barnett Pearce, *Interpersonal Communication: Making Social Worlds* (New York: HarperCollins, 1994).

4. Vernon Cronen, Barnett Pearce, and Carl Tomm, "A Dialectical View of Personal Change," in Kenneth Gergen and Keith Davis, eds., *The Social Construction of the Person* (New York: Springer-Verlag, 1985), 203–224.

5. Linda Harris and Vernon Cronen, "A Rules-Based Model for the Analysis and Evaluation of Organizational Communication," *Communication Quarterly* 27 (1979): 12–28.

6. Claude Steiner, *Scripts People Live: Transactional Analysis of Life Scripts* (New York: Grove Press, 1990).
7. Life Scripts from Changing Minds was referenced on February 4, 2013, from: http://changingminds.org/explanations/models/life_scripts.htm.
8. Human Genome Project Information was referenced on January 14, 2013, from: http://www.ornl.gov/hgmis/home.shtml.

7   CommunicationP hysics: What Holds Patterns Together

1. Art Kleiner, "Building the Skills of Insight," *Strategy + Business*, January 7, 2013, http://www.strategybusiness.com/article/00154?gko=d4421&cid=TL2 0130117&utm_campaign=TL20130117 (accessed on January 17, 2013).
2. Stephen Littlejohn, *Theories of Human Communication*, 5th ed. (Belmont, CA: Wadsworth Publishing, 1996).
3. In CMM, the hierarchy concept is more complicated. With the actual communication act at the bottom of the hierarchy, they include relationship context, episode context, self-concept context, and archetype context. Relationship context assumes that there are existing expectations between individuals who are members of a group. Episode context refers to a specific event in which the communication act unfolds. Self-concept context relates to one's sense of self. And archetype context is the image of one's system of beliefs about general truths within communication exchanges. Barnett Pearce, *Making Social Worlds: A Communication Perspective* (Wiley-Blackwell, 2008).
4. Erin Biba, "What Is Time? One Physicist Hunts for the Ultimate Theory," *Wired*, February 26, 2010, http://www.wired.com/wiredscience/2010/02 /what-is-time/.

8   Communication Design: Deconstructing and Re-Making Patterns

1. "Vitruvius," retrieved on February 7, 2011, from penelope.uchicago. edu. Referenced on February 3, 2013, from: http://en.wikipedia.org/wiki /Architecture#cite_note-elements-5.

9   Learning to See Patterns, Episodes, and Turns in Communication

1. *Maps and Mapmaking*, interview with Jerry Brotton on The Forum. Referenced on January 18, 2013, from: http://www.bbc.co.uk/programmes /p011qhpc.
2. Eric Eisenberg and H. Lloyd Goodall, *Organizational Communication* (New York: St. Martin's Press, 1997), 35.

10   Identifying High-Priority Patterns

1. Jesse Sostrin, "Establishing and Validating a Conceptual Framework of Barriers to Workplace Learning and Performance: A Q-method Study," doctoral dissertation, Fielding Graduate University, Santa Barbara, California, 2008.
2. Jesse Sostrin, *Beyond the Job Description: What Managers and Employees Can Do to Navigate the True Demands of the Job* (New York: Palgrave-Macmillan, 2013).
3. Jerry Gilley and Ann Maycunich, *Beyond the Learning Organization: Creating a Culture of Continuous Growth* (New York: Perseus, 2000).
4. Jim Collins, *Good to Great* (New York: HarperCollins, 2001).

12   Introduction to the Practice of Re-Making Communication at Work

1. Wendy Jaffe, "The Remodeling Balancing Act," *LA Times*, June 3, 2001, http://articles.latimes.com/2001/jun/03/realestate/re-5852 (accessed on January 18, 2013).
2. Alain de Botton, "A Kinder, Gentler Philosophy of Success," http://www.ted.com/talks/alain_de_botton_a_kinder_gentler_philosophy_of_success.html (accessed on January 7, 2013).
3. Kingsley Davis, *Human Society* (New York: Macmillan, 1942).
4. Stephen Axley, "Managerial and Organizational Communication in Terms of the Conduit Metaphor," *Academy of Management Review* 9 (1984): 428–437.
5. Professors Barnett Pearce and Vernon Cronen wrote extensively about various sequences for using the concepts and tools of CMM. Subsequently students of CMM have conducted research and practice projects that have extended CMM into a variety of fields, including counseling, mediation, community development, and more. Many of the early efforts to bridge the theory and implementation gap for people with no background in communication were unsuccessful. I created this basic flow to help my coaching and consulting clients understand and use CMM.

13   Single-Step Practices for Re-Making Communication at Work

1. Many of these single-step processes draw from the rich and diverse tradition of bringing the coordinated management of meaning (CMM) theory into real-world practice. On most of them my adaptations involved simplifying the language, application, and meaning of the various tools.
2. Leon Festinger, *A Theory of Cognitive Dissonance* (Stanford, CA: Stanford University Press, 1957).

3. Barnett Pearce and Kim Pearce, "Extending the Theory of the Coordinated Management of Meaning (CMM) through a Community Dialogue Process," *Communication Theory* 10.4 (November 2000): 405–423, 411.
4. In their book, *How the Way We Talk Can Change the Way We Work*, authors Robert Kegan and Lisa Laskow Lahey elegantly describe the power of competing commitments that often cause us to work against ourselves when two or more conflicting priorities are held simultaneously. Robert Kegan and Lisa Laskow Lahey, *How the Way We Talk Can Change the Way We Work* (San Francisco: Jossey-Bass, 2001).

14   M-A-I-D: A Guide for Re-Making Patterns of Communication and Interaction

1. "Effective Partnerships," *Economic Strategies and Innovation in Medium Sized Cities from European Union's Program for Sustainable Urban Development*. Retrieved on February 19, 2013, from http://urbact.eu/fileadmin/Projects/ESIMEC/outputs_media/ESIMeC_recipe_1_-_partnership_working_01.pdf.

16   Where to Begin: Individual, Team, and Organizational Starting Lines

1. Walter Fisher, "Narration as a Human Communication Paradigm: The Case of Public Moral Argument," *Communication Monographs* 51 (1984): 1–22.
2. Adi Ignatius, "Leading for the Long-Term at Amazon," *Harvard Business Review IdeaCast*, January 3, 2013 (referenced on January 20, 2013, from: http://blogs.hbr.org/ideacast/2013/01/jeff-bezos-on-leading-for-the.html.).
3. Kurt Lewin, "The Research Center for Group Dynamics at Massachusetts Institute of Technology," *Sociometry* 8.2 (1945): 126–136.

17   How toA ccelerate Your Progress: Guided Coaching for the Essentials

1. Barnett Pearce, *Interpersonal Communication: Making Social Worlds* (New York: Harper Collins College Publishers, 1994).
2. Sonni Brown maintains a website that has more information about the Doodle Revolution and her campaign for global visual literacy: http://sunnibrown.com/doodlerevolution/.
3. The five "whys" is a question-asking technique used to explore the cause-and-effect relationships underlying a particular problem. It was made popular in the 1970s by the Toyota Production System.
4. Dan Snow, *In the Company of Stones* (New York: Workman, 2001).
5. Martin Covington, *Making the Grade: A Self-Worth Perspective on Motivation and School Reform* (Cambridge, England: Cambridge University Press, 1992).

6. Barry Dym, Stephen Jenks, and Michael Sonduck, "Coaching Entrepreneurs," in *Executive Coaching: Practices and Perspectives*, eds. Catherine Fitzgerald and Garvey Berger (Palo Alto, CA: Davies-Black Publishing, 2002).

18 Re-Making Leadership and Organizational Culture with Communication

1. The Institute of Cultural Affairs' Technology of Participation® introduces more detail about the shift from hierarchical to facilitative leadership approaches. Within the facilitative style of leadership, there are numerous variations with relative emphasis placed on different aspects of values, practices, and organizational needs. Learn more at: http://www.ica-usa.org/.
2. Fredric Jablin, *Organizational Entry, Assimilation, and Exit* in Handbook of Organizational Communication, eds. Fredric Jablin, Linda Putnam, K. Roberts, and L. W. Porter (Newbury Park, CA: Sage Publications, 1987), 679–740.
3. Terrence Deal and Allan Kennedy, *Corporate Cultures: The Rites and Rituals of Corporate Life* (Harmondsworth: Penguin Books, 1982).
4. Amatai Etzioni, *Modern Organizations* (Englewood Cliffs, NJ: Prentice-Hall, 1964), 1.
5. Michael Papa, Tom Daniels, and Barry Spiker, *Organizational Communication: Perspectives and Trends* (Los Angeles, CA: Sage, 2008), 2.
6. Daniel Katz and Robert Kahn, *The Social Psychology of Organizations*, 2nd ed. (New York: John Wiley & Sons, 1978), 428.
7. Peter Senge, *The Fifth Discipline: The Art and Practice of the Learning Organization* (New York: Doubleday, 1990).
8. Chris Argyris and Donald Schon, *Organizational Learning: A Theory of Action Perspective* (Reading, MA: Addison-Wesley, 1978).

19 Sharing the Book's Lessons with the "Hard-to-Reach"

1. Christopher McDougall, *Born to Run: A Hidden Tribe, Superathletes, and the Greatest Race the World Has Never Seen* (New York: Knopf, 2009).

Appendix 2: Pattern Profiles

1. Martin Covington, *Making the Grade: A Self-Worth Perspective on Motivation and School Reform* (Cambridge, England: Cambridge University Press, 1992).
2. Robert Merton, *Social Theory and Social Structure* (New York: Free Press, 1968).
3. Edward Thorndike, "A Constant Error in Psychological Ratings," *Journal of Applied Psychology* 4.1 (March 1920): 25–29.
4. Jerry Gilley and Amy Coffern, *Internal Consulting for HRD Professionals: Tools, Techniques, and Strategies for Improving Organizational Performance* (New York: McGraw-Hill, 1994).

5. Joshua Rubinstein, David Meyer, and Jeffery Evans, "Executive Control of Cognitive Processes in Task Switching," *Journal of Experimental Psychology: Human Perception and Performance* 27.4 (2001): 763–779.

6. Paula Caproni, *Management Skills for Everyday Life* (Upper Saddle River, NJ: Pearson, 2005).

7. Luc de Brabandere, *The Forgotten Half of Change* (Chicago, IL: Dearborn, 2005).

8. Chris Argyris, *Reasoning, Learning and Action: Individual and Organizational* (San Francisco, CA: Jossey-Bass, 1982).

9. Howard McClusky, "Education for Aging: The Scope of the Field and Perspectives for the Future," in *Learning for Aging*, eds. Stanley Grabowski and Dean Mason (Washington, DC: Adult Education Association of the USA, 1974), 324–355.

10. Richard Wurman, David Sume, Loring Leifer, and Karen Whitehouse, *Information Anxiety 2* (Indianapolis, IN: Hayden/Que, 2001).

11. Julie Norem and Nancy Cantor, "Defensive Pessimism: Harnessing Anxiety as Motivation," *Journal of Personality and Social Psychology* 52 (1986): 1208–1217.

12. Chris Argyris, *Overcoming Organizational Defense. Facilitating Organizational Learning* (Boston: Allyn and Bacon, 1990).

13. Karen Watkins and Victoria Marsick, *Sculpting the Learning Organization: Lessons in the Art and Science of Systemic Change* (San Francisco: Jossey-Bass, 1993).

14. Paula Caproni, *Management Skills for Everyday Life* (Upper Saddle River, NJ: Pearson, 2005).

15. Jeffrey Pfeffer and Robert Sutton, *The Knowing-Doing Gap: How Smart Companies Turn Knowledge into Action* (Boston, MA: Harvard Business School Publishing, 2000).

16. Sidney Rosen and Abraham Tesser, "On Reluctance to Communicate Undesirable Information: The MUM Effect," *Sociometry* 33 (1970): 253–263.

17. John Kotter, *Leading Change* (Boston: Harvard Business School Press, 1996).

Bibliography

Argyris, Chris. *On Organizational Learning*. Malden: Blackwell Business, 1999.
———. *Overcoming Organizational Defense. Facilitating Organizational Learning*. Boston: Allyn and Bacon, 1990.
———. *Reasoning, Learning and Action: Individual and Organizational*. San Francisco, CA: Jossey-Bass, 1982.
Argyris, Chris, and Donald Schon. *Organizational Learning: A Theory of Action Perspective*. Reading: Addison-Wesley, 1978.
Axley, Stephen. "Managerial and Organizational Communication in Terms of the Conduit Metaphor." *Academy of Management Review* 9 (1984): 428–437.
Caproni, Paula. *Management Skills for Everyday Life*. Upper Saddle River: Pearson, 2005.
Collins, Jim. *Good to Great*. New York: HarperCollins, 2001.
Covington, Martin. *Making the Grade: A Self-Worth Perspective on Motivation and School Reform*. Cambridge: Cambridge University Press, 1992.
Craig, Robert. "Communication Theory as a Field." *Communication Theory* 9.2 (1999): 199–161.
Cronen, Vernon, Barnett Pearce, and Carl Tomm. "A Dialectical View of Personal Change." In *The Social Construction of the Person*, edited by Kenneth Gergen and Keith Davis, 203–224. New York: Springer-Verlag, 1985.
Davis, Kingsley. *Human Society*. New York: Macmillan, 1942.
de Brabandere, Luc. *The Forgotten Half of Change*. Chicago: Dearborn, 2005.
Deal, Terrence, and Allan Kennedy. *Corporate Cultures: The Rites and Rituals of Corporate Life*. Harmondsworth: Penguin Books, 1982.
DeVito, Joseph. *The Interpersonal Communication Book*. New York: Longman, 2001.
Eisenberg, Eric, and Goodall Lloyd. *Organizational Communication*. New York: St. Martin's Press, 1997.
Etzioni, Amatai. *Modern Organizations*. Englewood Cliffs: Prentice-Hall, 1964.
Festinger, Leon. *A Theory of Cognitive Dissonance*. Stanford: Stanford University Press, 1957.
Fey, Tina, *Bossypants*. New York: Little, Brown and Co., 2011.
Fisher, Walter. "Narration as a Human Communication Paradigm: The Case of Public Moral Argument." *Communication Monographs* 51 (1984): 1–22.
Gilley, Jerry, and Amy Coffern. *Internal Consulting for HRD Professionals: Tools, Techniques, and Strategies for Improving Organizational Performance*. New York: McGraw-Hill, 1994.

Gilley, Jerry, and Ann Maycunich. *Beyond the Learning Organization: Creating a Culture of Continuous Growth.* New York: Perseus, 2000.

Harris, Linda, and Vernon Cronen. "A Rules-Based Model for the Analysis and Evaluation of Organizational Communication." *Communication Quarterly* 27 (1979): 12–28.

Jablin, Fredric. "Organizational Entry, Assimilation, and Exit." In *Handbook of Organizational Communication,* edited by Fredric Jablin, Linda Putnam, K. Roberts, and L. W. Porter, 679–740. Newbury Park: Sage Publications, 1987.

Katz, Daniel, and Robert Kahn. *The Social Psychology of Organizations.* New York: John Wiley & Sons, 1978.

Kegan, Robert. *In Over Our Heads: The Mental Demands of Modern Life.* Cambridge: Harvard University Press, 1994.

Kegan, Robert, and Lisa Laskow Lahey. *How the Way We Talk Can Change the Way We Work.* San Francisco, CA: Jossey-Bass, 2001.

Kiechel, Walter. "A Manager's Career in the New Economy." *Fortune,* April 4, 1994. 68–72.

Kotter, John. *Leading Change.* Boston: Harvard Business School Press, 1996.

Lewin, Kurt. "The Research Center for Group Dynamics at Massachusetts Institute of Technology." *Sociometry* 8.2 (1945): 126–136.

Littlejohn, Stephen. *Theories of Human Communication.* Belmont: Wadsworth Publishing, 1996.

McClusky, Howard. "Education for Aging: The Scope of the Field and Perspectives for the Future." In *Learning for Aging,* edited by Stanley Grabowski and Dean Mason, 324–355. Washington, DC: Adult Education Association of the USA, 1974.

McDougall, Christopher. *Born to Run: A Hidden Tribe, Superathletes, and the Greatest Race the World Has Never Seen.* New York: Knopf, 2009.

Merton, Robert, *Social Theory and Social Structure.* New York: Free Press, 1968.

Mezirow, Jack. *Learning as Transformation: Critical Perspectives on a Theory in Progress.* San Francisco, CA: Jossey-Bass, 2000.

Norem, Julie, and Nancy Cantor. "Defensive Pessimism: Harnessing Anxiety as Motivation." *Journal of Personality and Social Psychology* 52 (1986): 1208–1217.

Papa, Michael, Tom Daniels, and Barry Spiker. *Organizational Communication: Perspectives and Trends.* Los Angeles: Sage, 2008.

Pearce, Barnett. *Interpersonal Communication: Making Social Worlds.* New York: Harper Collins College Publishers, 1994.

Pearce, Barnett, Jesse Sostrin, and Kim Pearce. *CMM Solutions Field Guide for Consultants.* San Mateo: Lulu Press, 2011.

Pearce, Barnett, and Kim Pearce. "Extending the Theory of the Coordinated Management of Meaning through a Community Dialogue Process." *Communication Theory* 10.4 (November 2000): 420.

Pfeffer, Jeffrey, and Robert Sutton. *The Knowing-Doing Gap: How Smart Companies Turn Knowledge into Action.* Boston: Harvard Business School Publishing, 2000.

Rosen, Sidney, and Abraham Tesser. "On Reluctance To Communicate Undesirable Information: The MUM Effect." *Sociometry* 33 (1970): 253–263.

Rubinstein, Joshua, David Meyer, and Jeffery Evans. "Executive Control of Cognitive Processes in Task Switching." *Journal of Experimental Psychology: Human Perception and Performance* 27.4 (2001): 763–779.

Rummler, Geary, and Alan Brache. *Improving Performance: How to Manage the White Space in the Organization Chart.* San Francisco: Jossey Bass Business and Management Series, 1995.

Senge, Peter. *The Fifth Discipline: The Art and Practice of The Learning Organization.* New York: Doubleday, 1990.

Snow, Dan. *In the Company of Stones.* New York: Workman, 2001.

Sostrin, Jesse. "Establishing and Validating a Conceptual Framework of Barriers to Workplace Learning and Performance: A Q-method Study." Doctoral dissertation, Fielding Graduate University, Santa Barbara, California, 2008.

Sostrin, Jesse. *Beyond the Job Description: What Managers and Employees Can Do to Navigate the True Demands of the Job.* New York: Palgrave-Macmillan, 2013.

Steiner, Claude. *Scripts People Live: Transactional Analysis of Life Scripts.* New York: Grove Press, 1990.

Thorndike, Edward. "A Constant Error in Psychological Ratings." *Journal of Applied Psychology* 4.1 (March 1920): 25–29.

Vaill, Peter. *Learning as a Way of Being.* San Francisco, CA: Jossey-Bass, 1996.

Watkins, Karen, and Victoria Marsick. *Sculpting the Learning Organization: Lessons in the Art and Science of Systemic Change.* San Francisco, CA: Jossey-Bass, 1993.

Watzlawick, Paul, Janet Beavin, and Don Jackson. *The Pragmatics of Human Communication: A Study of Interactional Patterns, Pathologies, and Paradoxes.* New York: Norton, 1967.

Weick, Karl. *The Social Psychology of Organizing.* Reading: Addison-Wesley, 1979.

Wurman, Richard, David Sume, Loring Leifer, and Karen Whitehouse. *Information Anxiety 2.* Indianapolis: Hayden/Que, 2001.

Index